IMAGES
of America

JACKSONVILLE
ARKANSAS

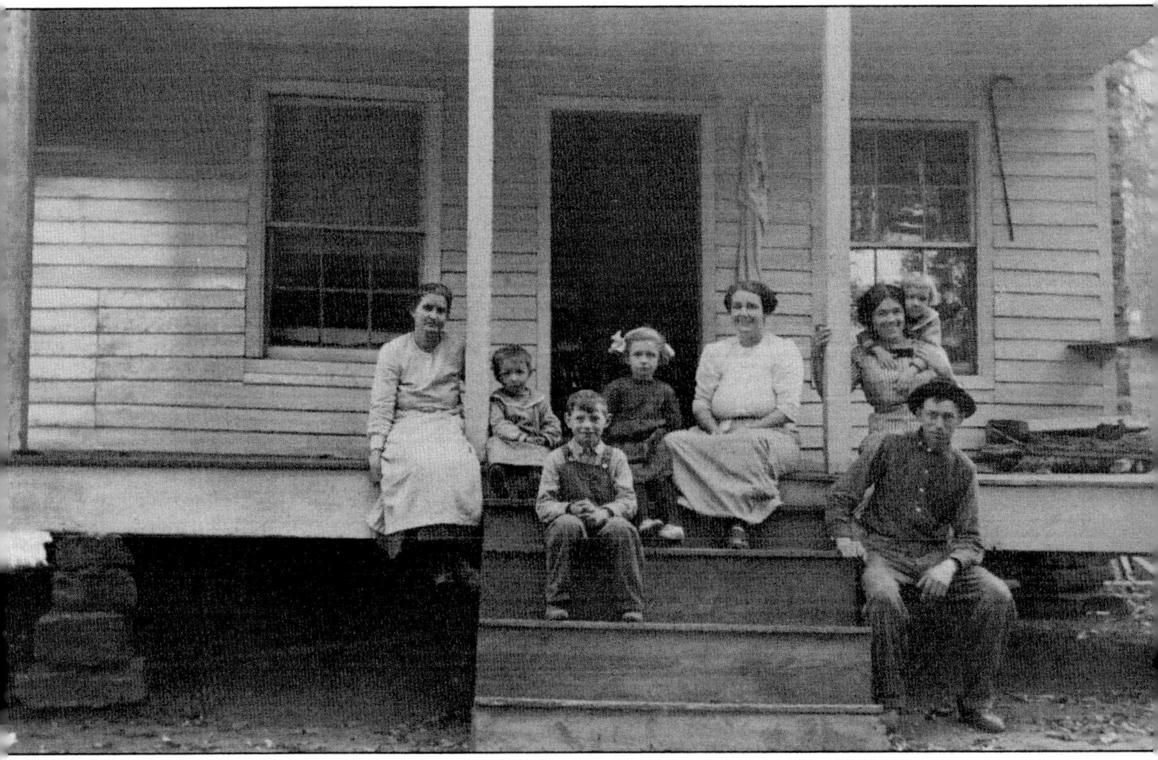

This family is sitting on their porch about 1920. (Jeanne McCain Duke.)

IMAGES
of America

JACKSONVILLE ARKANSAS

Kay Danielson

ARCADIA
PUBLISHING

ISBN 978-0-7385-0837-5

Published by Arcadia Publishing
Charleston, South Carolina

Printed in the United States of America

Library of Congress Catalog Card Number: 00-108401

For all general information contact Arcadia Publishing at:
Telephone 843-853-2070
Fax 843-853-0044
E-mail sales@arcadiapublishing.com
For customer service and orders:
Toll-Free 1-888-313-2665

Visit us on the Internet at www.arcadiapublishing.com

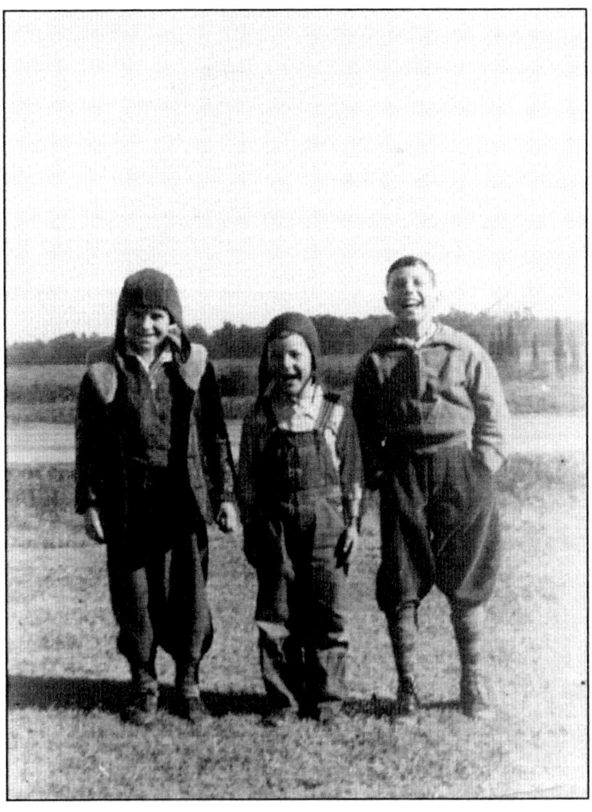

These three happy boys are pictured about 1930. (Marie Harpole Hackett.)

Contents

Acknowledgments		6
Introduction		7
1.	The Early 1800s and the Civil War	9
2.	1870 through the 1920s	11
3.	The 1930s	49
4.	The 1940s	69
5.	The 1950s and Beyond	57

ACKNOWLEDGMENTS

I want to thank the many people in the Jacksonville community who went through old boxes and opened the family scrapbooks to share their unique parts of history. The pictures came with stories that brought smiles, laughter, and a few tears.

Two publications, *The History of Jacksonville 1818–1976*, and *Siftings from Jacksonville's History 1820 to 1980*, have been most helpful to the author.

And many thanks to my husband, Jack Danielson, who was a constant source of information and new leads.

INTRODUCTION

Jacksonville has never been a tourist town, and therefore there are few available public images of the area. But there is a rich history tucked away in old boxes and scrapbooks. The people of Jacksonville brought forth those treasured family photographs, some creased and ragged, others pristine as new, to tell the story. Some images show a likeness, dress, and personality in a studio setting, but most are the result of a family member taking a picture to record some special moment in their lives. Much of the town's story is in the background of those pictures—Main Street as it used to be, current fashions, the car models, buildings that have disappeared, and people who have gone. This history of Jacksonville is from those family albums.

One

THE EARLY 1800S AND THE CIVIL WAR

In the early 1800s, what was to become the Arkansas Territory was known to the Caddo, Cherokee, Osage, and Quapaw Native Americans. Other Indian groups migrated westward through the area in an attempt to avoid white settlers who were populating their former homelands.

Twelve miles northeast of the Arkansas River at La Petit Roche, the land was forested with rises and wet lowlands with bayous that, once drained and cleared, were well-suited for raising corn and cotton. Temperatures ranged from brief, cool winters to long, hot, and humid summers.

The first known white settlers came about 1820, traveling in flat-bottomed boats on the Bayou Meto. Twenty-three people of the Gray family cleared land at the current 294 and Military Road site, and the area became known as Graytown and later Gray Township. Little more than a dirt track running from Memphis to Little Rock, the rough road was improved in 1828, which encouraged more traffic.

With the Relocation Act of 1830, most of the Cherokee, Creek, Choctaws, and Chickasaws were forced out of the Carolinas and Georgia to march westward to Oklahoma on the Trail of Tears. One of the branches of that trail went through the Arkansas Territory on the Military Road. In 1836, Arkansas was admitted to the Union as a slave state.

In the early 1860s, there were about two hundred people in the area. When the question of secession rose, most men, following their beliefs, donned gray uniforms and joined units to fight the Civil War. While the conflict scarred many areas of the south, Graytown saw only a brief battle at Reed's Bridge in 1863, a few weeks before the fall of Little Rock.

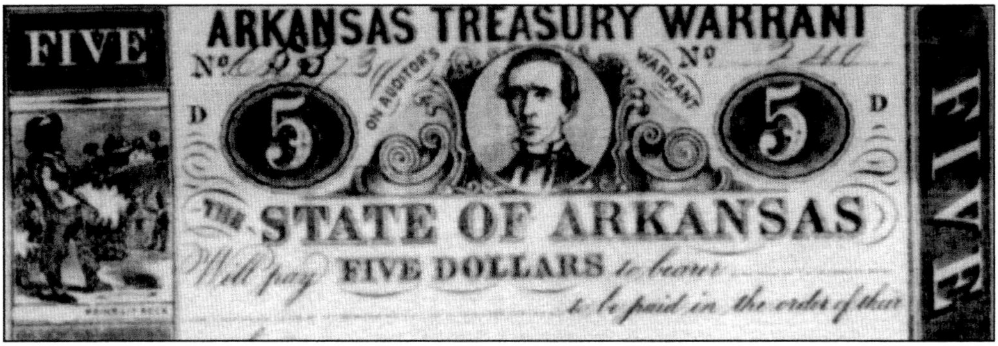

Pictured is a $5 Arkansas Treasury Warrant from 1863. In order to raise funds to finance the war, southern states issued paper money rather than levy a tax. This warrant promised to pay eight percent interest at the end of the successful war. (Mack McIntire.)

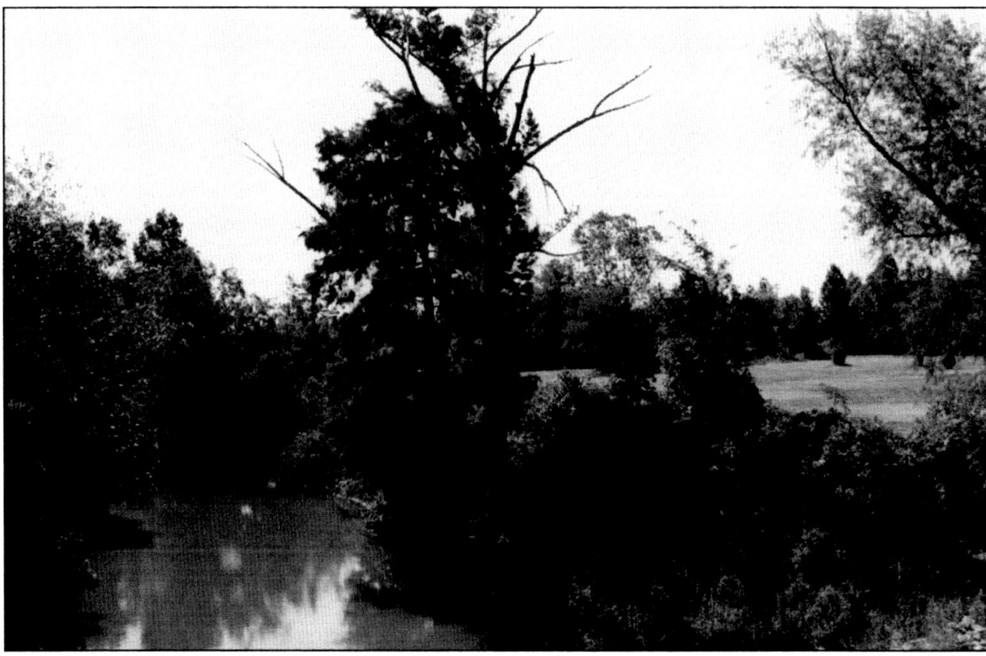

This quiet little piece of the Bayou Meto saw the only Civil War action in Graytown (later known as Jacksonville) on a hot and clammy August 26, 1863. Marching on the Military Road toward Little Rock, 6,000 Union troops met 4,000 Confederate soldiers, and they skirmished where a small wooden bridge crossed the muddy water. The Union forces had to find another passage when the bridge was burned, but they captured Little Rock a few weeks later. Now the field beyond the Bayou Meto is preserved as the historic Reed's Bridge Civil War Battlefield on Highway 161. (Author's photograph.)

Two

1870 Through 1920

After the war, the Cairo and Fulton Railroad really opened the area to settlement. The town of Jacksonville was platted in 1872, when Nicholas W. and Elizabeth Jackson granted a right of way to the railroad, extracting thc promise of a train depot in the town. More people came to the area, but it remained a small rural community well into the next century.

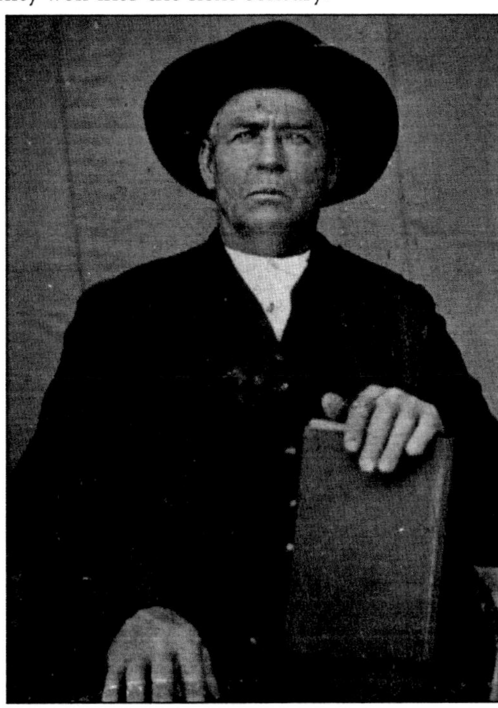

Nicholas W. Jackson and his wife, Elizabeth, were not the first settlers in the area, but in 1870 they deeded land for a right of way to the Cairo and Fulton Railroad for $300. The resulting train depot opened the doors for more settlers to the area that was platted and named Jacksonville. (Nixon Library, Jacksonville.)

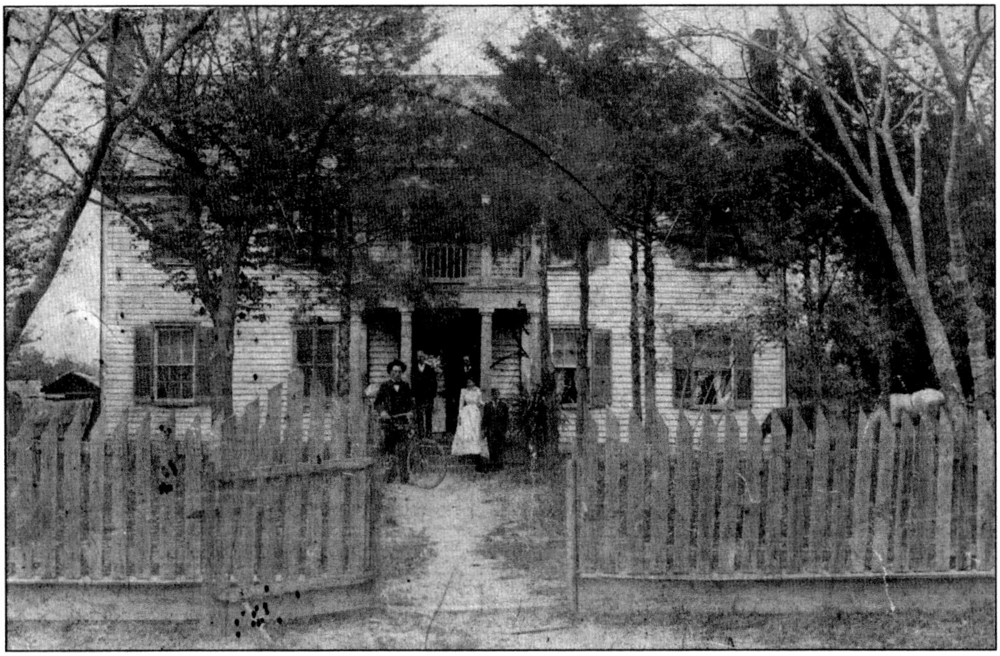

The Jackson home on South First Street is shown here about 1900. (Nixon Library, Jacksonville.)

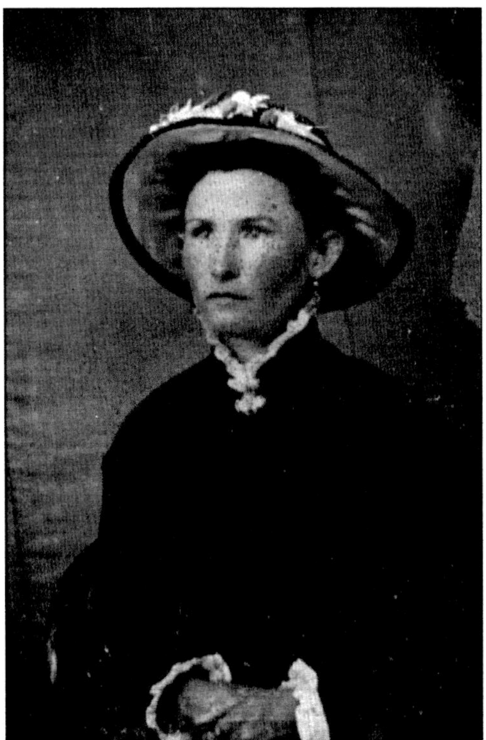

Mary Davidson Jackson (a widow) was the second wife of Nicholas W. Jackson. They had two children, Thompson and Laura. (Nixon Library, Jacksonville.)

Thompson Jackson was the son of Nicholas W. Jackson's second wife, Mary Davidson. This photograph dates to 1898. (Nixon Library, Jacksonville.)

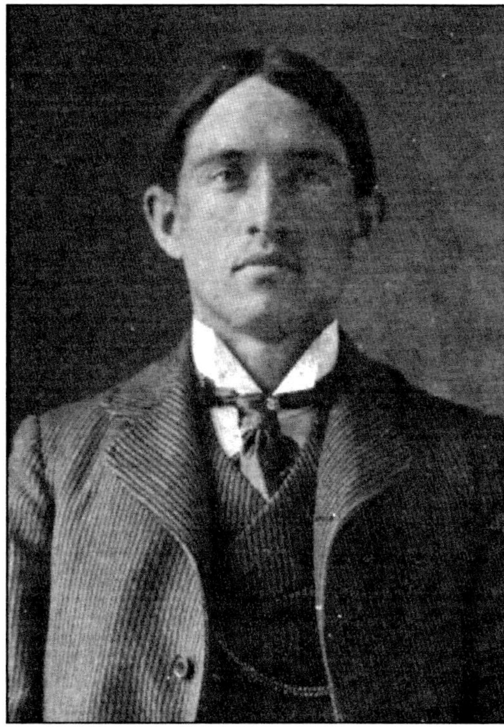

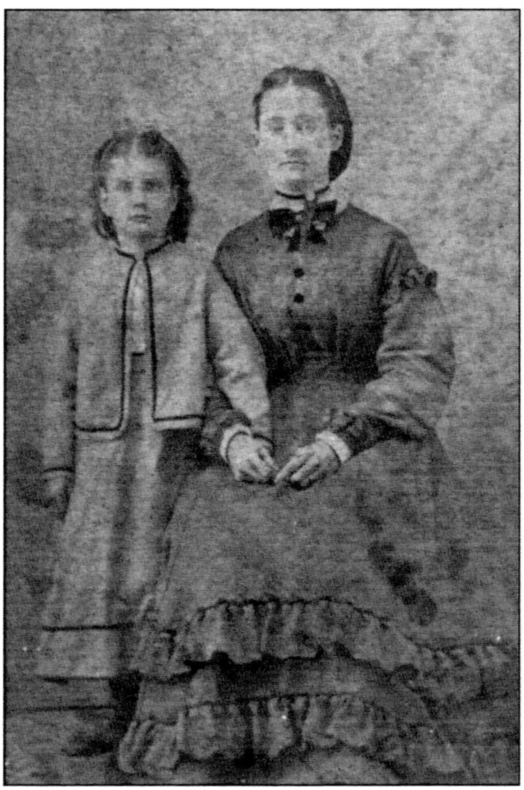

After the Civil War, many early settlers left established homes and families in the southeastern states to head west for new opportunities. This mother and daughter had a studio picture taken in Sommersville, Tennessee, before leaving for the unknown. (Tommy Dupree.)

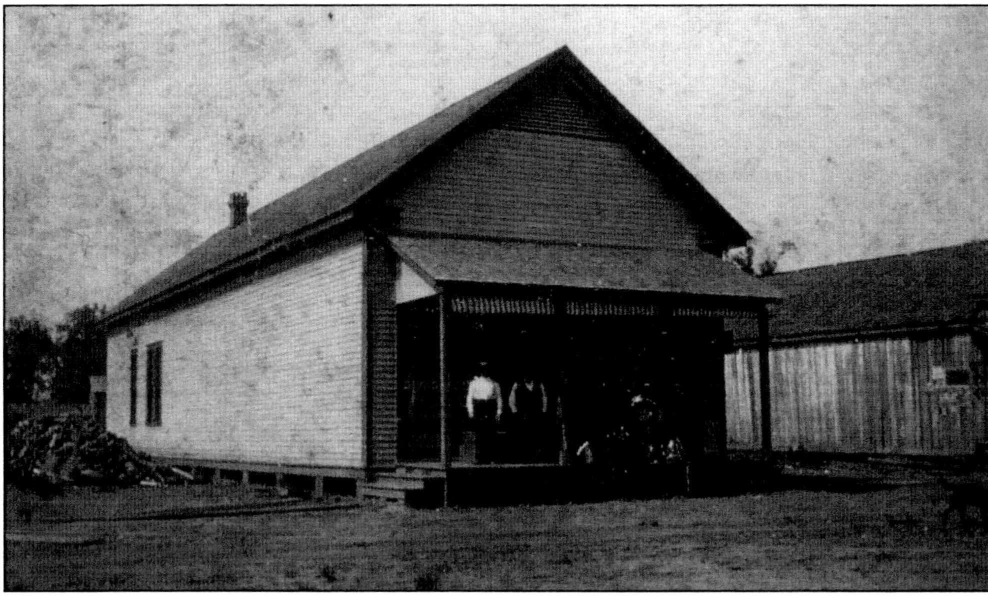

Late in the 19th century, the general store was the hub of Jacksonville's small community. Located at the northwest corner of Main and Front Streets, Jeff Ramsey's establishment offered shoes, clothing, and dry goods around 1895. (Jacksonville Historical Society.)

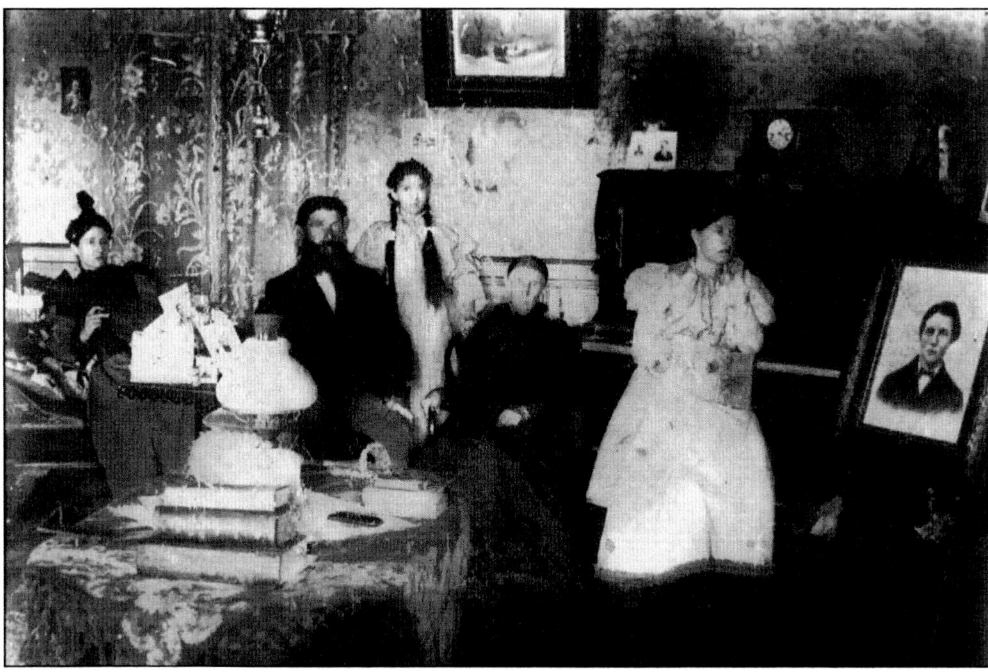

Little is known about the Roderweis family except that John Louis Roderweis was born in Phulinger, Germany, on November 27, 1846, and came to Arkansas in 1880. The Roderweis house, located northwest of town, was one of the most elaborate in the Jacksonville area, and it still stands today. John was an amateur woodworker, and his family left a few pieces of furniture and these photographs to the Arkansas Territorial Restoration for future generations to enjoy. (Arkansas Territorial Restoration.)

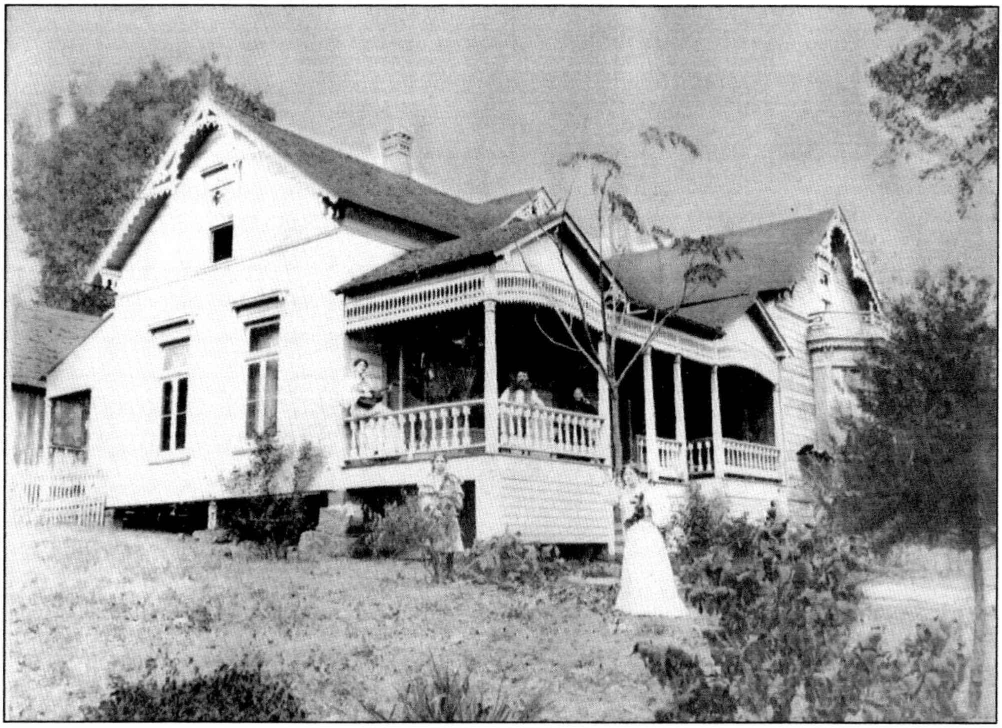

The Roderweis house is pictured here about 1890. (Arkansas Territorial Restoration.)

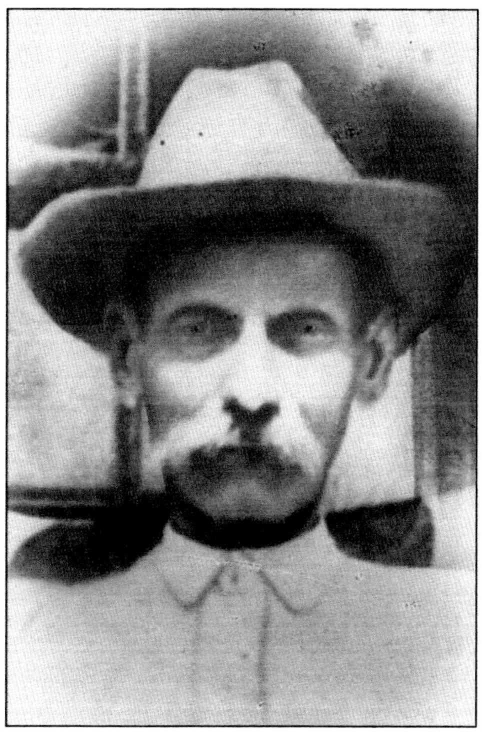

Joe Lamb, born in 1849, was a farmer all his life and had a dozen children with two wives. (Mary Alice Lamb Cole.)

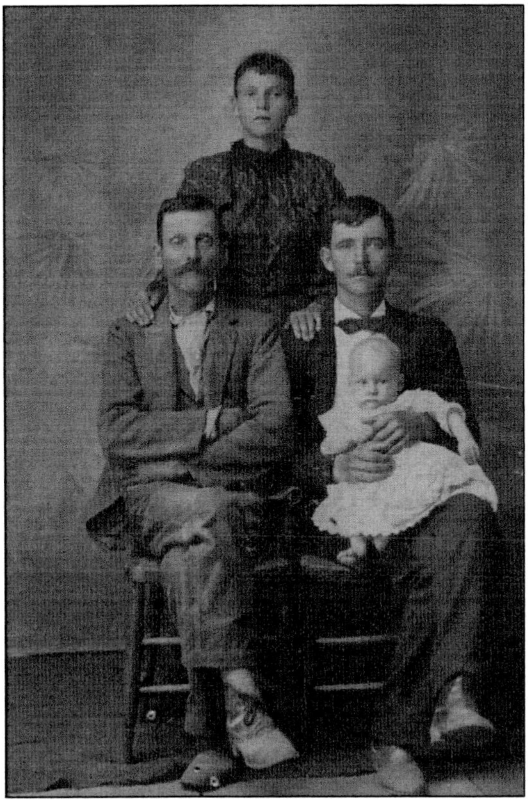

Joe Lamb, on the left, is shown with his daughter Maggie Crook, her husband Jim Crook, and their baby Joe Crook, about 1890. (Mary Alice Lamb Cole.)

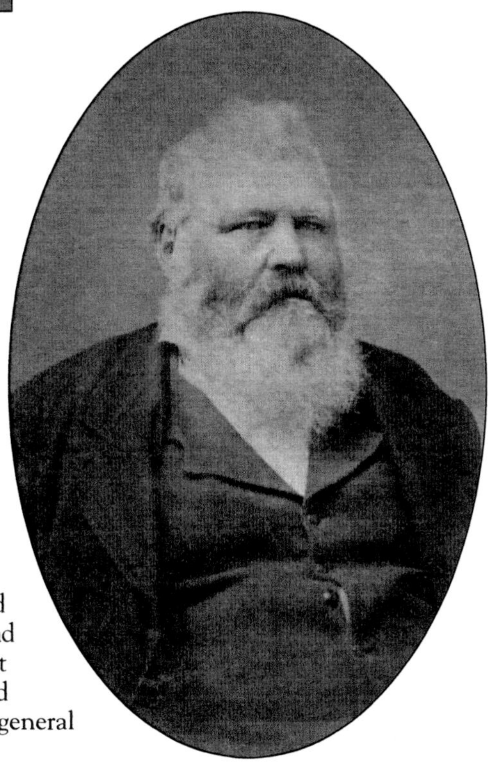

Mancil Euclid Stone married Mary Ferguson and settled in Gray Township around 1858. They had five children. Stone had a limited education, but he had a thriving farm, a profitable gristmill, and cotton gin. He and his son, Elihu, established a general merchandise store in 1881. (Tommy Dupree.)

The Dupree family left Oakland, Tennessee, for Jacksonville when Peter Warren Dupree was six years old. Educated at Hendrix College, he married Leonora Stone on July 30, 1901, and joined his father-in-law, E.C. Stone, in business. The venture later became the P.W. Dupree General Mercantile Business. (Tommy Dupree.)

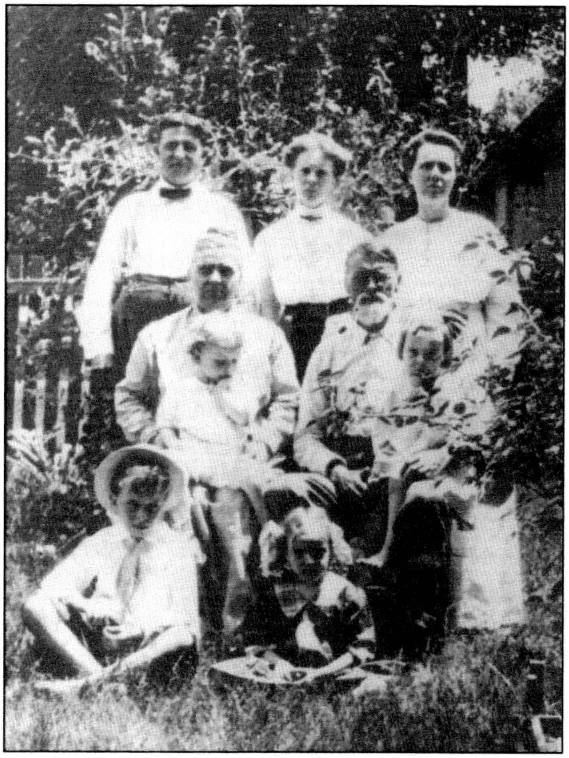

This photograph, taken about 1915, shows boys in a tree by Jacksonville School. Built in 1897 on the current Jacksonville Elementary grounds, this school first housed nine grades but expanded to include a full twelve. The building was replaced in 1925. (George Herman Taylor.)

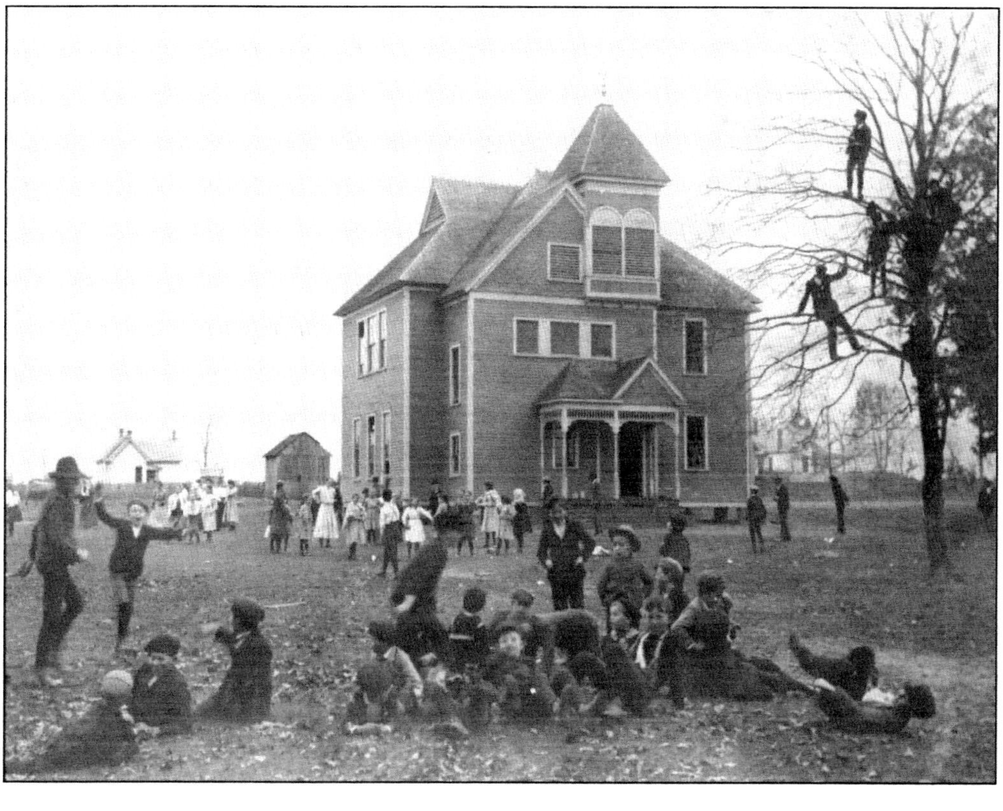

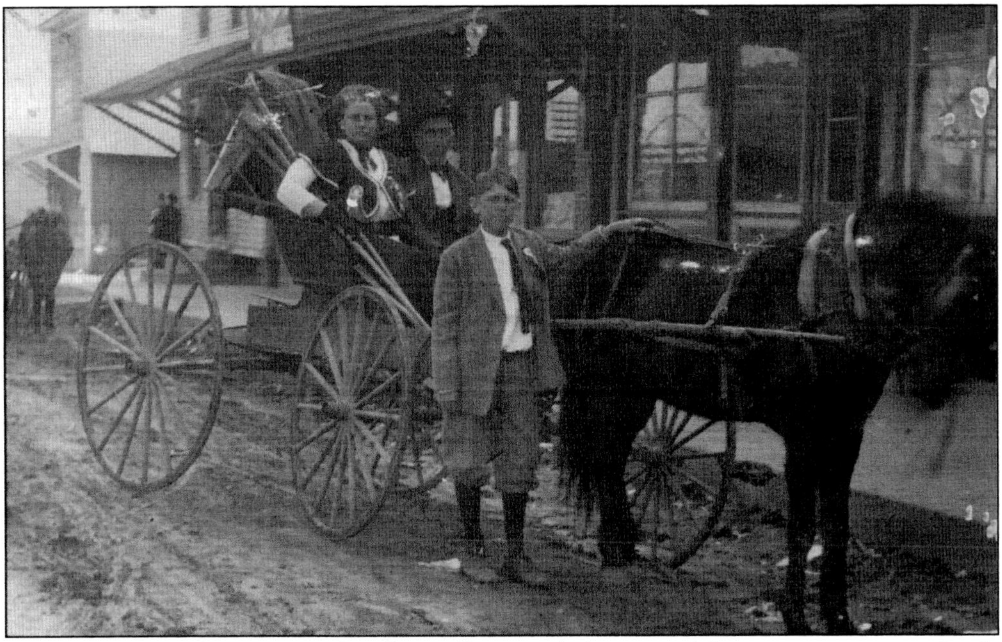

For most families living in rural Jacksonville around the turn of the century, a trip to Little Rock for supplies was a major undertaking. (Mary Alice Lamb Cole.)

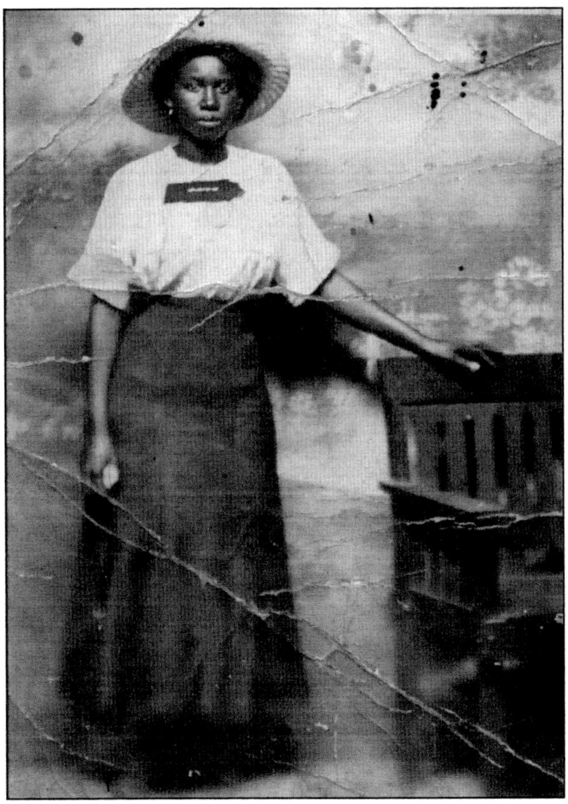

Exie Carter and her family lived at Center and Oak Streets about 1910. She had six children, was active in church, and was a seamstress. Many of the quilts she made survive today. (James Carter.)

Inez Taylor is shown here about 1910. (James Carter.)

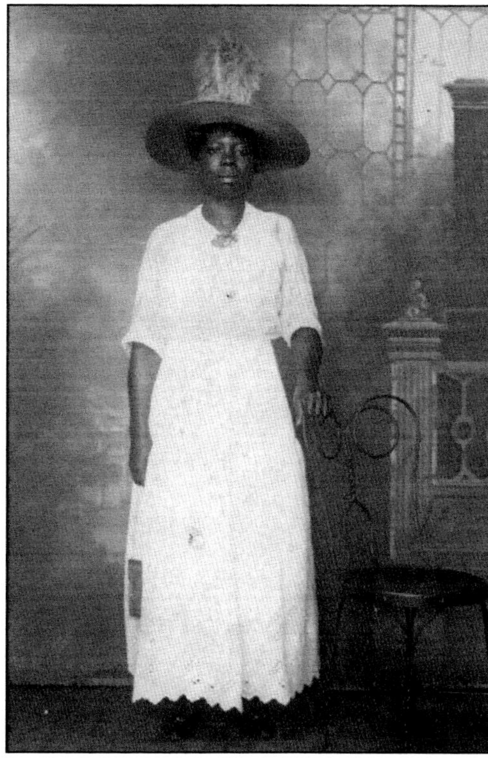

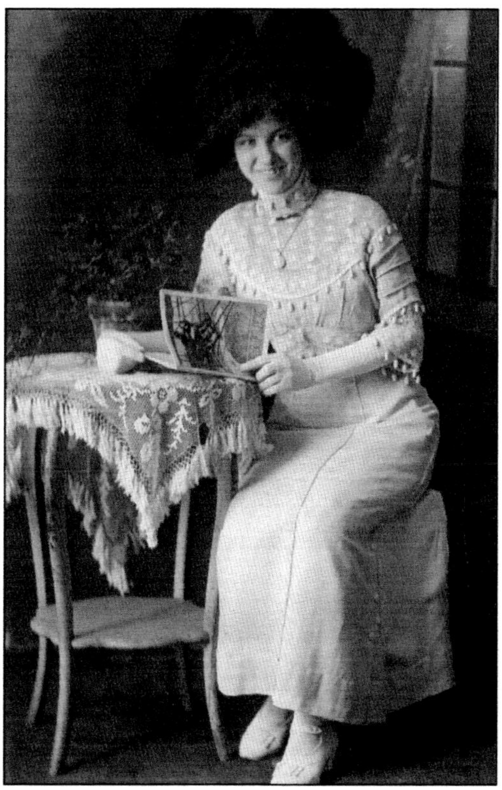

This fashionable young woman sat for her studio portrait in the early 1900s. (Jeanne McCain Duke.)

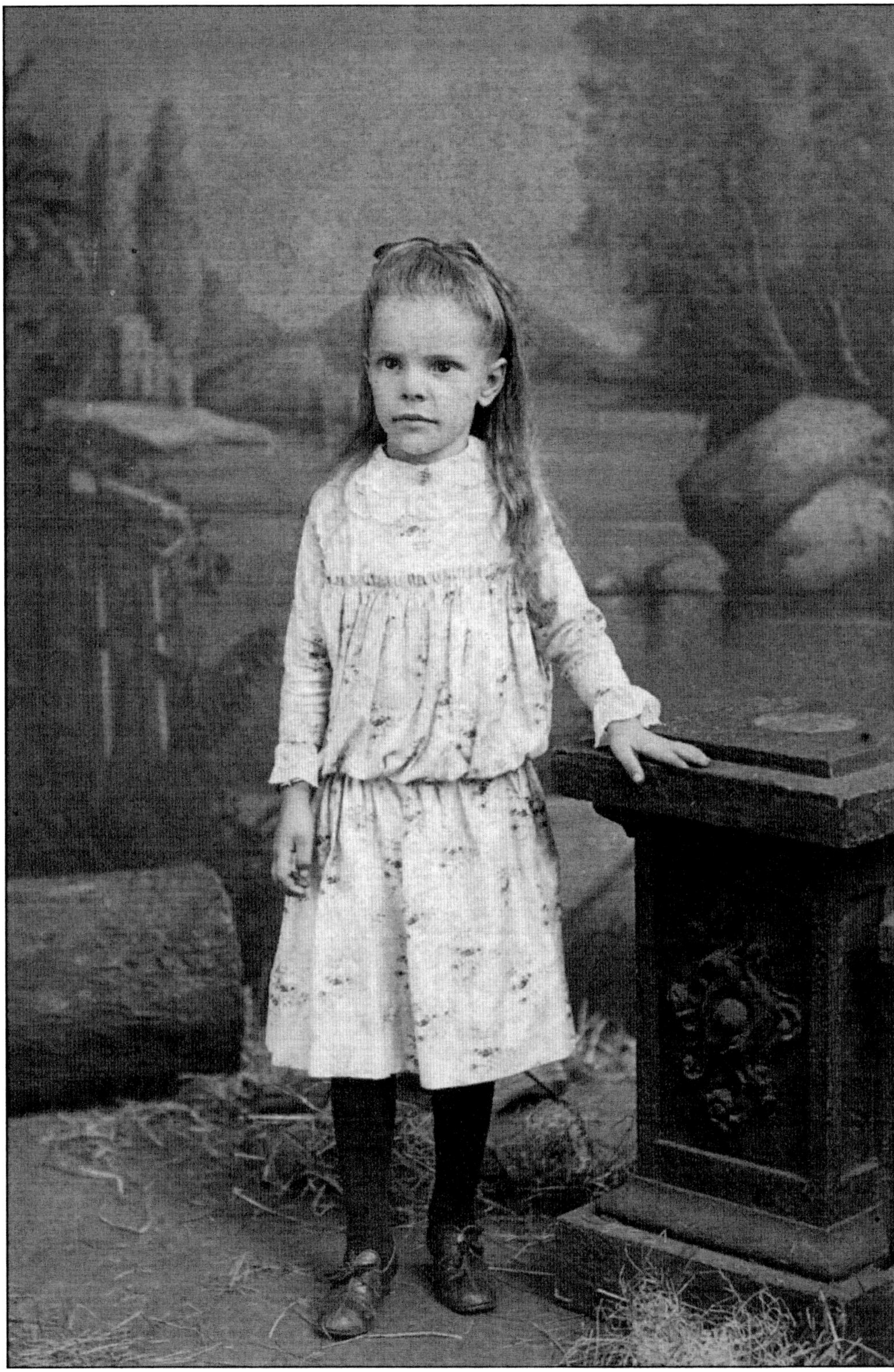

Here we see Leonora Stone about 1890. (Tommy Dupree.)

Perhaps it was their wedding photograph, but this unknown couple chose a studio setting with a rough floor and a tree trunk. She holds pictures from an album and he, the Bible, about 1890. (Jean McCain Duke.)

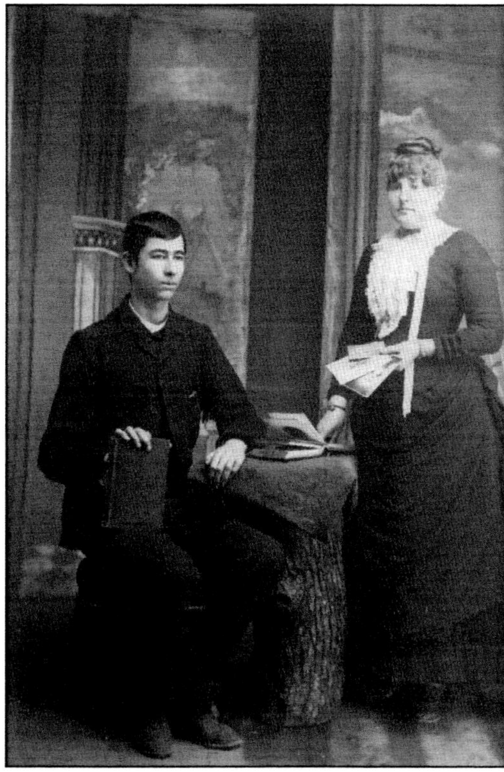

This Jacksonville Telephone Company certificate dates to 1904. A telephone was installed in 1890 in the P.W. Dupree store, but the town didn't have a switchboard until 1934. (Carroll Boyd.)

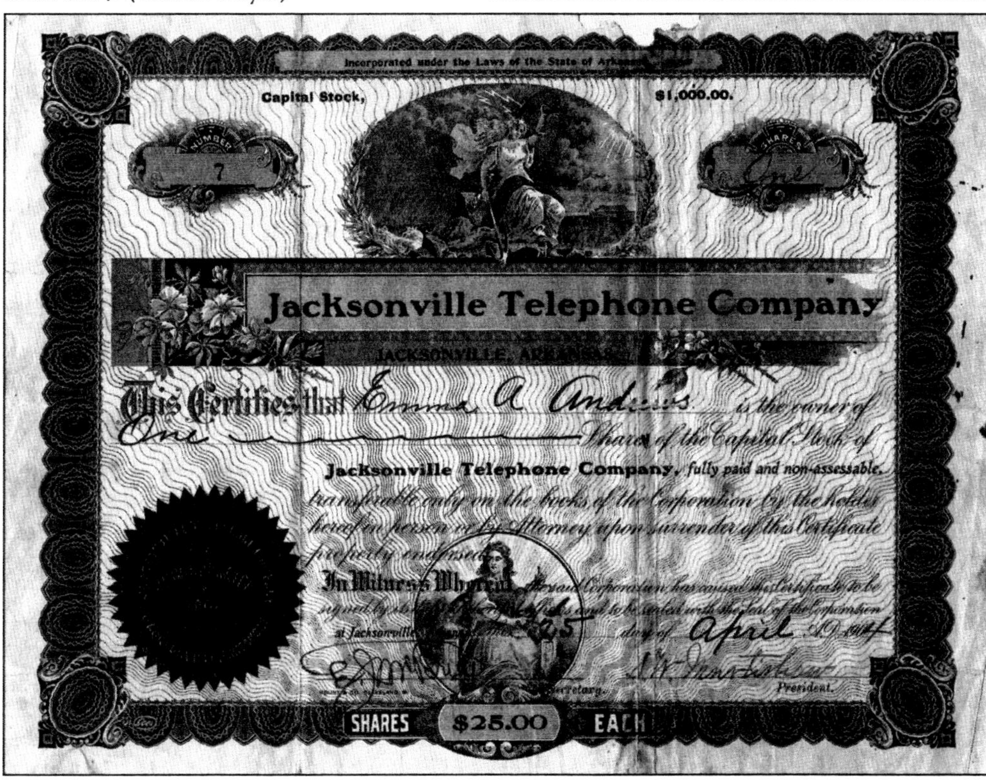

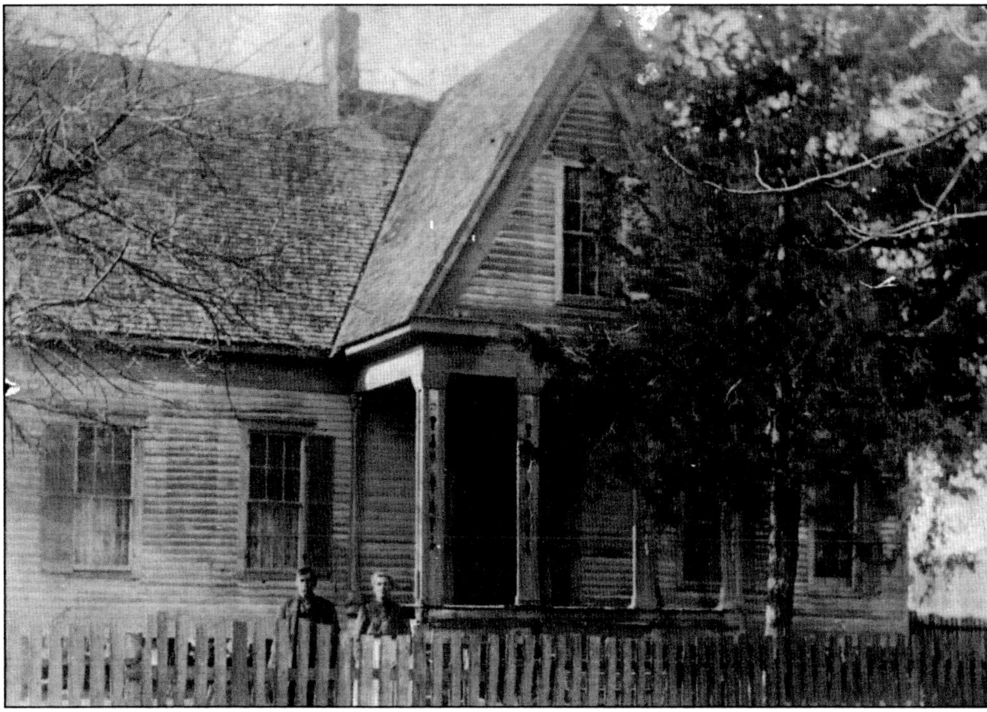

Grandma and Grandpa Madden are pictured here at their homestead, which was eventually destroyed to make room for the Little Rock Air Force Base (LRAFB). (Carroll Boyd.)

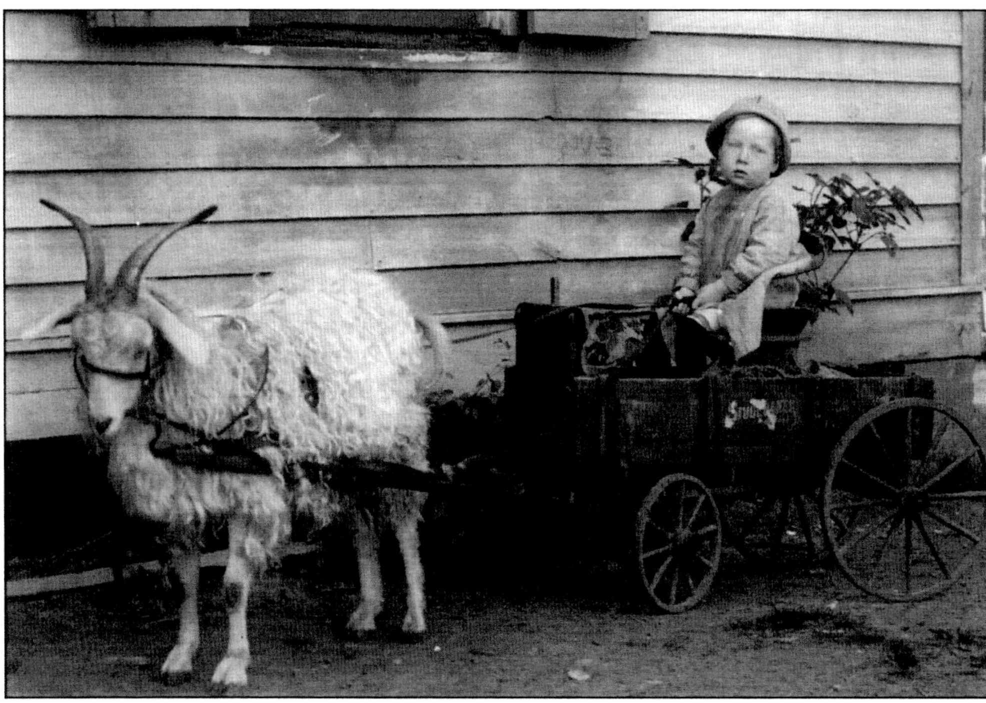

This could be a wild ride, but animal carts were not unusual in the days around the turn of the century when most amusements were homemade. (Jeanne McCain Duke.)

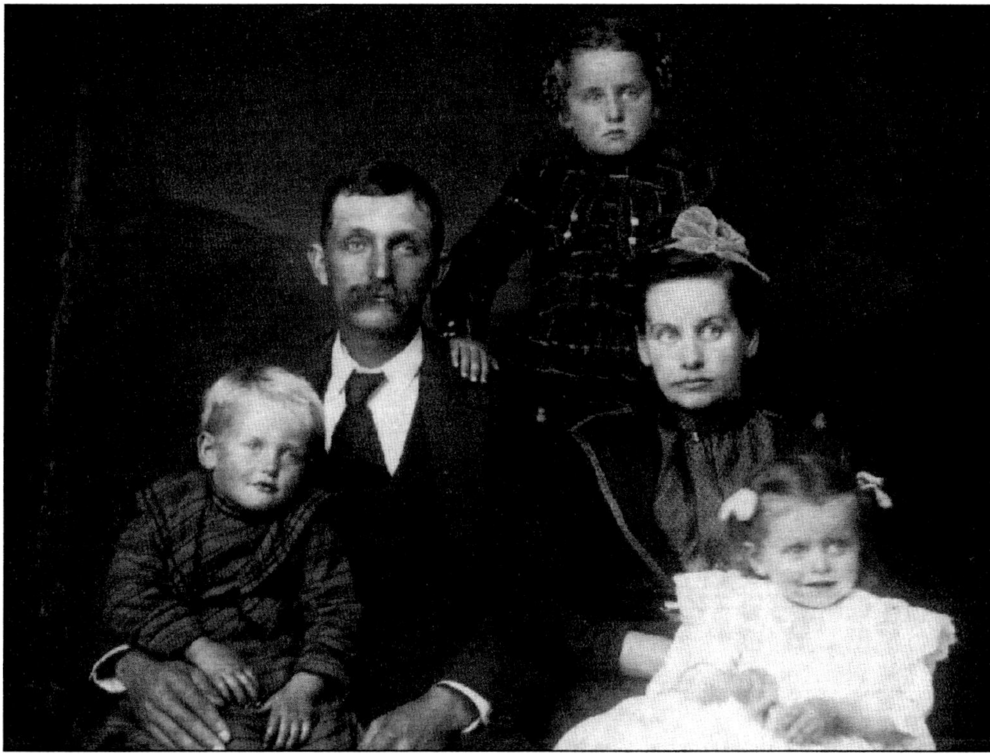

The Rufus Darby Boyd family sat for this photograph in 1902. Like most other young families in the area, R.D. Boyd settled in Jacksonville to farm, which he did for the next 50 years. (Pat Boyd.)

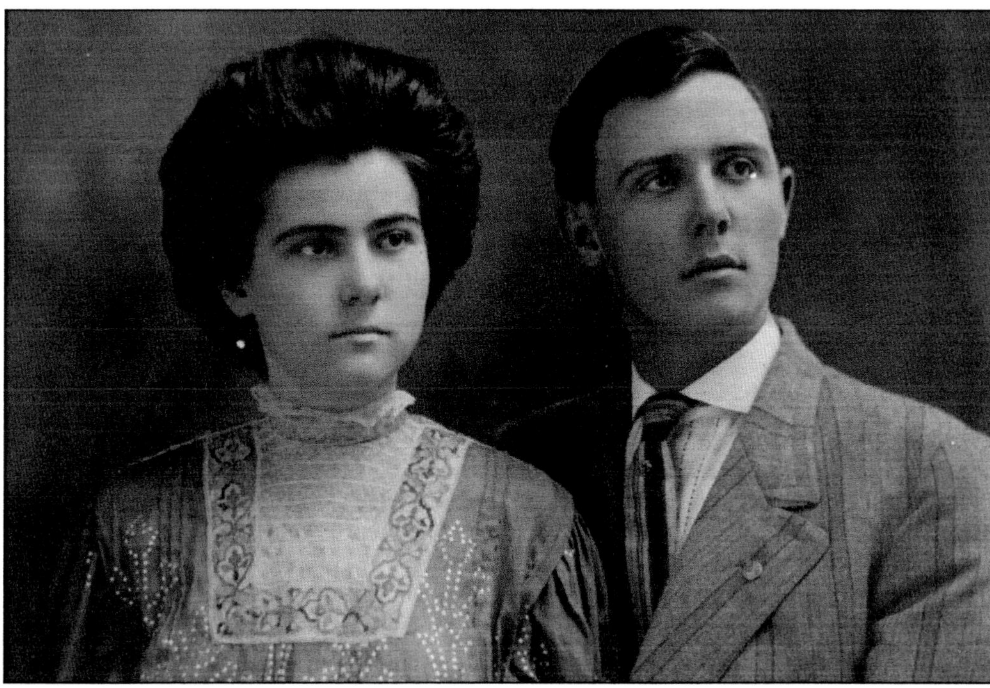

This couple is from the Dupree family about 1910. (Tommy Dupree.)

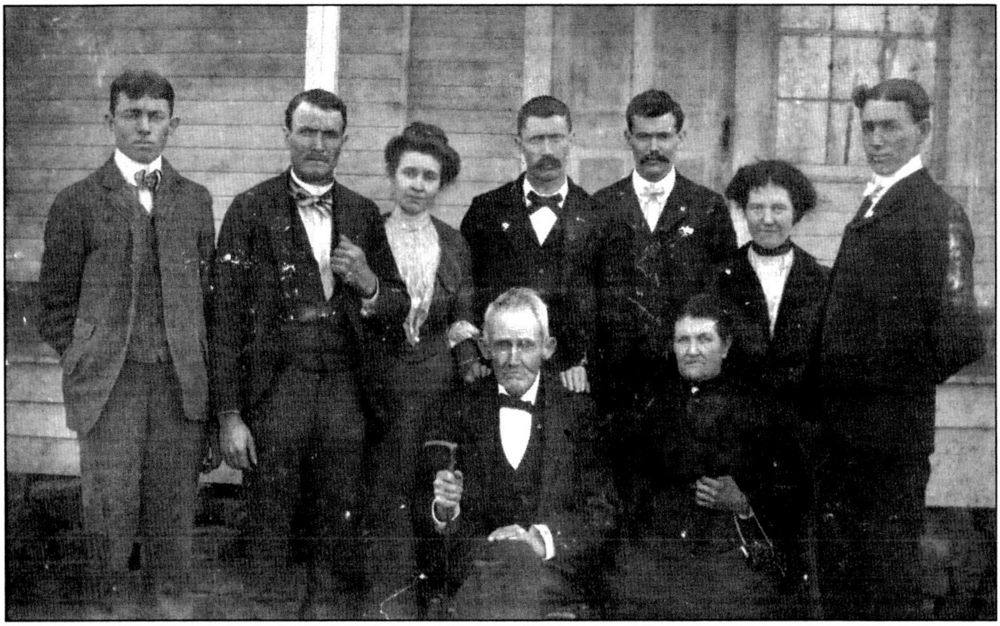

This 1903 photograph shows the McCain family. George Hamilton McCain (at far right) would establish a dairy farm in the 1940s. He supplied milk for much of the surrounding area until required pasteurization equipment made it prohibitive to continue in the business. (Jeanne McCain Duke.)

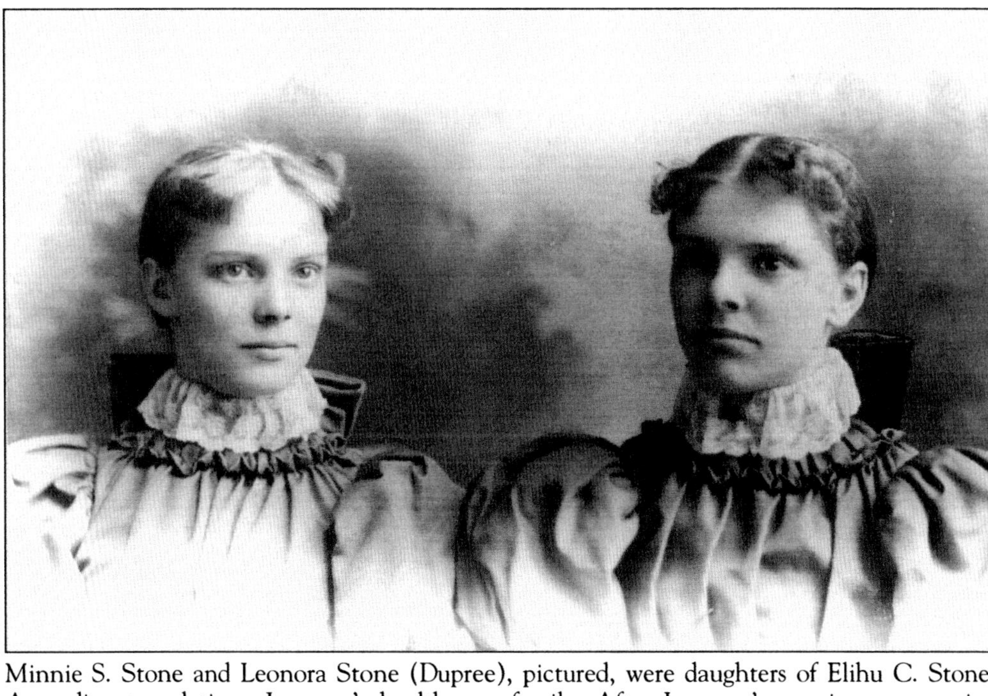

Minnie S. Stone and Leonora Stone (Dupree), pictured, were daughters of Elihu C. Stone. According to relatives, Leonora's health was fragile. After Leonora's marriage, unmarried Minnie came to help her sister's family and never left. (Tommy Dupree.)

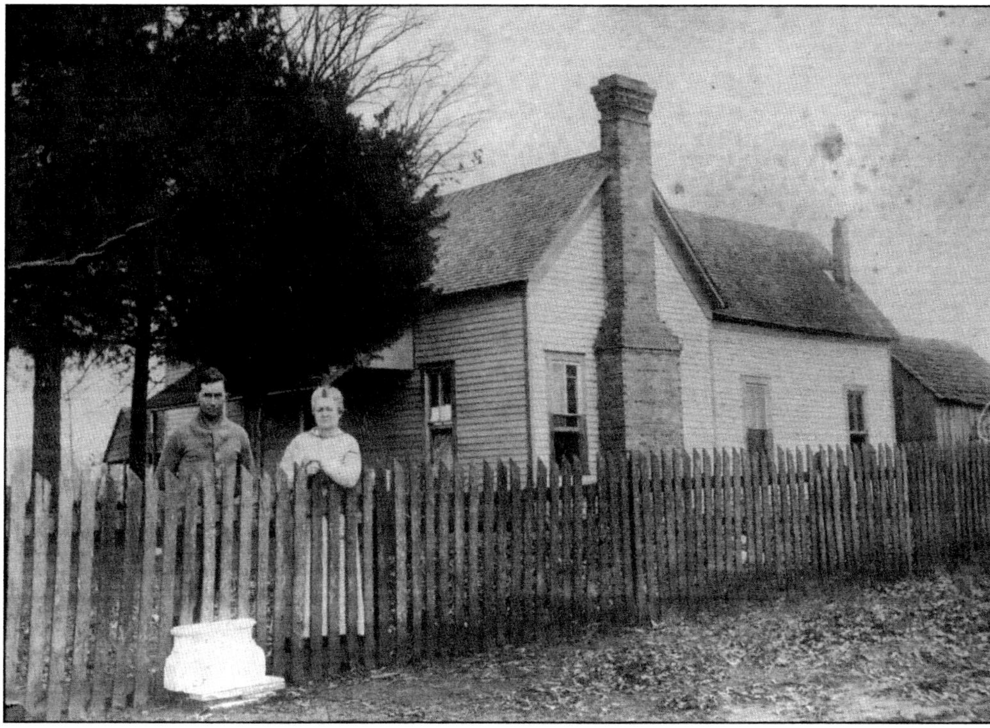

Grandmother Taylor is shown here with her son about 1920. (George Herman Taylor.)

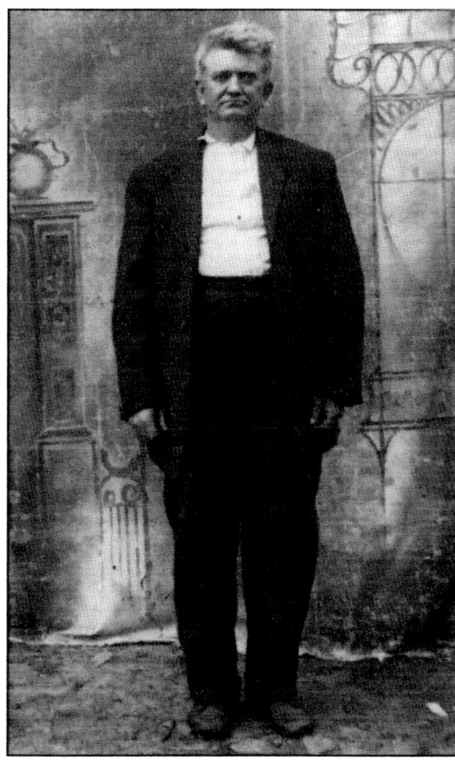

Here is Jim Webb in 1910. (Doyle Webb.)

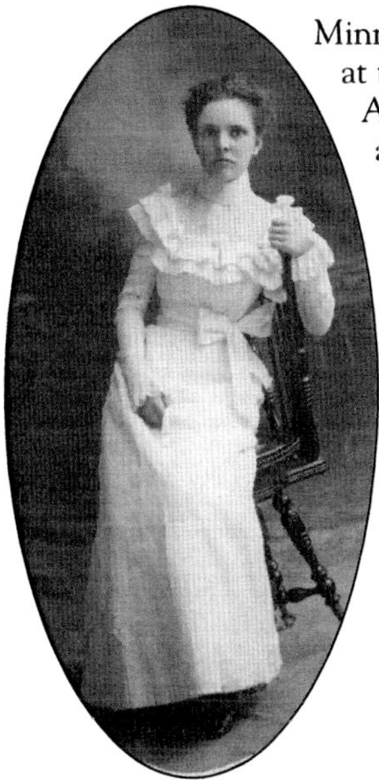

Minnie Stone was born in 1881. As an adult she helped with bookwork at the family store, was a member of the School Improvement Association (which later became the Parent, Teacher Association), and was involved in church activities. (Tommy Dupree.)

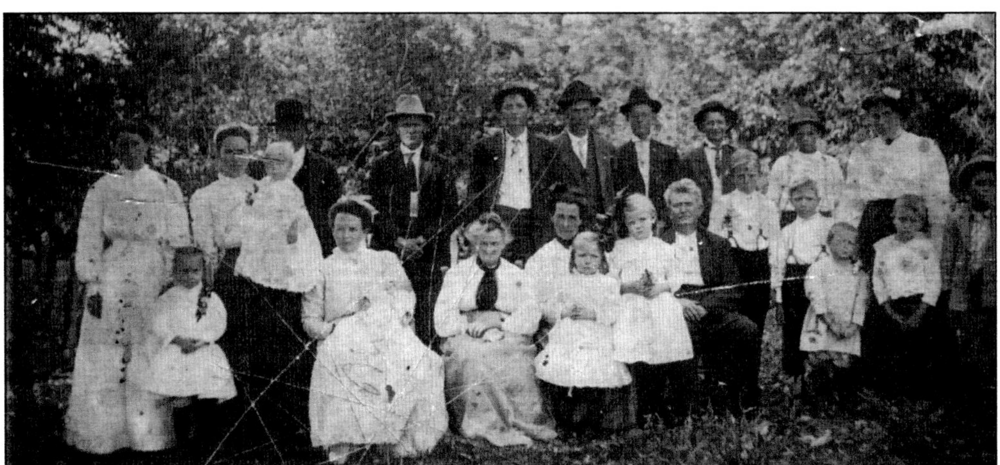

The Webb family is pictured here in 1911. This happy time was long before the economic Depression years would force some family members off their farms. Some of the descendants went on to merchandising in Jacksonville. (Doyle Webb.)

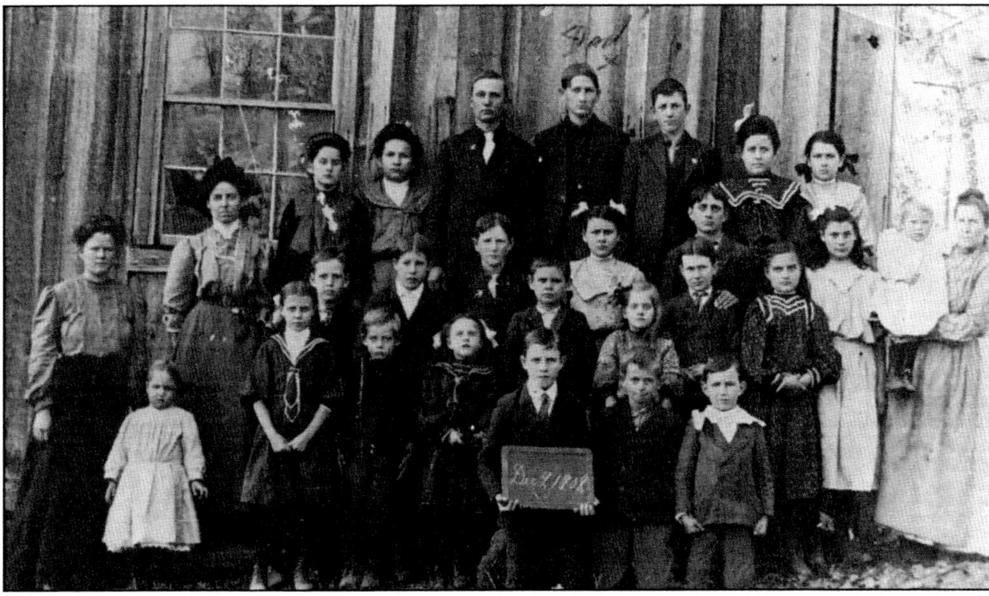

Harry Harpole is pictured in the top row, center, at the Tony Lonesome School in 1908. Schools were important to the community, and a collective effort to support a school system began as far back as 1870. (Opal Harpole Mallett.)

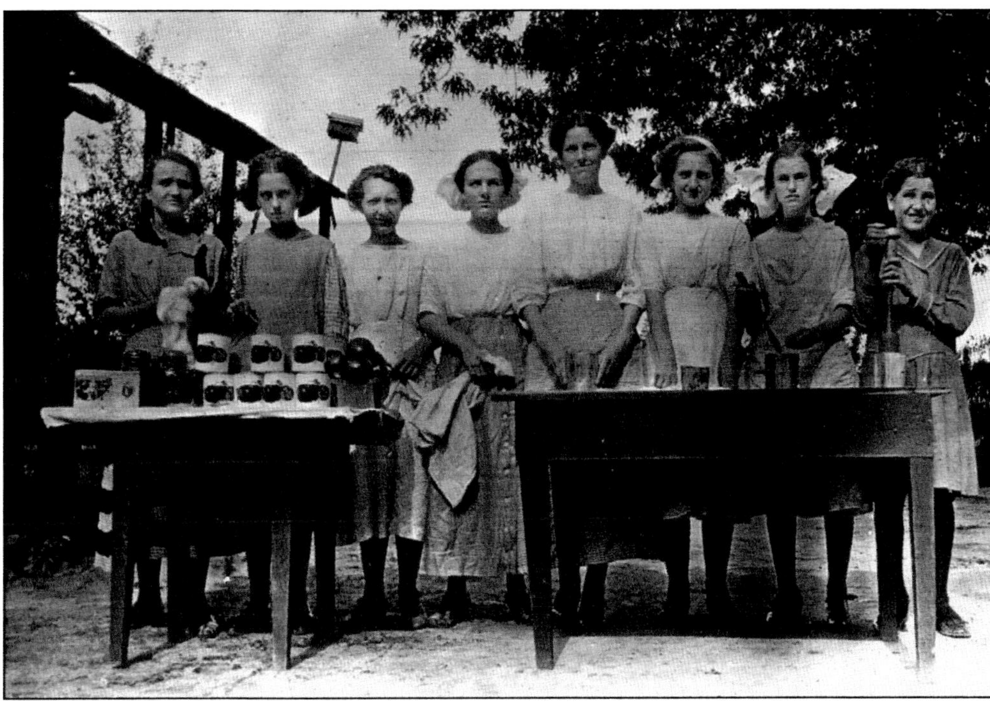

Mabel Brown Lamb helped to organize the 1912 Tomato and Poultry Club homemakers. A forerunner of the home extension clubs, the organization taught young women new methods to raise and preserve foods for home consumption and for sale. The homemaking group was a lifelong interest that came naturally to Brown. The oldest of seven children, she raised the rest of her siblings when her mother died. (Mary Alice Lamb Cole.)

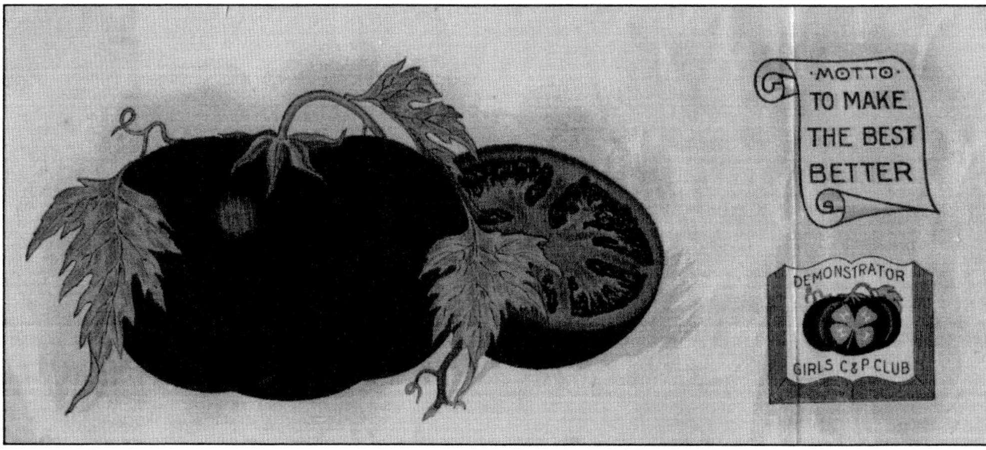

This is the Tomato and Poultry Club label. In addition to food preparation, the young women learned to sew clothing, make rugs, re-cover furniture, and construct quilts. The group financed community projects like providing lights and a stage curtain for the school and landscaping the parsonage of the First Baptist Church by selling quilts. (Mary Alice Lamb Cole.)

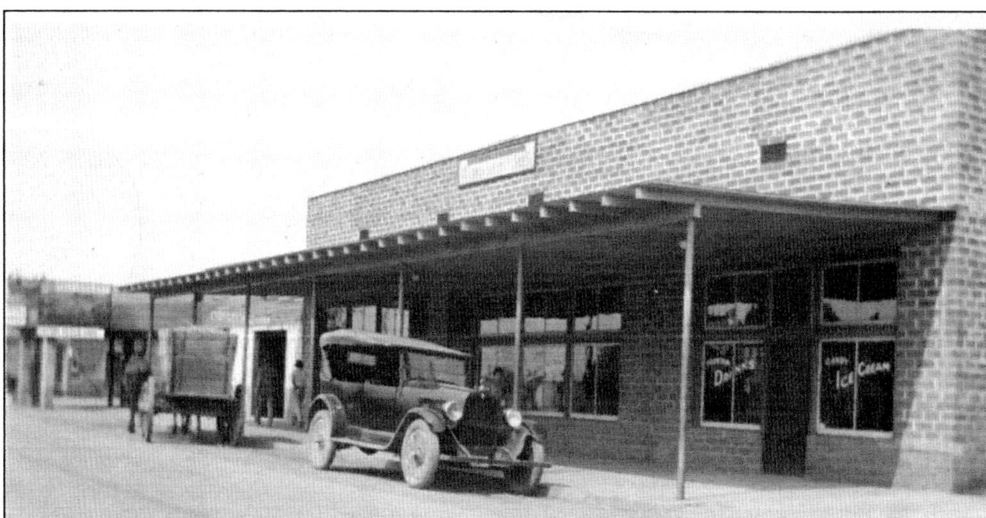

For many decades, Harpole's store on First Street was a Jacksonville institution. It was not their original establishment, however. That began in a barn-like structure at the turn of the century. (Opal Harpole Mallett.)

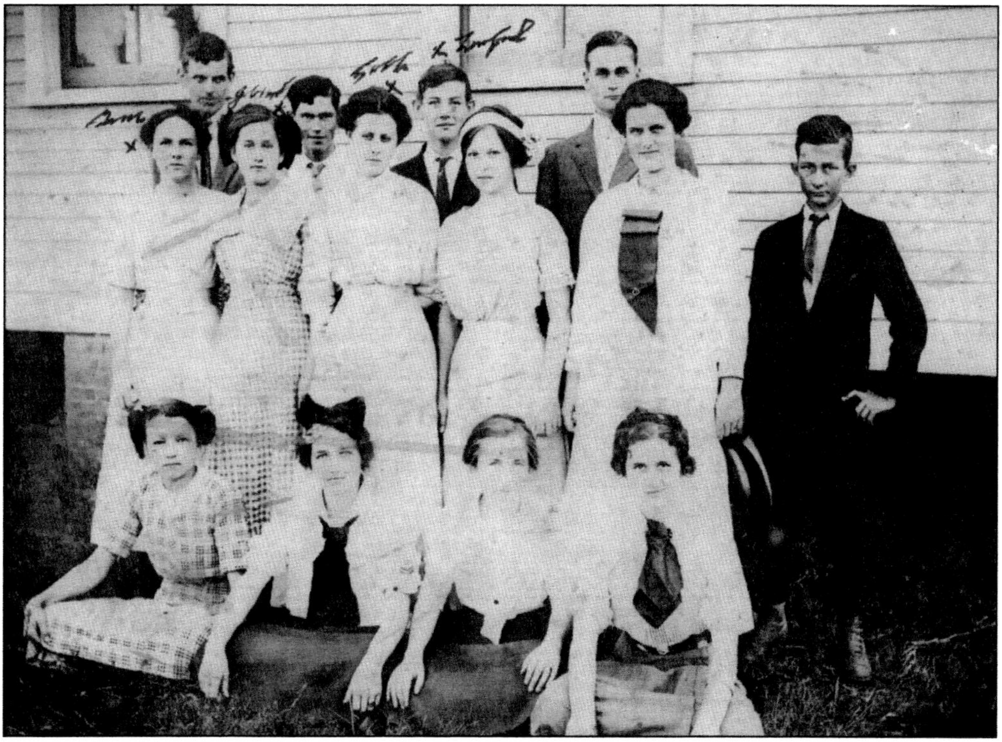

Here is the old Jacksonville School Class in 1912. (Opal Harpole Mallett.)

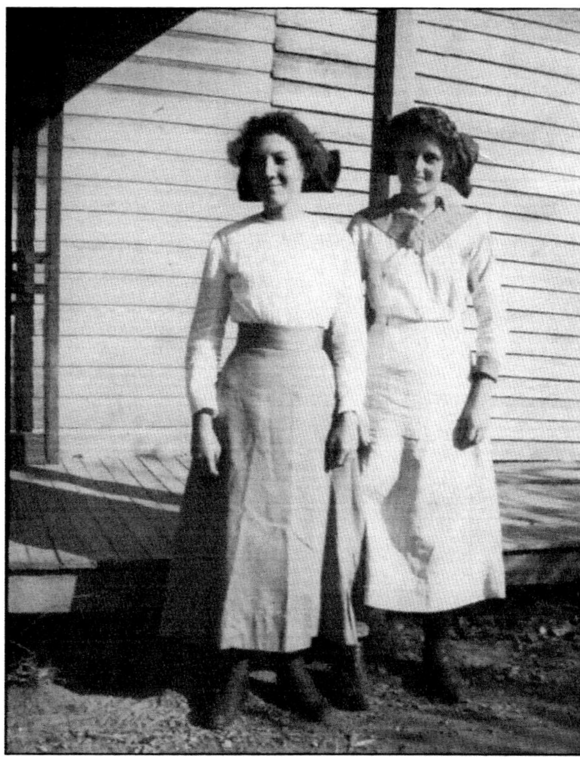

Mabel and Willie Brown stopped for this picture in 1913. (Mary Alice Lamb Cole.)

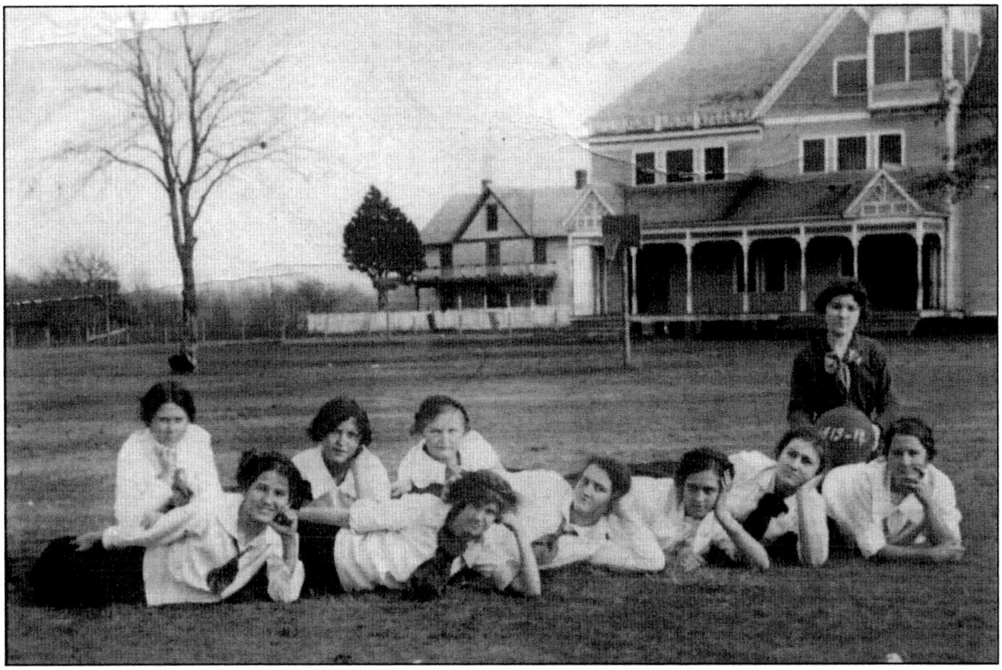

The Jacksonville School Class of 1913 girls' basketball team is pictured here. They are, from left to right, as follows: Belle Ray, Willie Williford, Penola Ray, Minnie Ray Douglass, Inez Douglass, Jewel Boyd, Callie Killingsworth, Tompie Stanphill, and Lenore Stanphill. (George Herman Taylor.)

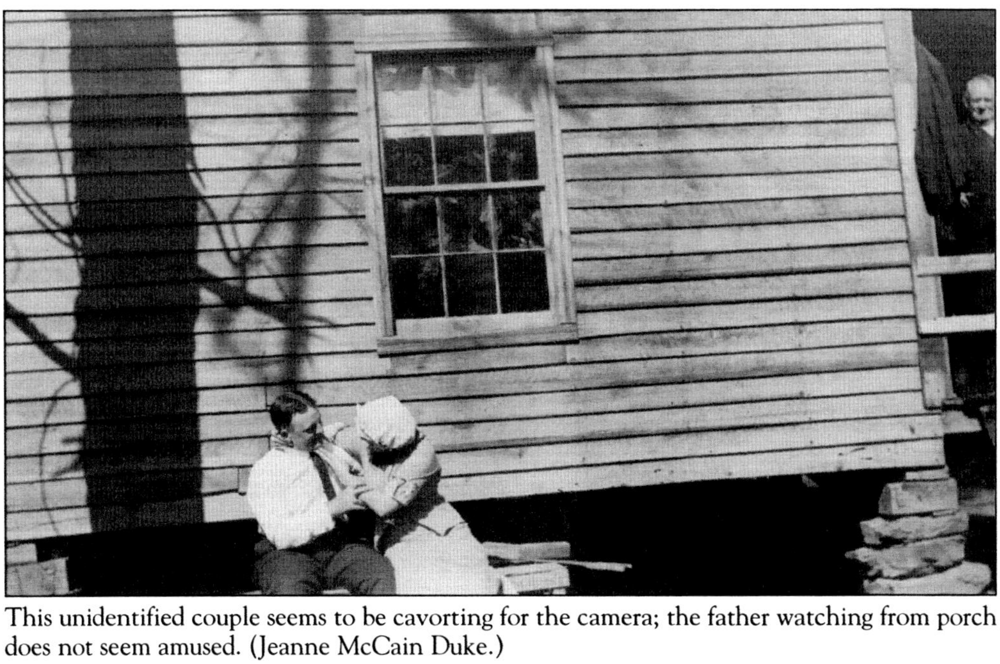

This unidentified couple seems to be cavorting for the camera; the father watching from porch does not seem amused. (Jeanne McCain Duke.)

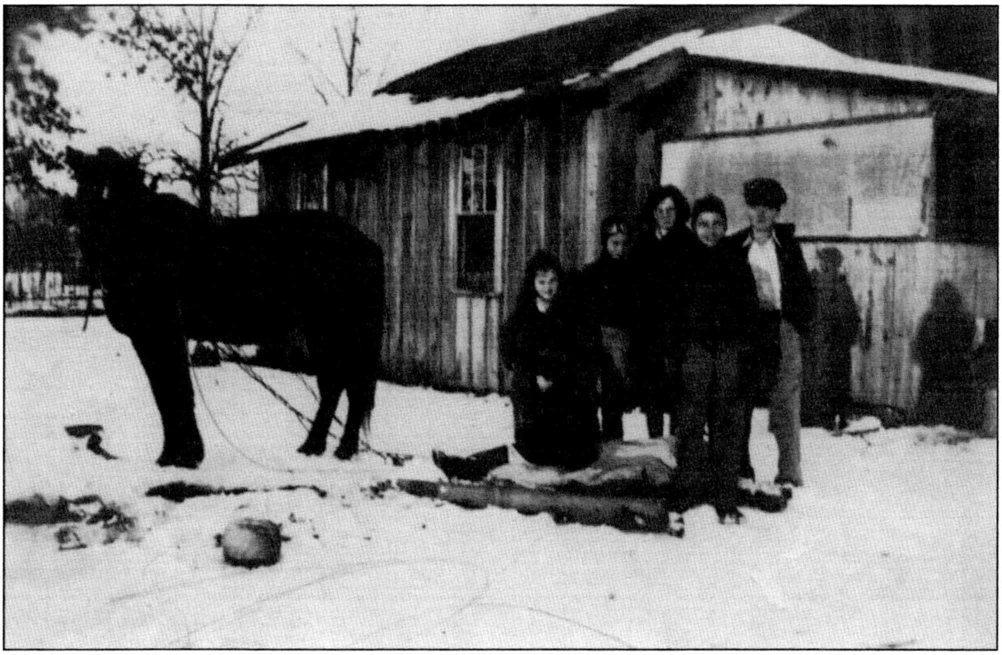

The horse-drawn sled was a boon for young people who had to get barrels of water from the spring or to bring in a Christmas tree from the woods. (Mary Alice Lamb Cole.)

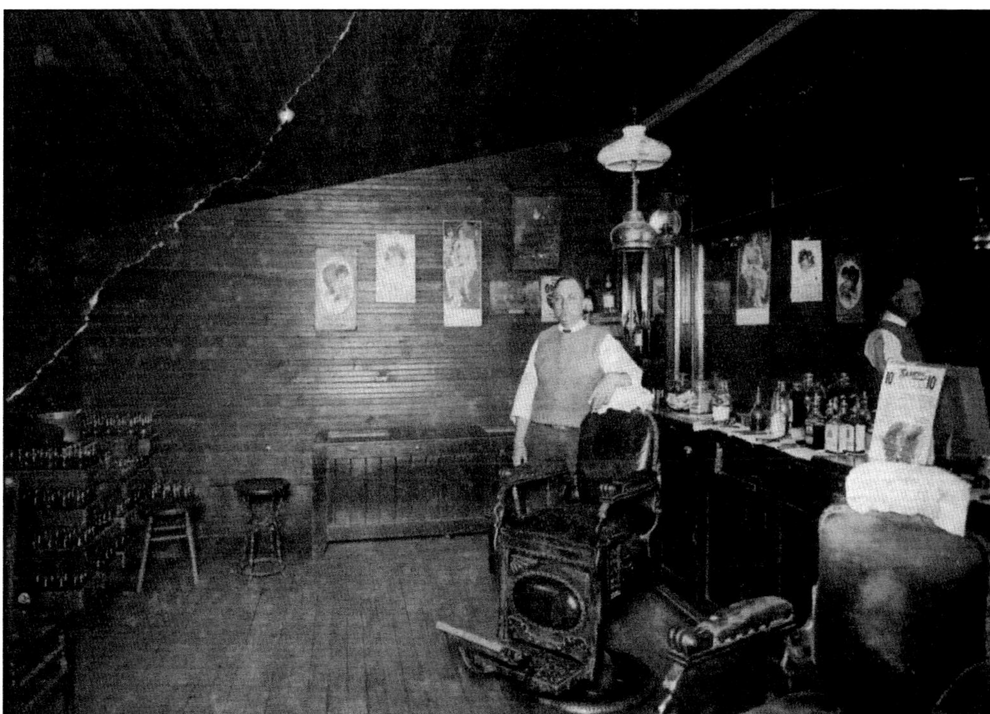

Harpole's Barber Shop was located in the First Street store behind the ice cream parlor in 1919. (Marie Harpole Hackett.)

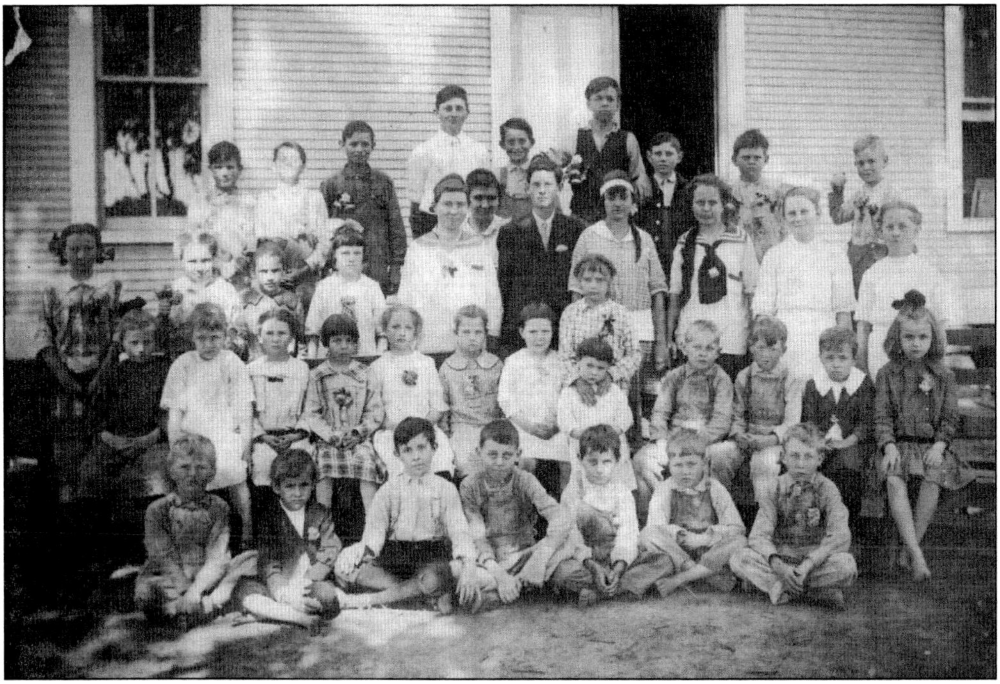

Here is the Vaughn School in 1912. (Jeanne McCain Duke.)

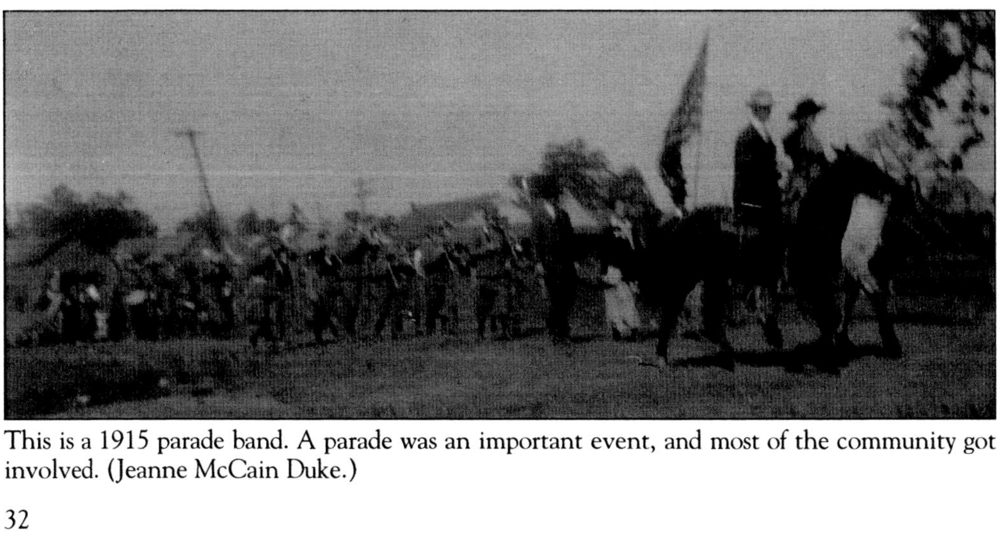

This is a 1915 parade band. A parade was an important event, and most of the community got involved. (Jeanne McCain Duke.)

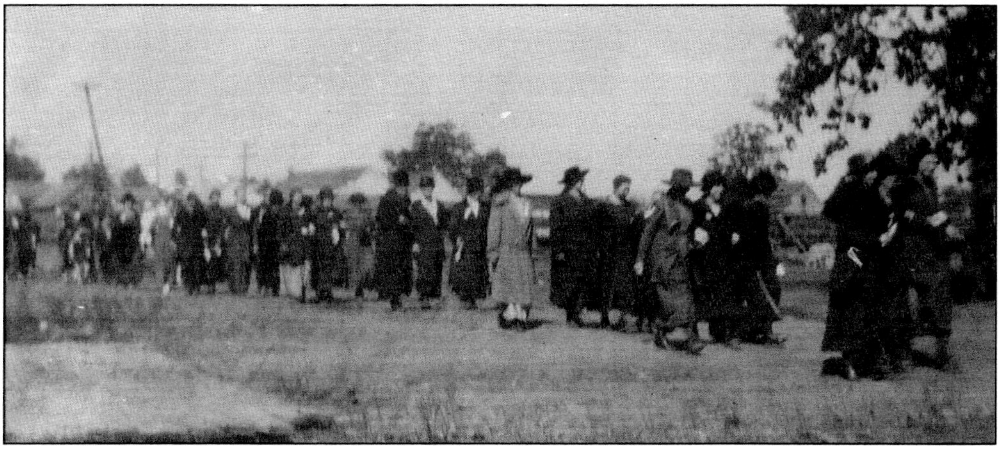

In this 1915 parade, are women marching for the vote? (Jeanne McCain Duke.)

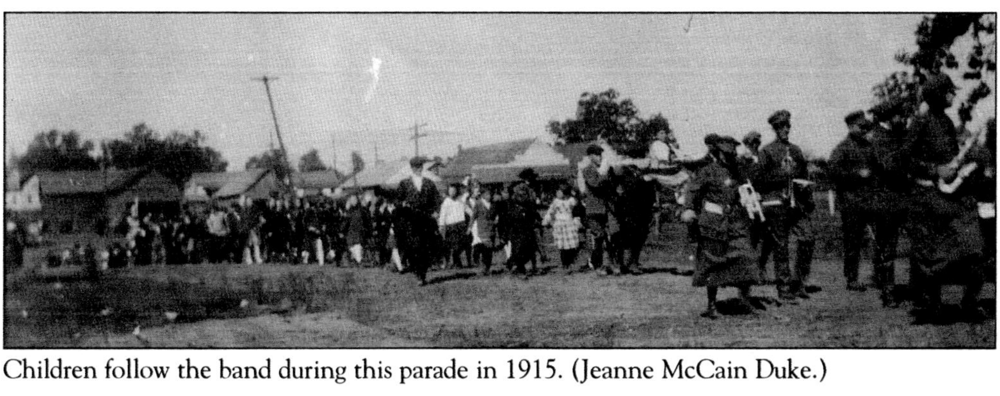

Children follow the band during this parade in 1915. (Jeanne McCain Duke.)

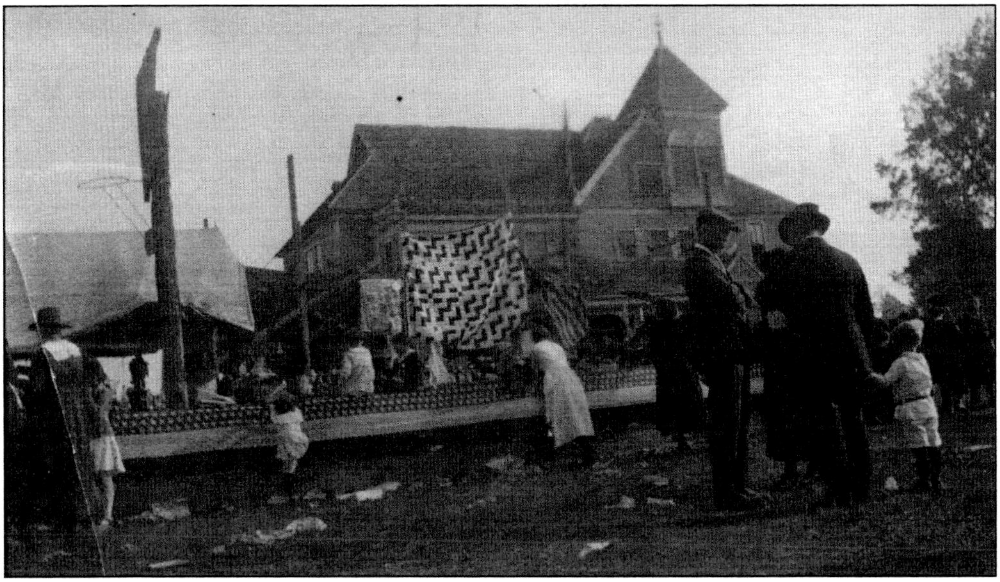

The Jacksonville School was the center of the community and a place of celebrations. The parade probably went down Main Street and ended at the school with a potluck supper. (Jeanne McCain Duke.)

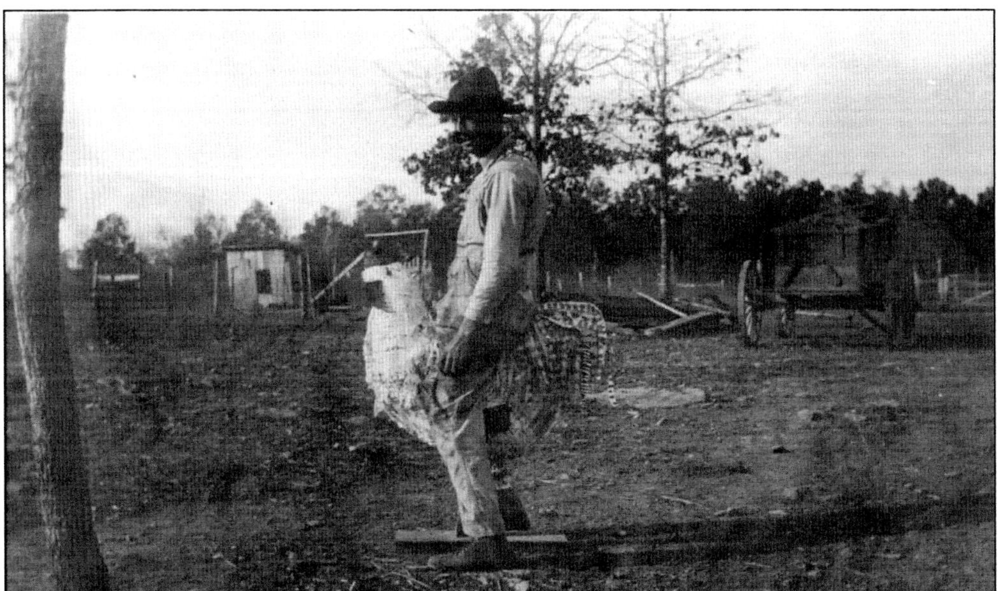

The particular significance of Chicken Man has been lost to history, but George Hamilton McCain did appear in the parade. (Jeanne McCain Duke.)

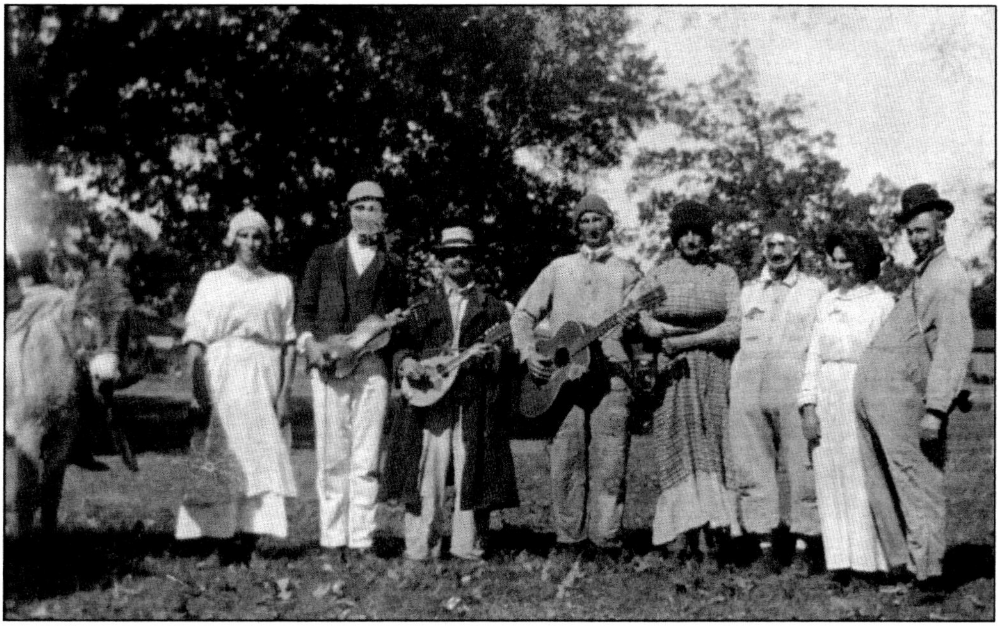

Time has erased just why these men dressed up for this 1915 parade, but it seems they were having a good time. (Jeanne McCain Duke.)

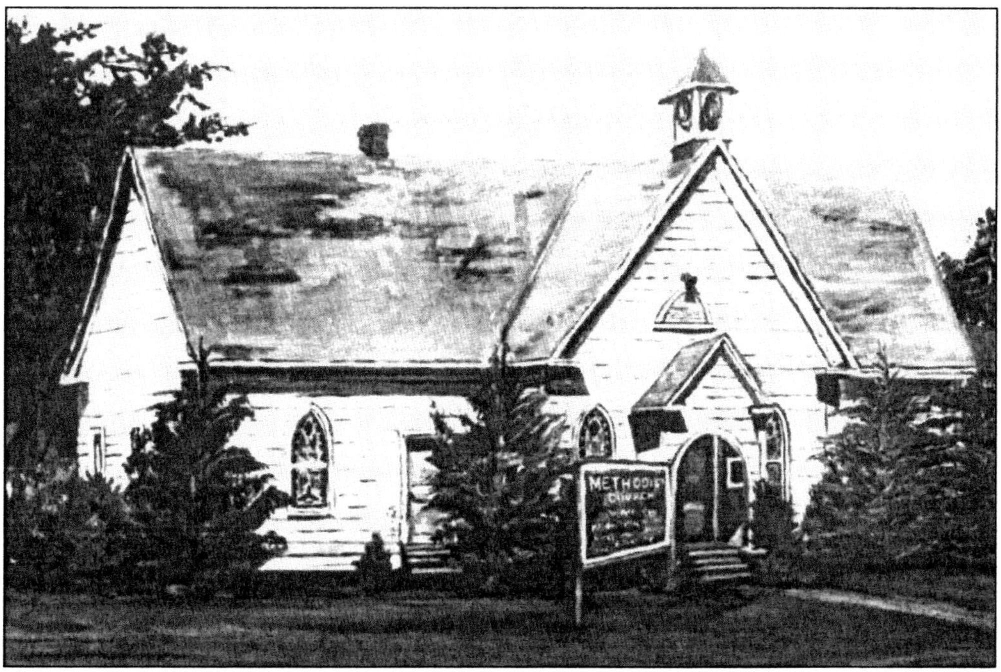

This is an old First United Methodist Church painting from the late 1800s. The church began in the 1840s, and was located in the Bayou Meto Cemetery. The building was also used as a school, for community functions, and as the Masonic Lodge. Around 1876, the logs from this structure were hauled by ox wagon to be used for the new church on Main Street. The church had two front doors, one for men and one for women, and there was segregated seating inside. The building was remodeled many times over the years and now only has one front door. (Carolyn Gray.)

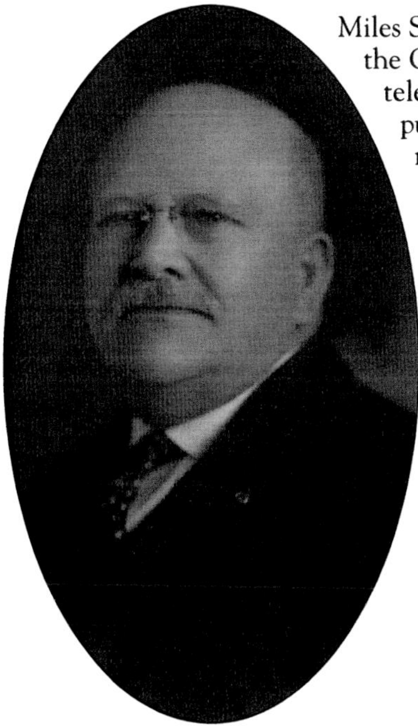

Miles Stone attended Jacksonville schools and then went to the Commercial College in Little Rock, where he taught telegraphy after completion of his studies. In 1885, he purchased the college, introduced new methods and regular office work into the studies, and wrote a series of textbooks for the innovative approach to teaching. (Tommy Dupree.)

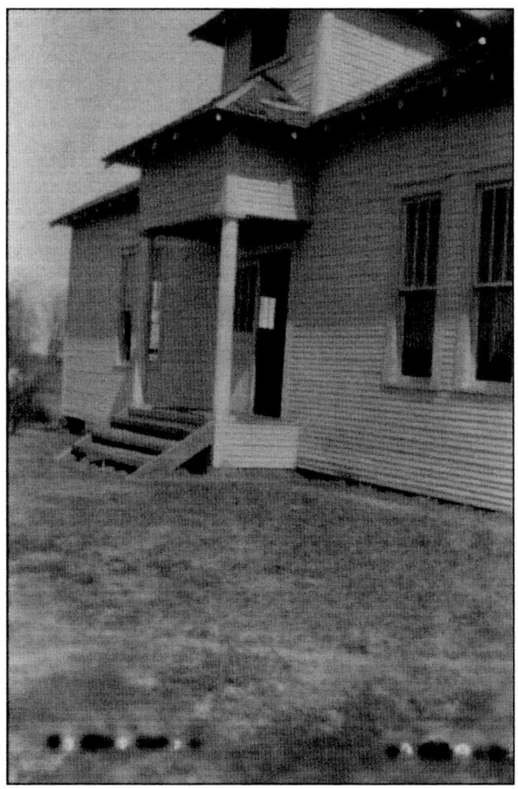

The First Baptist Church on Elm Street is shown with one of its many additions, about 1920. From the very beginning of the settlement, churches played an important part of community life. Some of the first churches included the First Baptist, First United Methodist, First Presbyterian, and Mt. Pisgah Baptist. (Mary Alice Lamb Cole.)

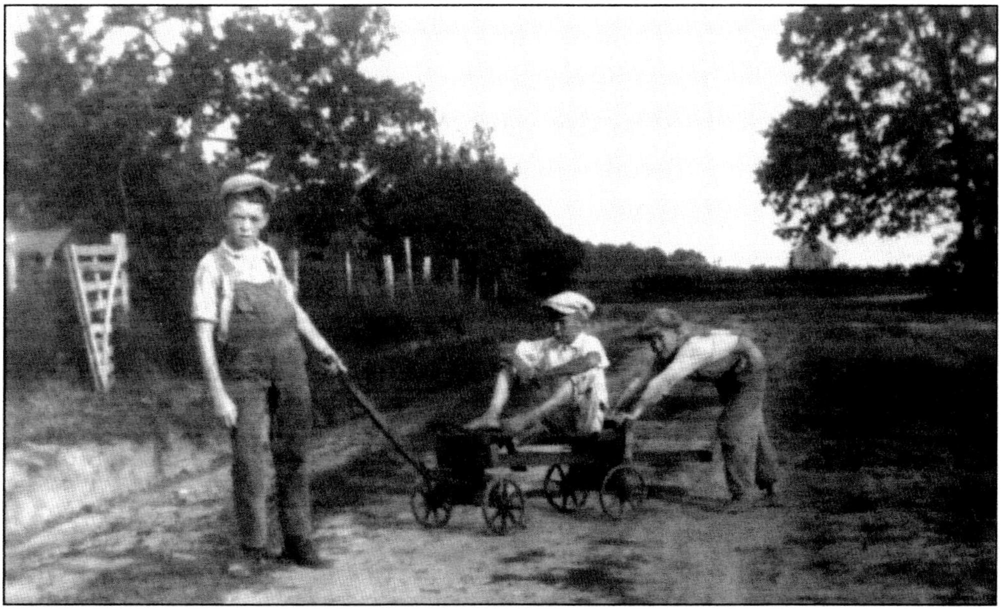

These boys pull a wagon on the streets of Jacksonville around 1925. They are, from left to right, as follows: Oscar Lorin Hudson, Walter Watson Nixon Jr., and Carroll Latta Hudson. (Esther Nixon.)

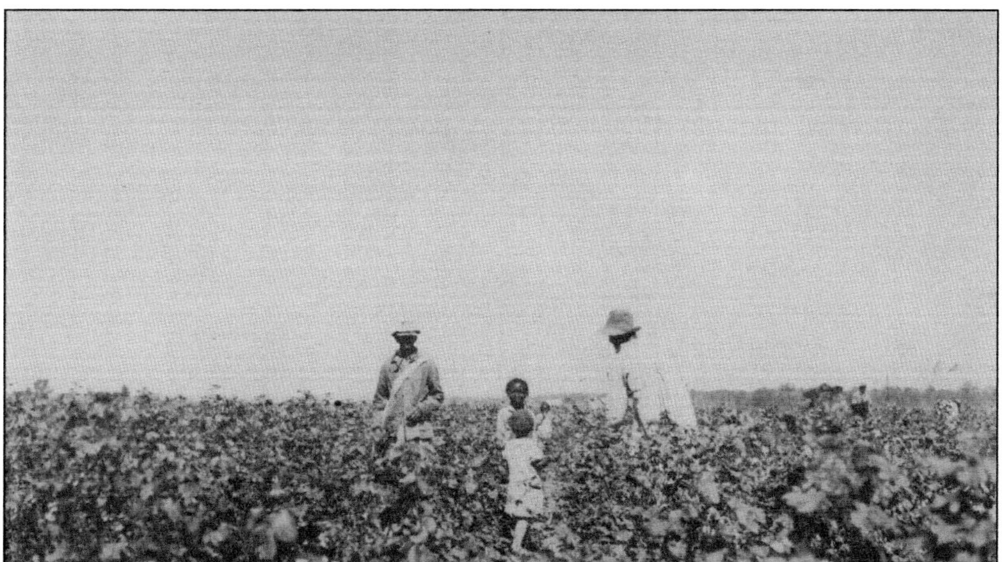

After the Civil War, some freed slaves were given land by former owners, while others were simply turned out to fend for themselves. Many became sharecroppers, clearing and farming the land for a portion of the yields. (Jeanne McCain Duke.)

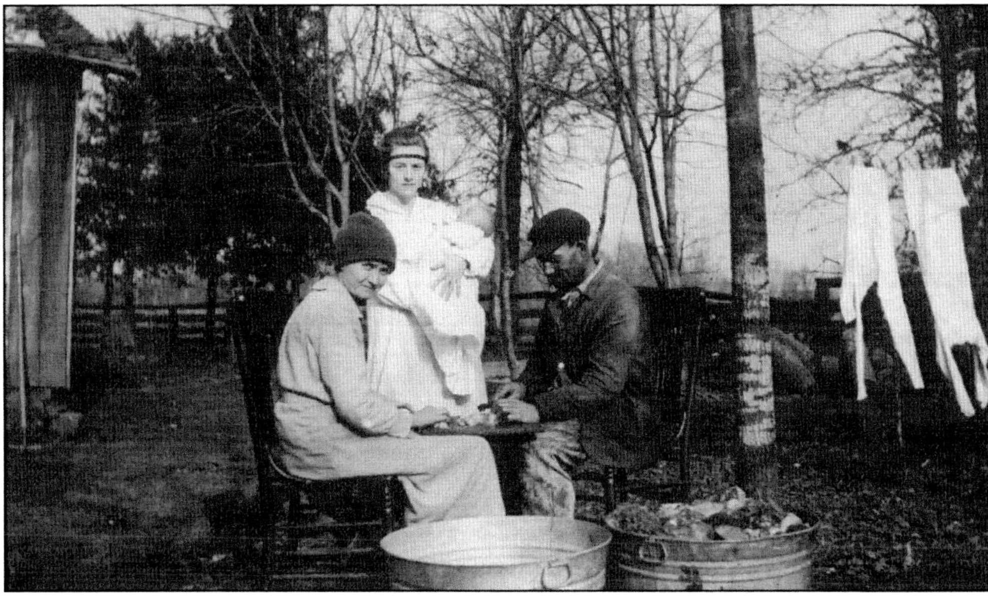

Butchering animals at home was part of rural life. These three people are sorting hog meat for curing and storage. (Jeanne McCain Duke.)

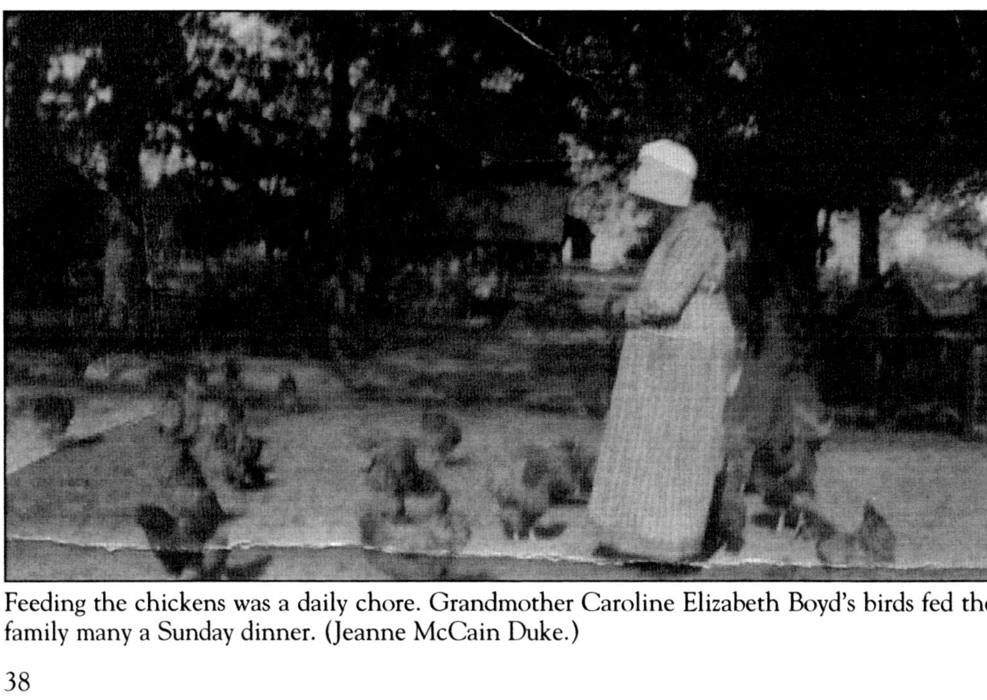

Feeding the chickens was a daily chore. Grandmother Caroline Elizabeth Boyd's birds fed the family many a Sunday dinner. (Jeanne McCain Duke.)

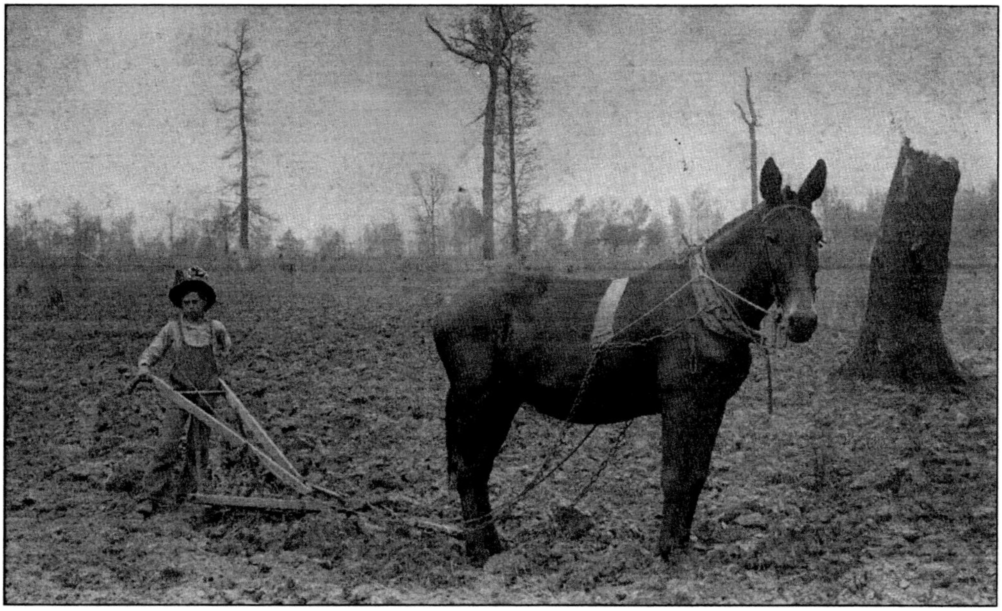

Children helped with all the chores in rural Arkansas. Harvey Lamb was skilled at plowing with a mule at a young age in 1909. (Mary Alice Lamb Cole.)

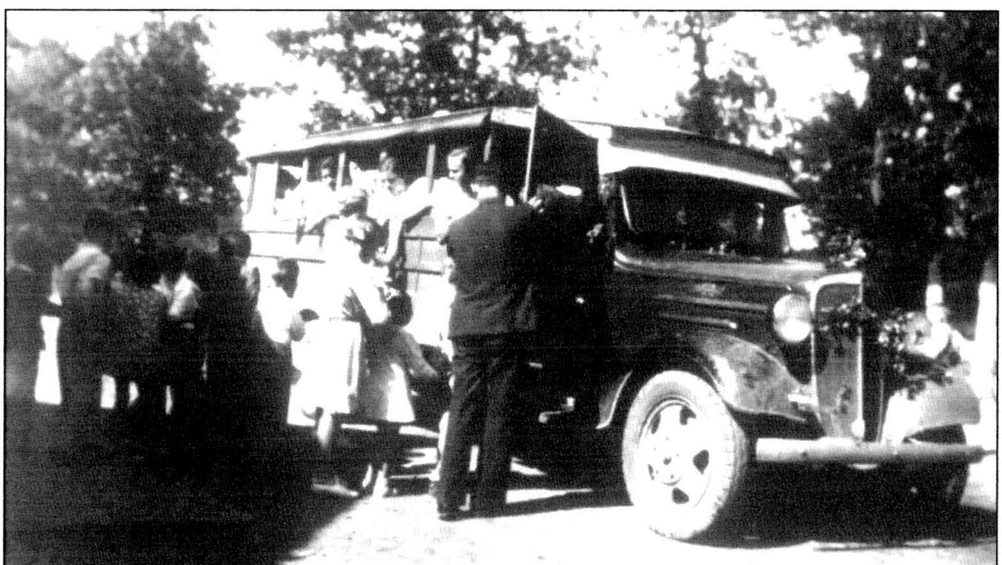

This Jacksonville school bus made the route and picked up children around 1925. According to one passenger, it was very cold in the winter, with no glass in the windows. (Jacksonville Historical Society.)

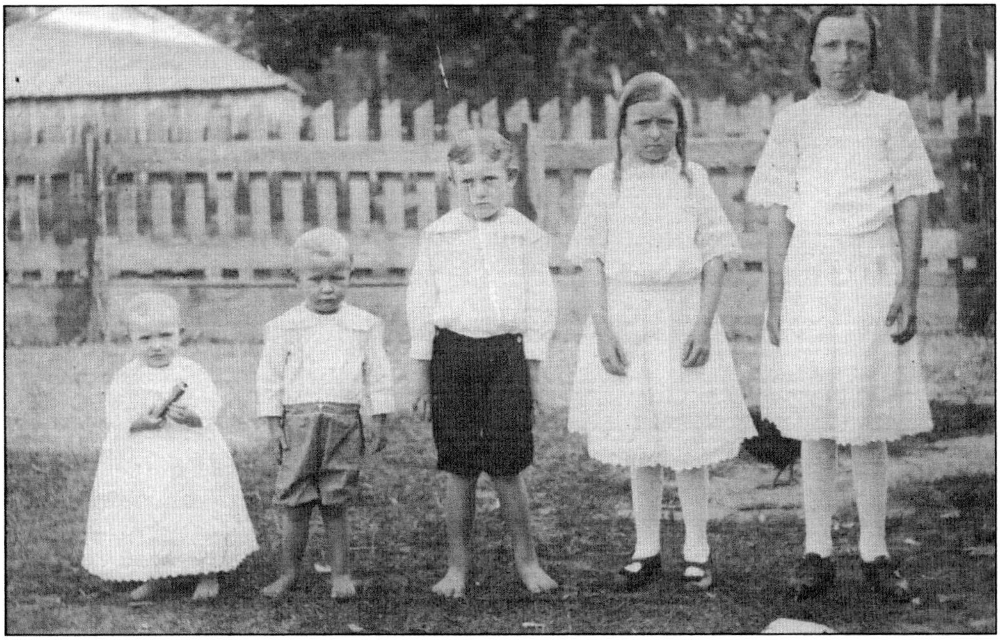

Not every picture-taking opportunity was a happy one. (Marie Harpole Hackett.)

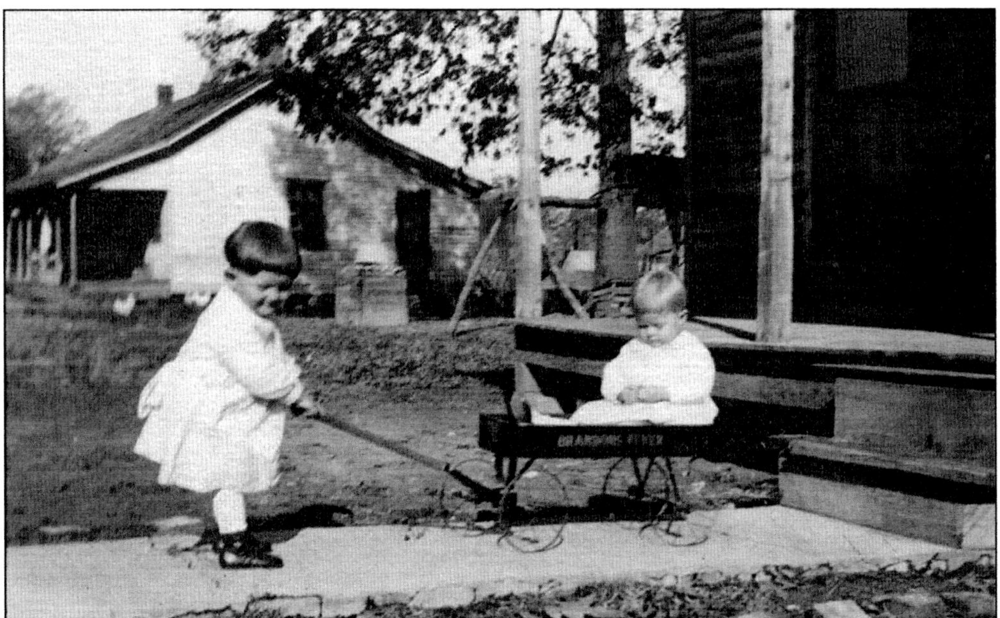

Marie (left) and Opal Harpole are shown here in 1920. (Marie Harpole Hackett.)

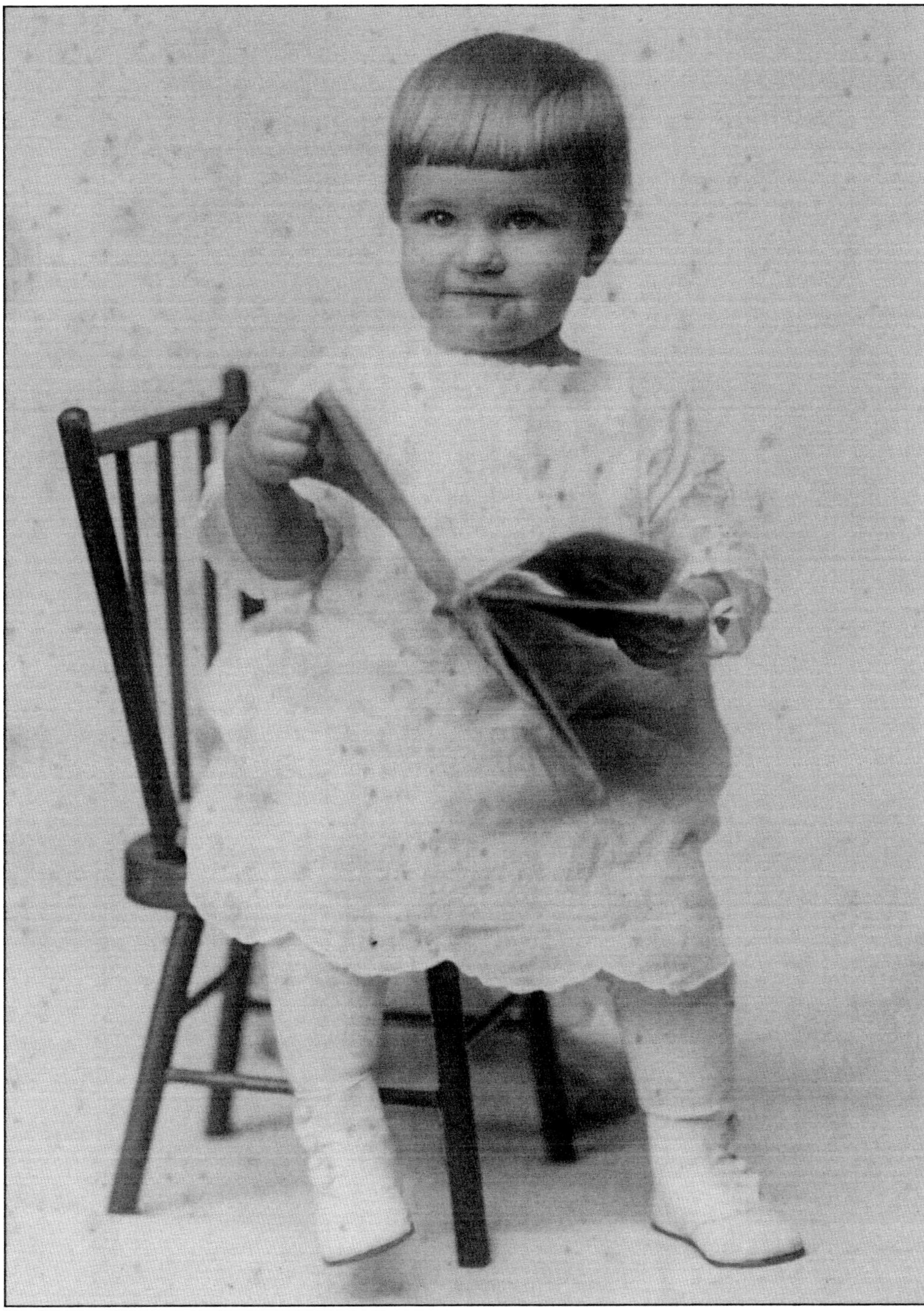

Murrell Taylor was to have a great impact on her community. A native of Jacksonville, she became a teacher and later served as principal of the elementary school, retiring after 38 years. Taylor also served on the board of the Jacksonville Elderly Activities Program and was involved with the First United Methodist Church activities. An elementary school was named in her honor. (George Herman Taylor.)

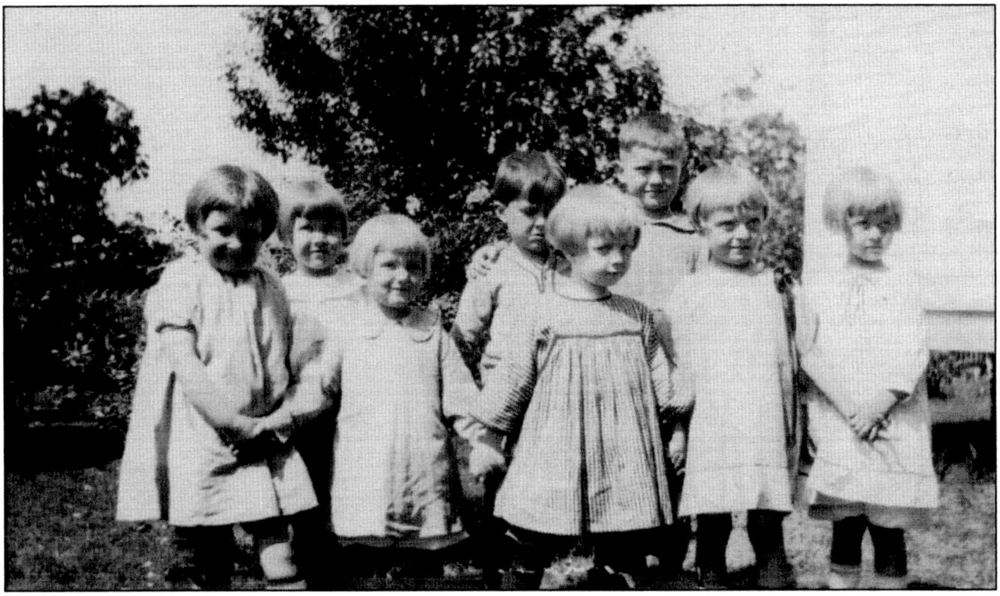

Jacksonville's first kindergarten class, shown here in 1923, seemed to have a uniform haircut code. Pictured, from left to right, are as follows: Opal Harpole Mallett, Mary Ann Nixon, Kathryn Beall, Jack Martin, unidentified, Bobby Henry, unidentified, and Marie Harpole Hackett. (Opal Harpole Mallett.)

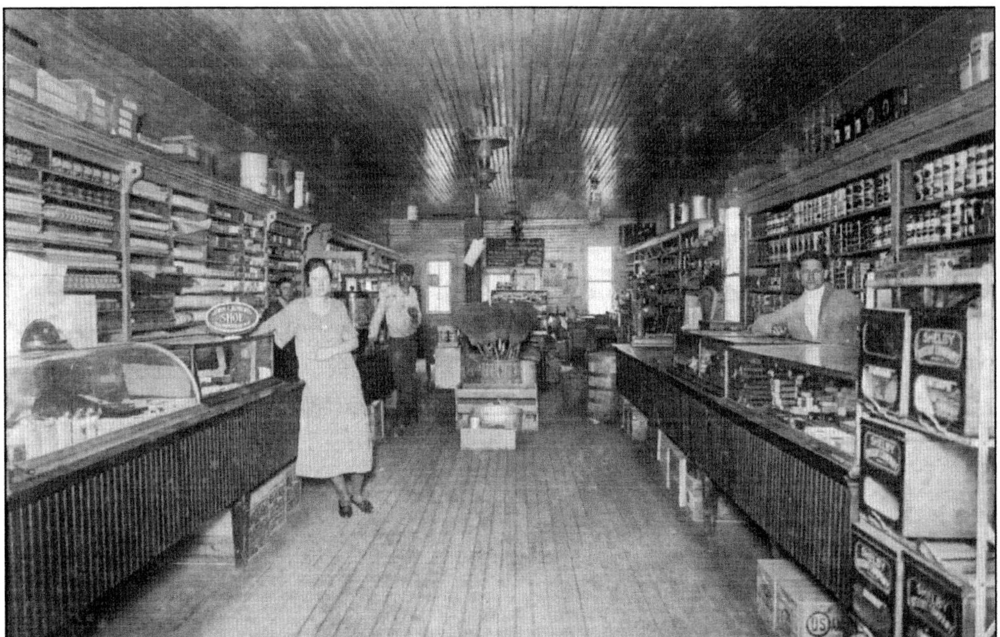

Harpole's Store changed with the decades, offering up-to-date goods for the Jacksonville community in 1919. Harry Harpole is shown at far right. (Opal Harpole Mallett.)

Harvey Lamb served in France during WW I. After the war he returned to his bride, Mabel Brown, and farmed and worked 23 years for Henry Brothers' store as a meat cutter. (Mary Alice Lamb Cole.)

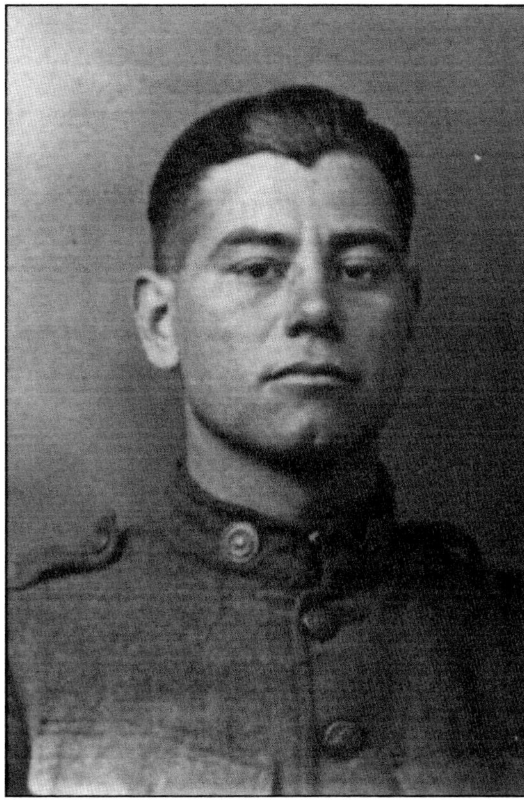

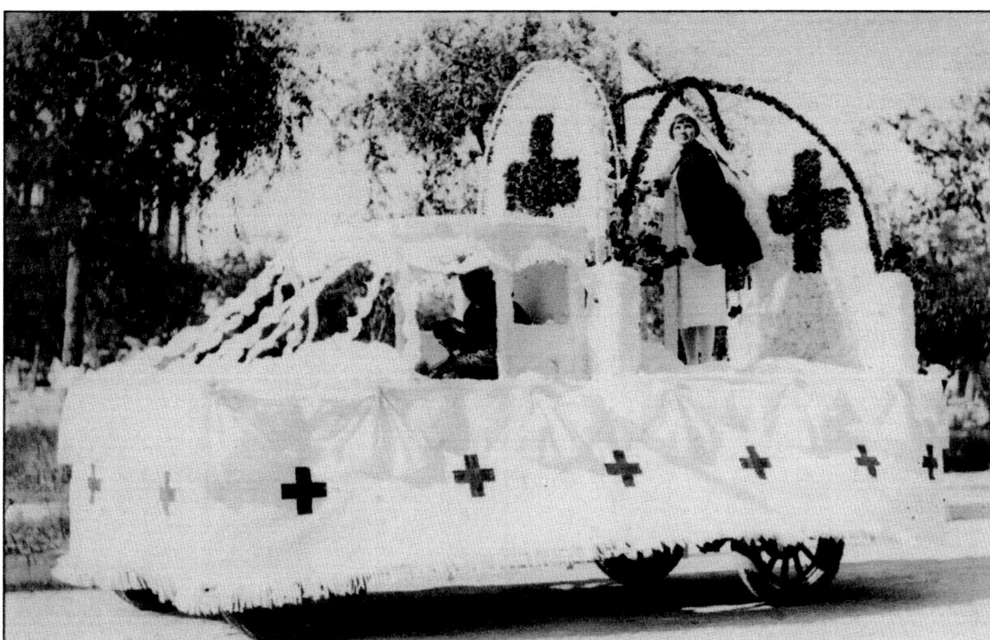

This is a WW I Red Cross parade float. (Jeanne McCain Duke.)

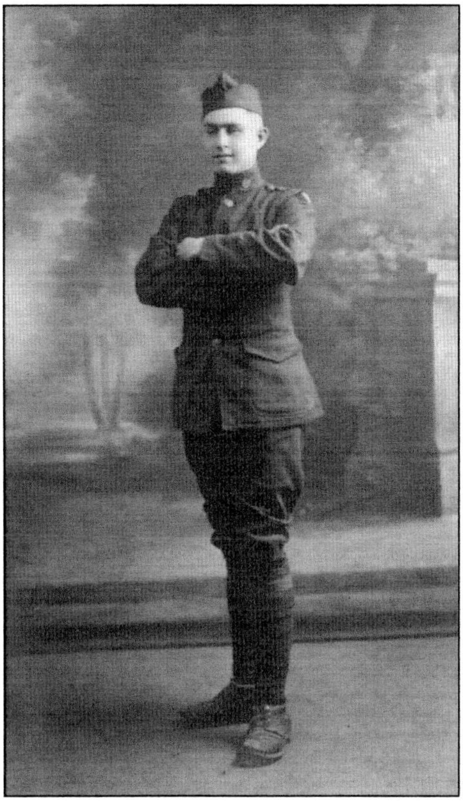

Haschal Boyd served in France during WW I. (Jeanne McCain Duke.)

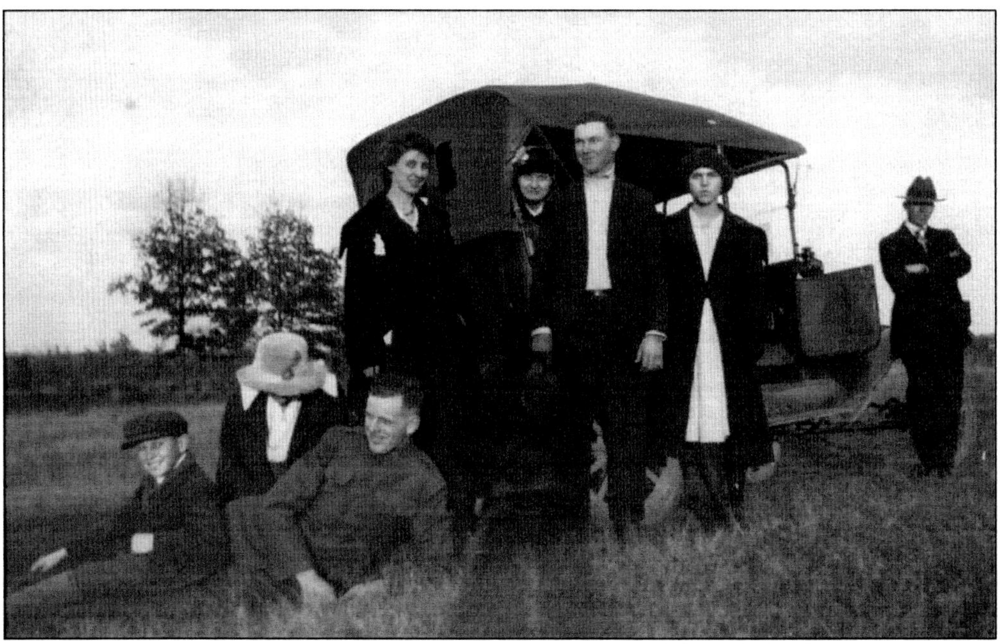

Leave time was all too short for the families and friends of WW I soldiers. (Jeanne McCain Duke.)

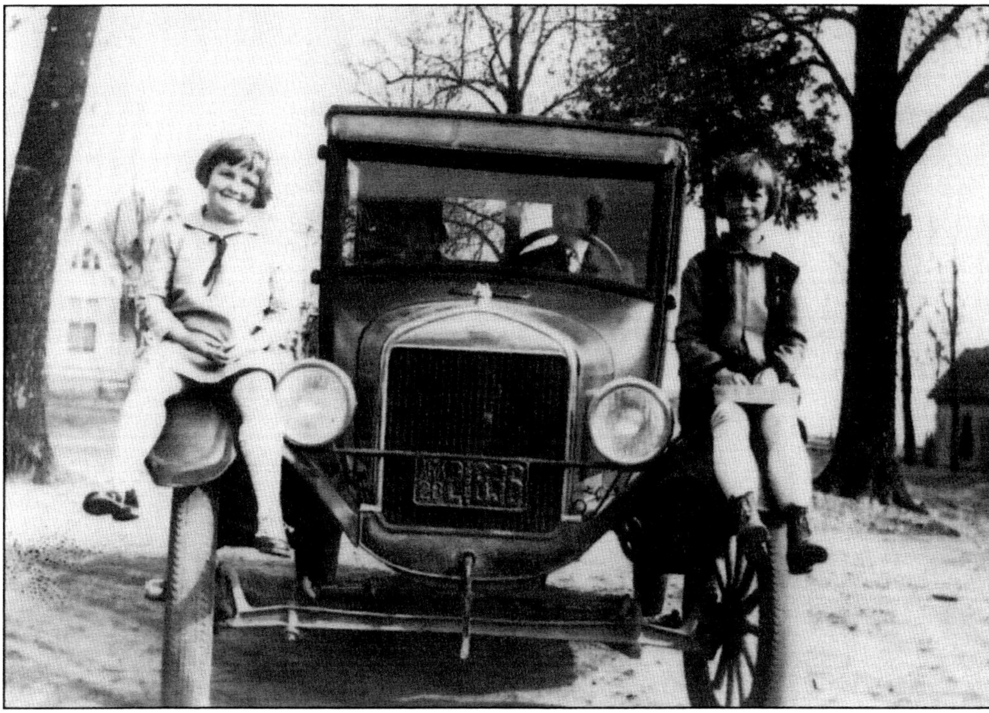

In rural America, cars were a prized possession and likely to be included in photographs, such as this one in 1928. (Marie Harpole Hackett.)

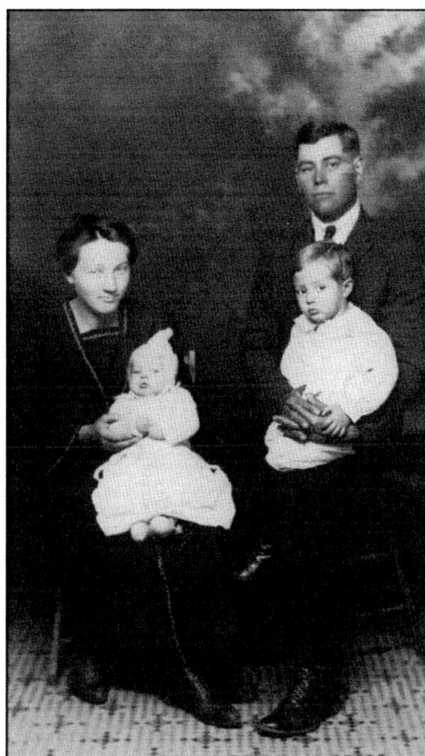

This 1923 photograph shows the Harvey Lamb family in 1923. Pictured, from left to right, are: Mabel, Marion, Virgil, and Harvey. (Mary Alice Lamb Cole.)

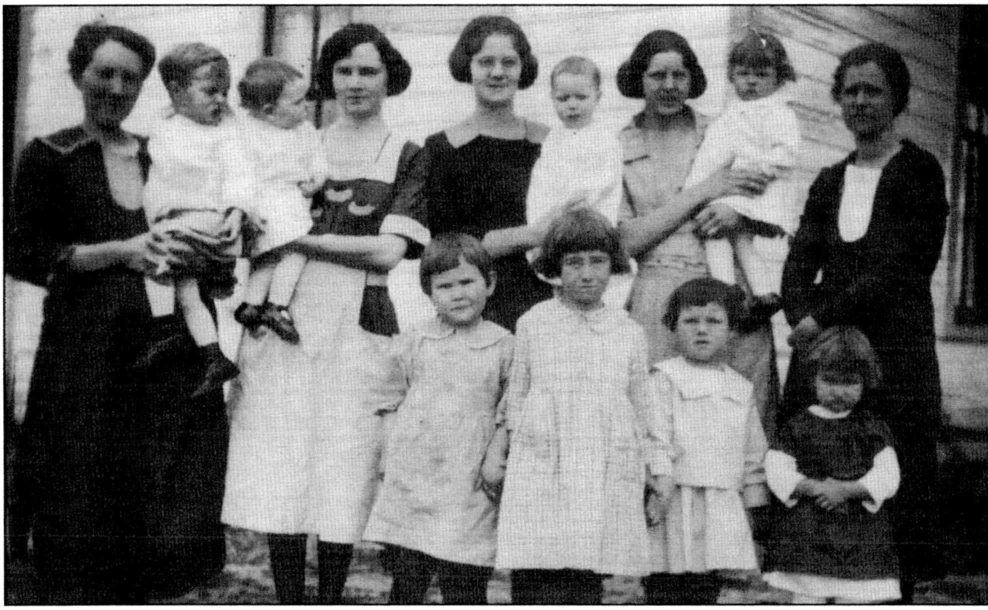

In this photograph taken of the Mothers of the Bayou Meto Club in 1928, Mabel Lamb and baby Marion are shown on the far left. The social companionship and educational opportunities the homemaker organizations offered were very important to the young mothers who couldn't get out much. "I feel like if I have not learned at least one thing—I have lost the day," wrote Mabel Lamb. (Mary Alice Lamb Cole.)

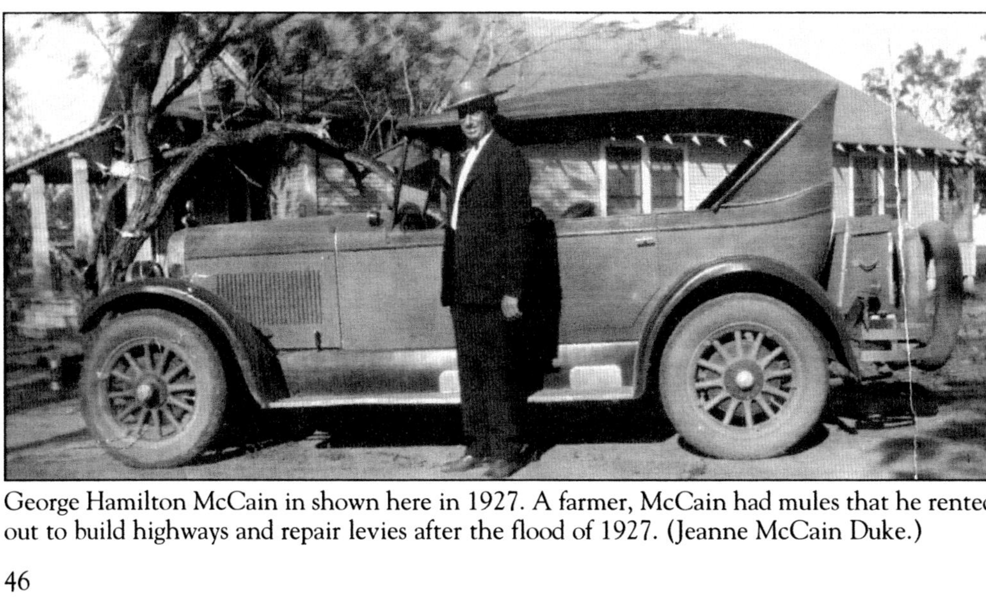

George Hamilton McCain in shown here in 1927. A farmer, McCain had mules that he rented out to build highways and repair levies after the flood of 1927. (Jeanne McCain Duke.)

This is the Spool Factory during the 1920s. Producing about 4,000 spools per day, this company received 2¢ per spool shipped. (Jacksonville Historical Society.)

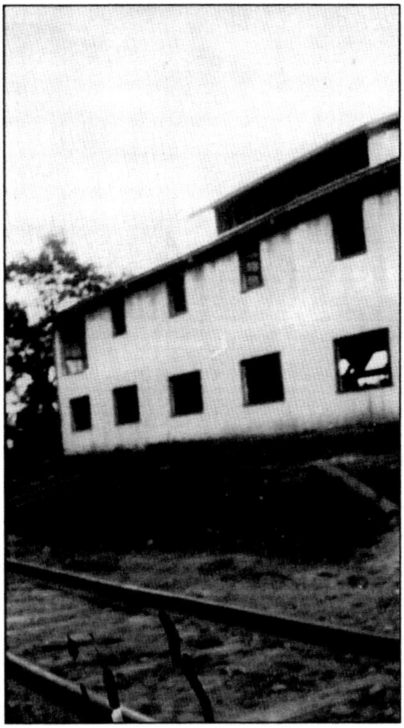

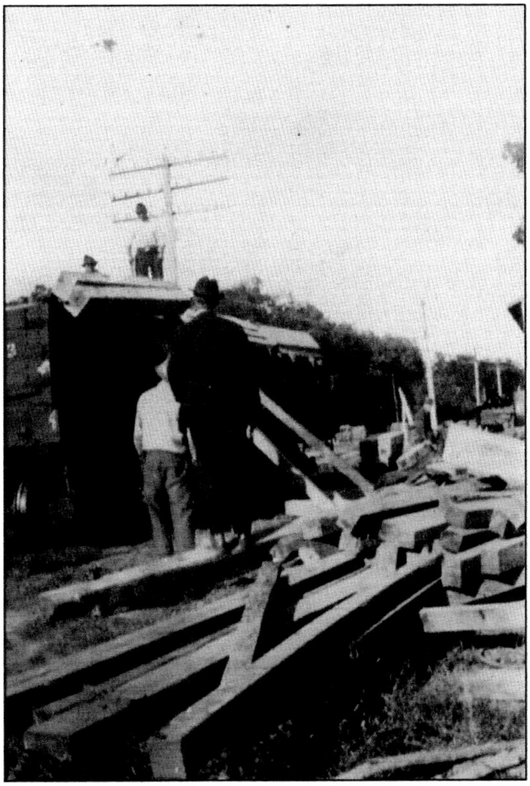

This 1920s photograph shows the Thompson Saw Mill. After the lumber was sawed, it was loaded into railroad cars and shipped out. Most of the timber production was cut into cross-ties to be used for rail bed foundations. (Jacksonville Historical Society.)

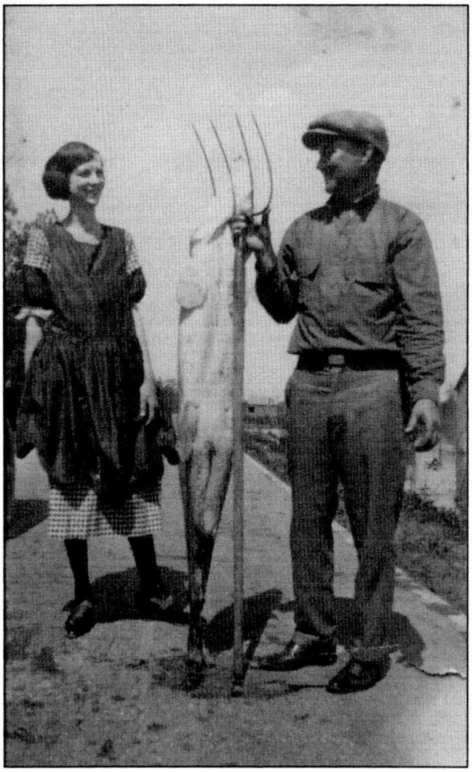

In the spring of 1927, rains swelled the Arkansas River and overflowed the banks. Alligator gar from the river went with the flow and were trapped in bayous and ditches around the area. The huge fish were caught and displayed proudly. (Jeanne McCain Duke.)

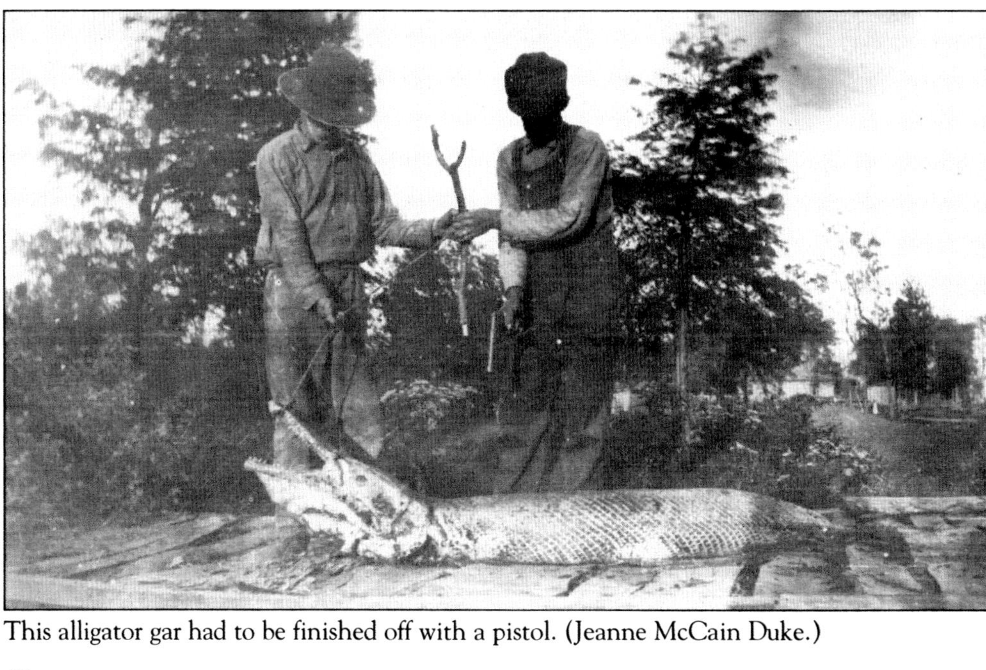

This alligator gar had to be finished off with a pistol. (Jeanne McCain Duke.)

Three

The 1930s

The Great Depression struck and was felt by the community, but life went on. In 1933, the Jacksonville school had to close several months early due to lack of money for coal and other operating costs.

Roosevelt enacted the CCC camps and from 1933 to 1942, young men between the ages of 17 and 24 left home, learned military discipline and a trade, built public projects, went to school, saw the country, and earned money to send home to their families. The camp at Jacksonville was one of the largest and finest in Arkansas, and the town had a population of about four hundred.

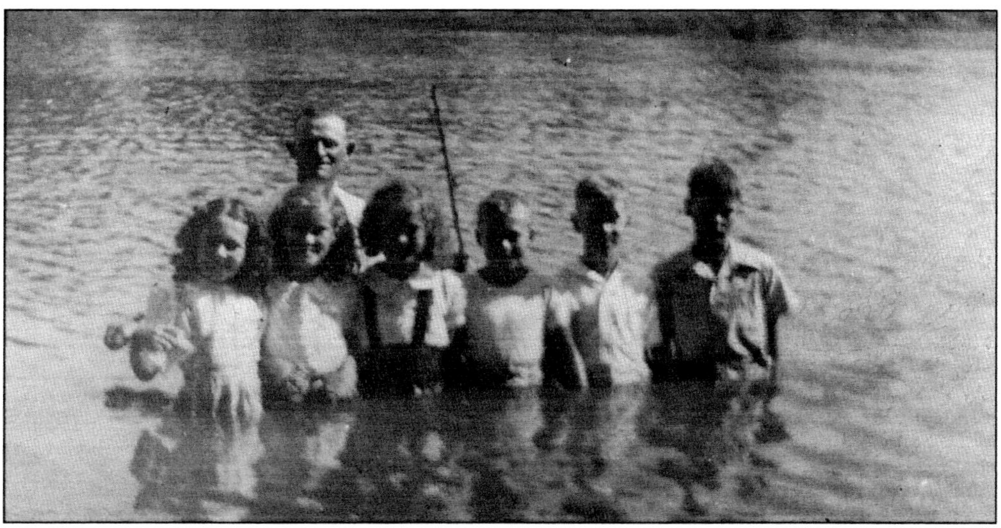

This baptism at Friendship Baptist Church took place in Sadler Pond during the 1930s. Immersion baptism is still practiced by some churches today. (Pat Boyd.)

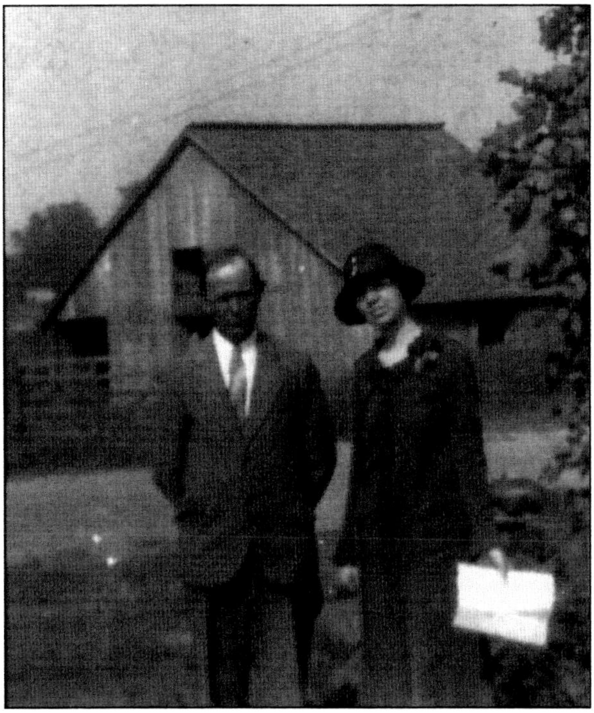

Walter and Hattie Nixon are pictured here about 1930. Walter was the postmaster for many years, delivering the mail in a horse-drawn wagon. Hattie was involved with many community projects and the First Presbyterian Church activities. (Esther Nixon.)

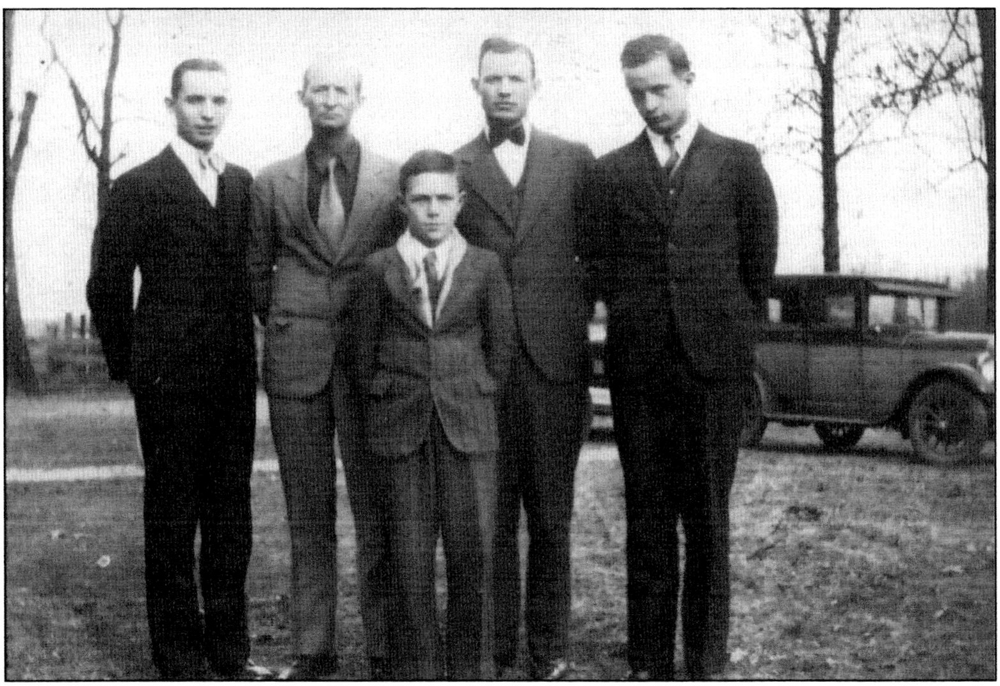

A young Kenneth Patrick Wilson is pictured with his brothers about 1930 on the Madden/Wilson homestead. Wilson was to play a big part in the development of Jacksonville after working his way through the University of Arkansas and serving in the Army. Instrumental in organizing the Jacksonville Chamber of Commerce, Wilson went on to start the Jacksonville State Bank and worked to secure the Little Rock Air Force Base for Jacksonville. (Larry Wilson.)

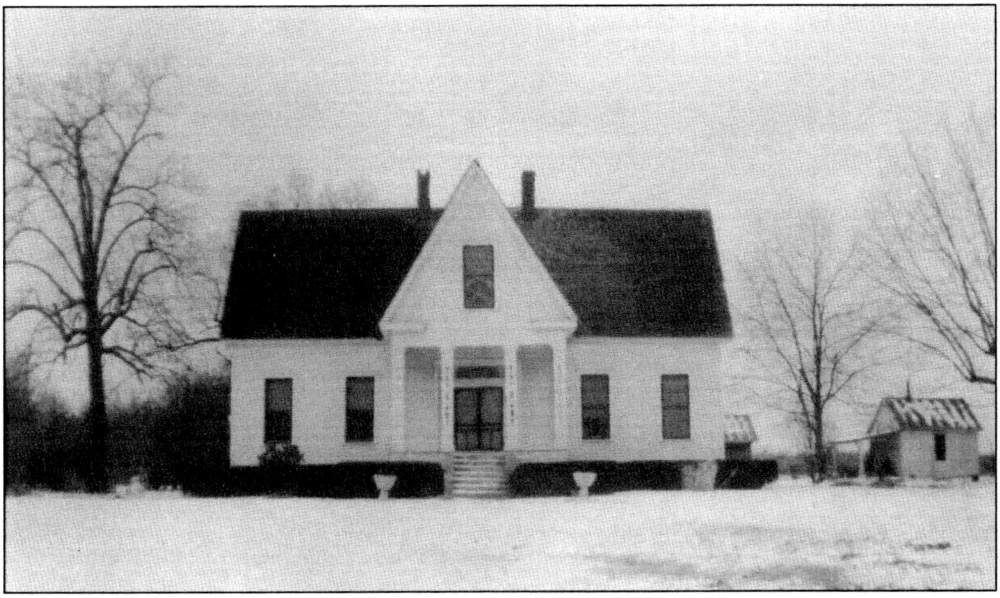

The Madden/Wilson homestead was one of the many home places forfeited to accommodate the Little Rock Air Force Base. (Larry Wilson.)

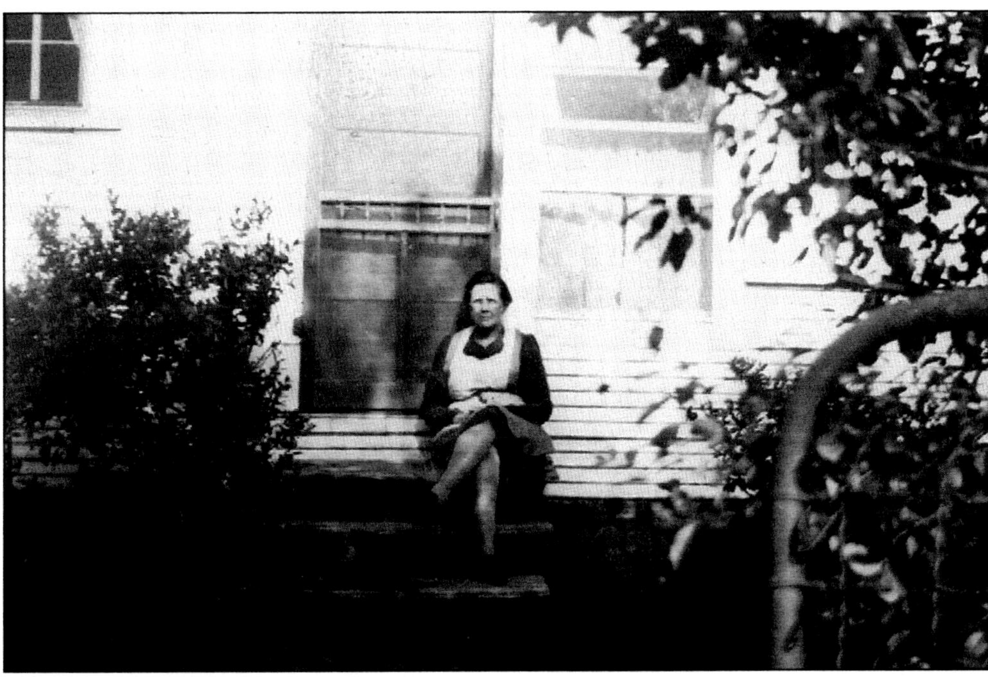

Callie Harpole is shown at 113 North Second Street during the 1940s. "The house was near the railroad tracks and during the Depression Grandma would feed the hungry men on that back porch," says Carolyn Gray. (Marie Harpole Hackett.)

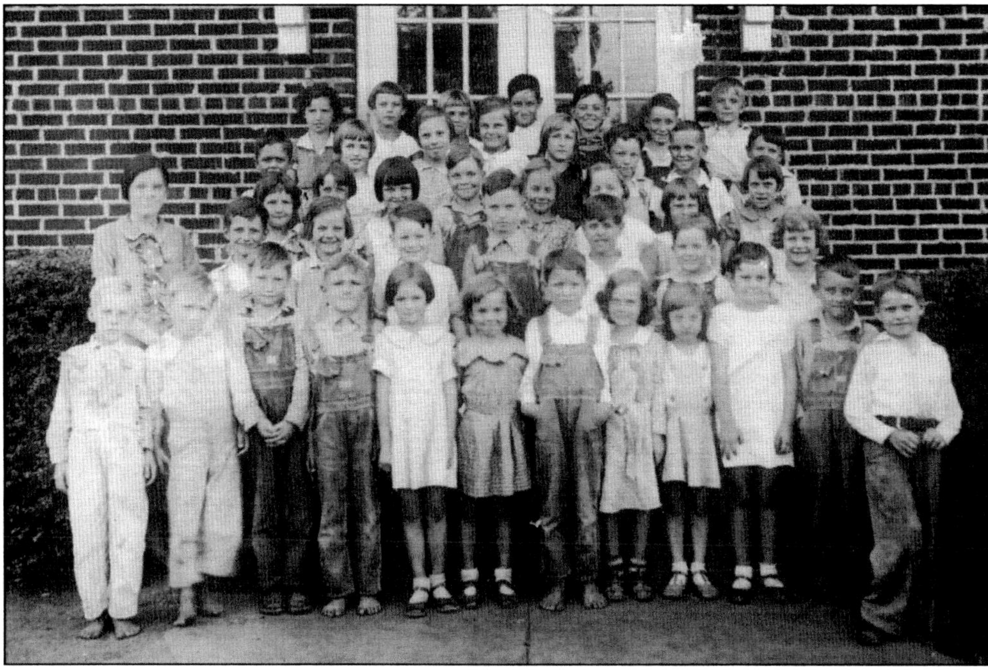

Jacksonville School second grade teacher Mrs. Murtishaw is pictured here in 1934. (Mary Alice Lamb Cole.)

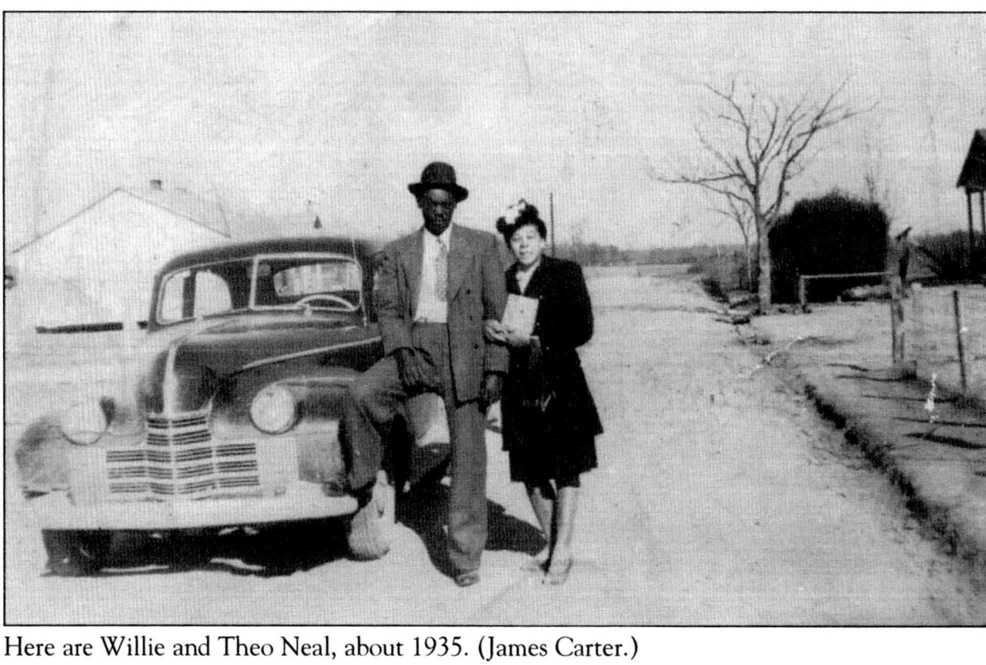

Here are Willie and Theo Neal, about 1935. (James Carter.)

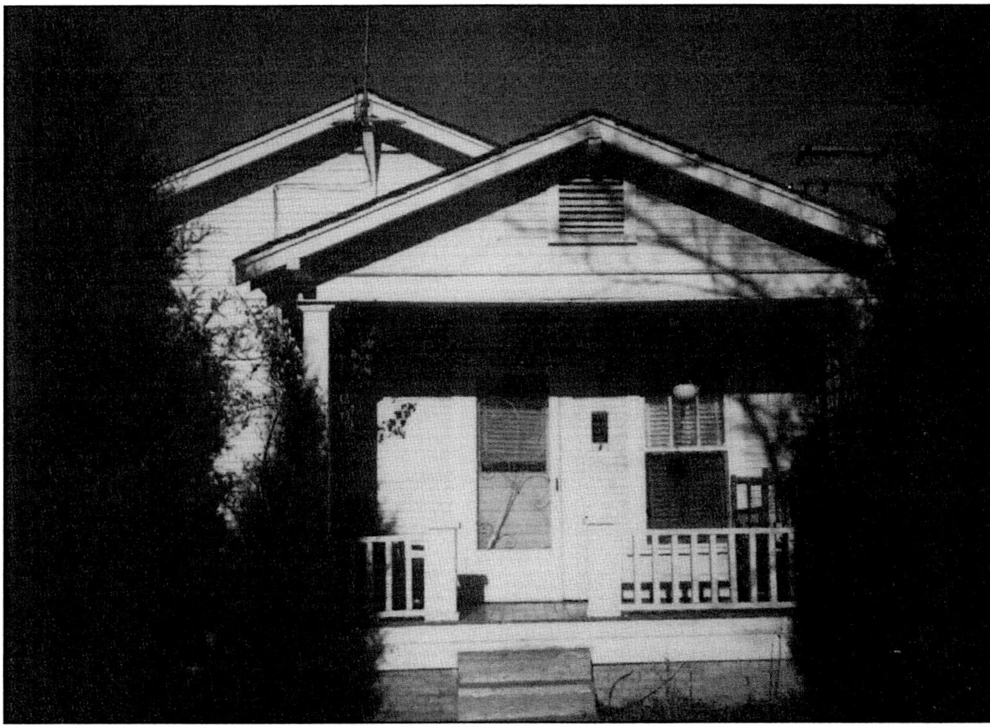

This is the first Telephone Exchange in Jacksonville in 1934. Located in the home of Mrs. Essie Chaney, the switchboard had 13 hookups, two of which were 5¢ pay stations. Miss Ruby Hardcastle (Hudson) was a telephone operator, and she got a room and $20 a month pay. (Nixon Library, Jacksonville.)

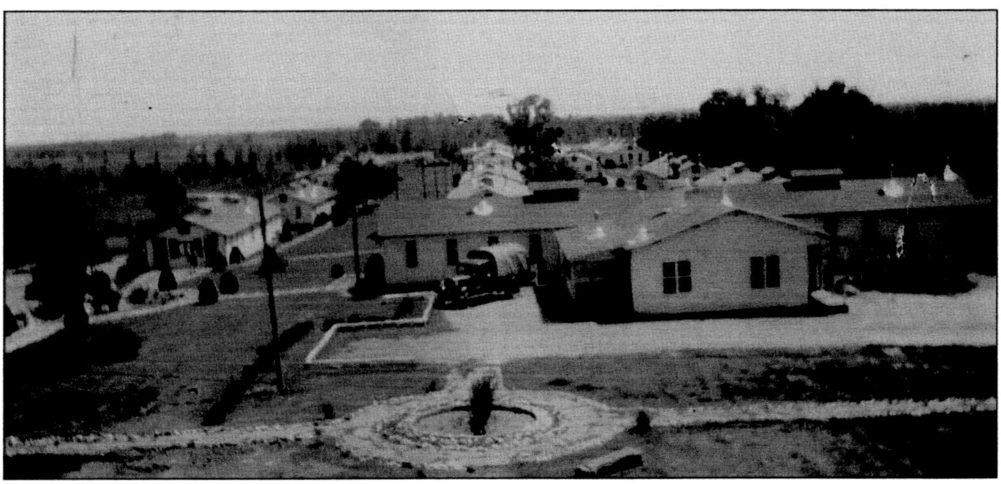

This is a Jacksonville CCC Camp. The Civilian Conservation Corp program was established April 4, 1933, by President Roosevelt, and within a month several camps were started in Arkansas. In the summer of 1935, there were 64 camps in Arkansas, and Jacksonville was considered one of the best. Young men between the ages of 17 and 24 were enlisted to learn a trade, do public works projects, attend school, and earn $30 a month, sending $25 of that pay home to their families. The program was run by the military and discontinued when WW II was imminent. (George Herman Taylor.)

COLD SANDWICHES

Chicken Sandwich 25, with Coffee .30
Lettuce and Mayonnaise ..... .15
Cold Ham Sand. Coffee or Milk .15
Cold Pork Sand. Coffee or Milk .15
Cold Beef Sand. Coffee or Milk .15
Cheese Sandwich, Coffee or Milk .15
Sardine Sandwich, Coffee or Milk 25

HOT SANDWICHES

Hot Beef or Pork with Coffee .. .15
Egg Sandwich, Coffee or Milk .15
Denver Sandwich, Coffee or Milk 15
Clubhouse with Coffee or Milk .30
Fried Ham with Coffee or Milk .15
Ham and Egg, Coffee or Milk .. .20
Hamburger Sand, Coffee or Milk .15

FISH AND OYSTERS

Fresh Eastern Oyster Stew 25
with Drink 30
Half Doz Raw Oysters 25
Half Doz Oysters Fried 30
Fresh Chinook Salmon 20
Fried Halibut Steak 25
Norway Mackerel 30
Cove Oyster Stew 25
Imported Sardines, Potato Salad .25
Pickled Herring, Potato Salad ...25
Steamed Finnan Haddie 25

-x- Saturday —— —

Split Pea Soup 5c
Homemade Chili ......

EN

Grilled Pork Chops wi
Fried Turkey Livers a
Turkey Hash . ...
Veal Stew with Green
Hamburger Loaf, Spa
Beef Tenderloin Steak
Pork Tenderloin, Fried
Fresh Side Pork, Appl
Hot Combination Dinn
Fried Halibut, Lemon
Pot Roast with Baked
Fried salmon, drawn b
Fried Sweet Potatoes a
Head Cheese and Potat
Roast beef with brown
Roast leg of pork with
½ dozen fried oysters,
Baked hash ....
Boiled Norway Macke
Pickled Norway herrin
Beef stew with vegetab
Fried Liver, Pan Gra
Fried Corn Meal Mush
Scrambled Brains and
Little Pig Sausage, Co
Vegetable Dinner, Po
Old Fashion Steak, P
Breaded Veal Cutlets,
Sirloin Steak Smother
Hamburger Steak, Br
Weiners and Sauerkra
Liver and Onions or
Homemade Sausage,
Pickled Pig Feet Pot

This menu dates from December 26, 1936. George Taylor traveled all over the country working with the CCC crews. He was in Spokane, Washington, on the day after Christmas and kept this

— Dec. 26, 1936 -x-

with Meals

.... 10

Sauce .... .25
n .... .25
.... .15
.... .20
.... .15
con .... .30
Potatoes .... .25
.... .20
.... .20
.... .25
.... .25
.... .20
on .... .15
.... .20
.... .20
.... .25
w .... .30
.... .10
ed Potato .... .30
o salad .... .25
.... .10
.... .15
con .... .15
.... .20
ravy .... .20
gg .... .20
y .... .20
Gravy .... .20
Onions........... .35
vy .... .15
otato Salad ...... .15
.... .20
Gravy .... .15
d .... .15

DESSERT SPECIALS

Cake or Pie and Coffee 15
Doughnuts or Rolls and Coffee ..10
Tomato Juice 10

Radishes or Green Onions 10

Sliced Tomatoes 10

EGGS and OMELETTES

Two Eggs Fried, Boiled
or Scrambled 15
Three Eggs 20
Minced Ham and Eggs 20
Ham and Eggs 25
Bacon and Eggs 25
Plain Omelette 20
Cheese or Ham Omelette 25
Green Pepper Omelette 25
Scrambled Brains and Eggs 20
Two Poached Eggs on Toast......20
Two Eggs Vienna Style..........35

STEAKS and CHOPS

Plain Steak 25
Pork Steak 25
Sausage, Homemade 15
Little Pig Sausage 20
Hamburger Steak 15
Pork Chops 25
Liver and Onions 20
Liver and Bacon 20
Liver and Eggs 20

menu. Prices have changed a little. (George Herman Taylor.)

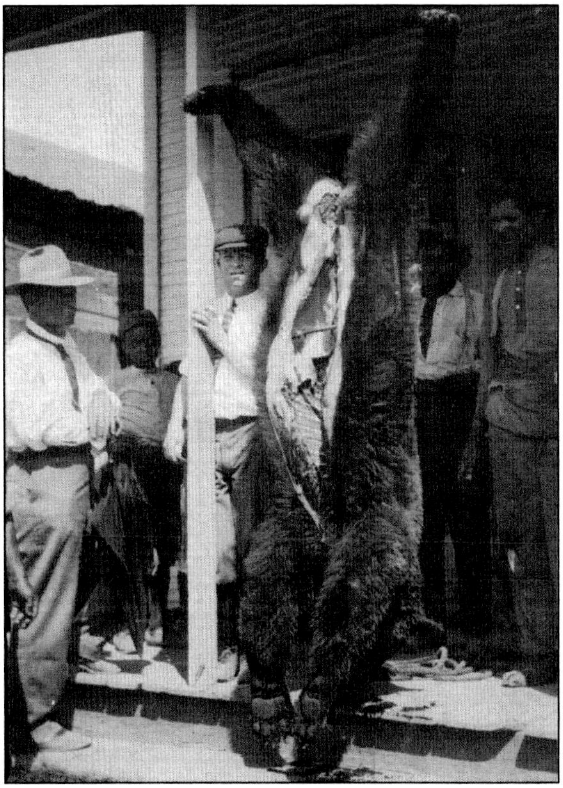

In the early part of the century, an occasional bear was taken and was quite a curiosity. (Jeanne McCain Duke.)

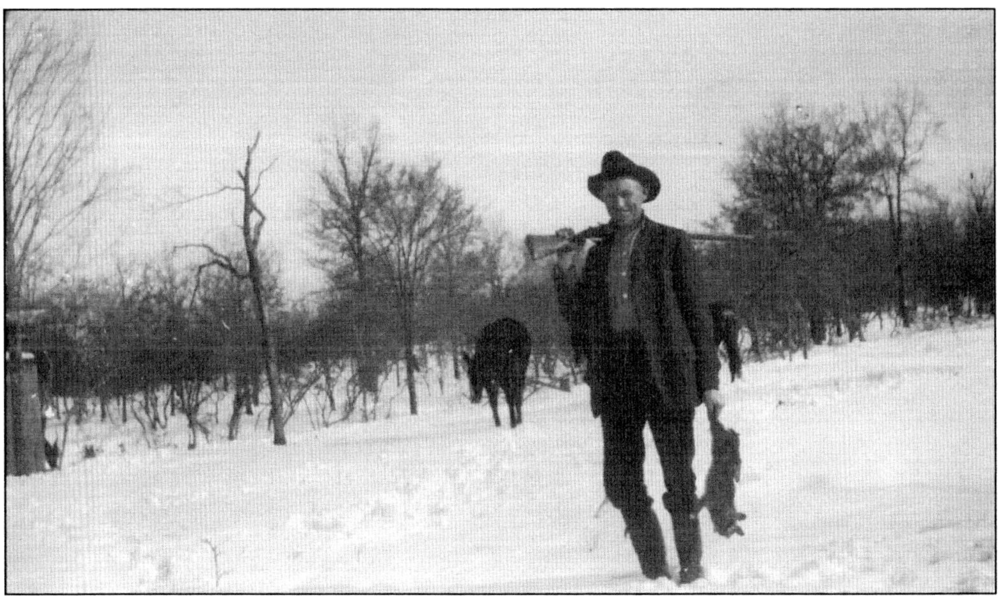

Wild rabbit was good eating any time of the year, but even more so in winter. (Jeanne McCain Duke.)

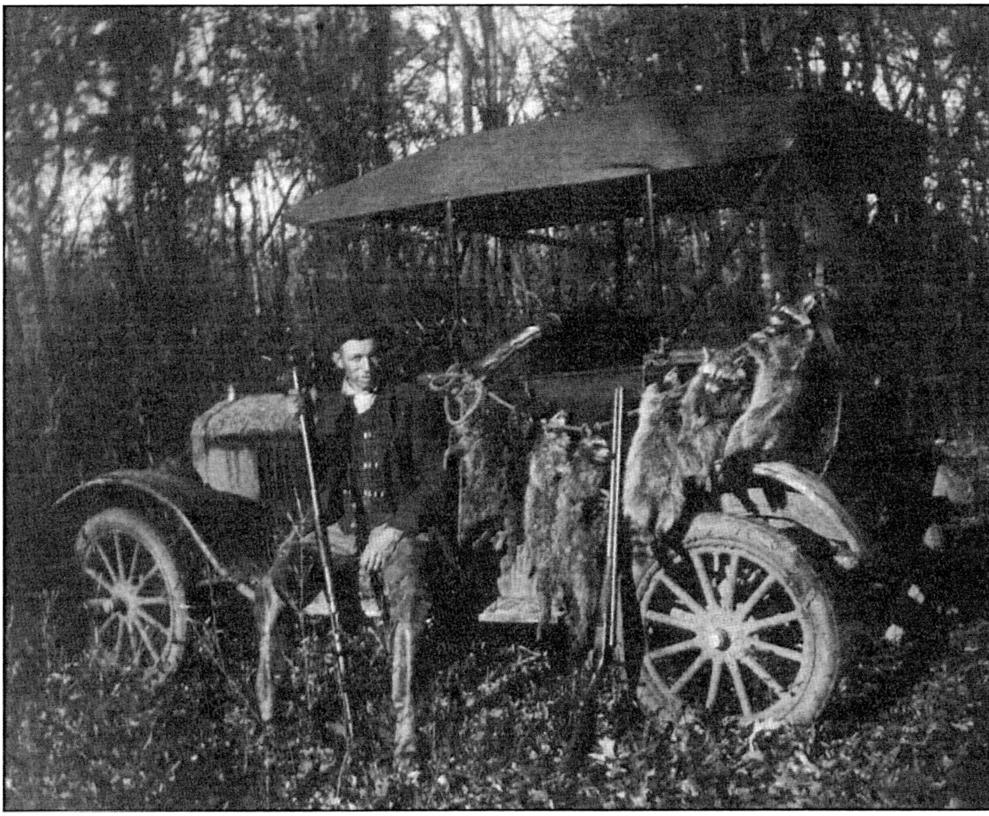

This hunter got a mess of raccoons for his all-night hunt. (Jeanne McCain Duke.)

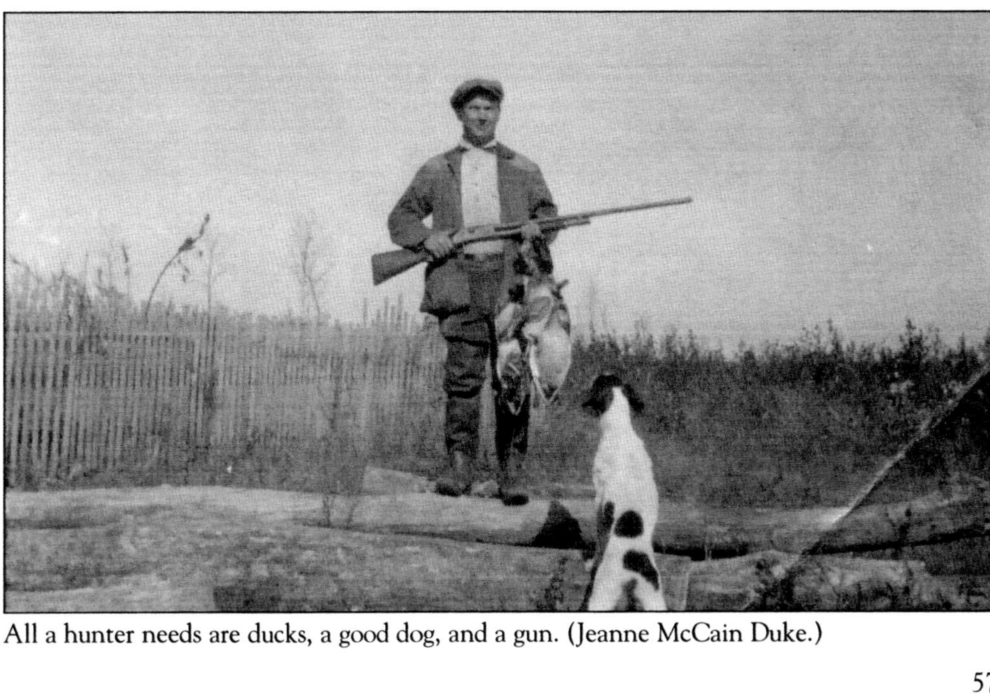

All a hunter needs are ducks, a good dog, and a gun. (Jeanne McCain Duke.)

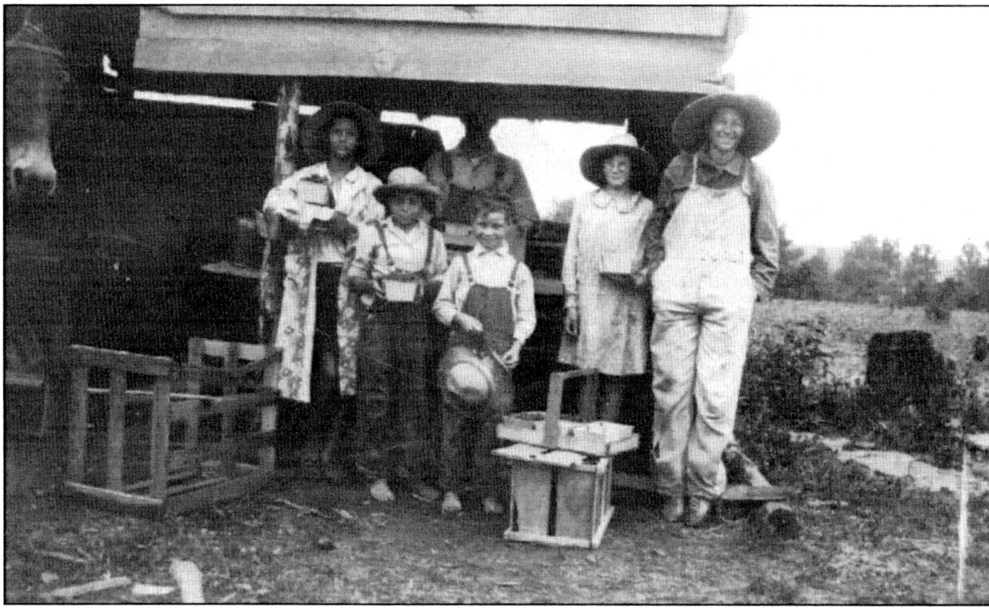

The Crook family picked strawberries for preserving in 1931. (Mary Alice Lamb Cole.)

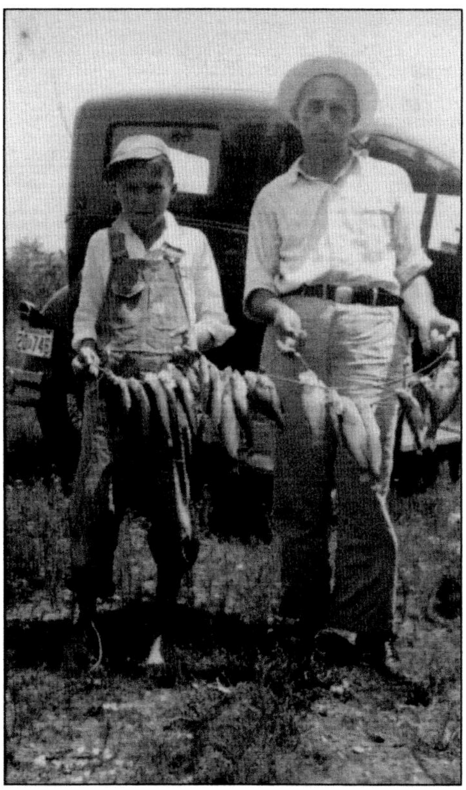

C.T. (left) and LeRoy Boyd pose after a successful fishing trip in 1939. (Carroll Boyd.)

Mabel Lamb is shown here with her prized, award-winning rooster in the 1930s. (Mary Alice Lamb Cole.)

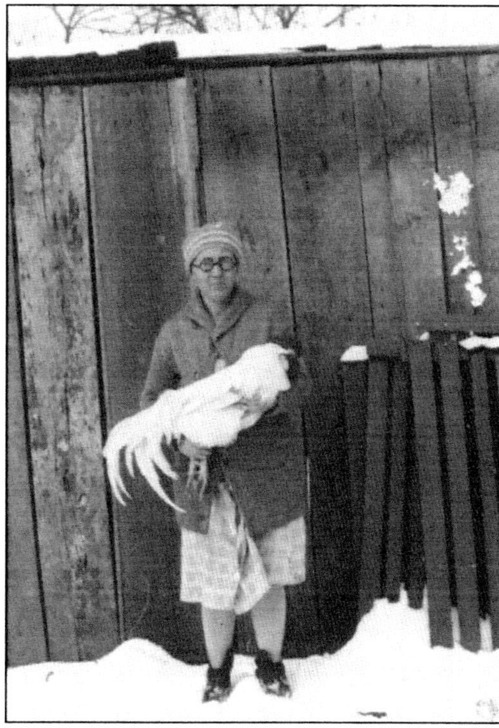

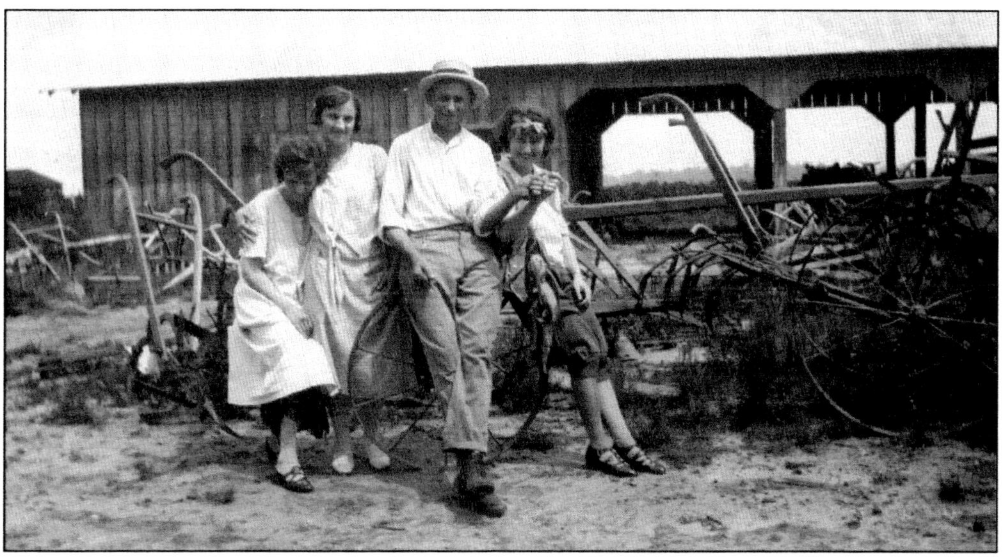

George McCain had several sharecropper tenants who used his cultivators for their crops. He is shown here with Dr. Sherer's daughters. (Jeanne McCain Duke.)

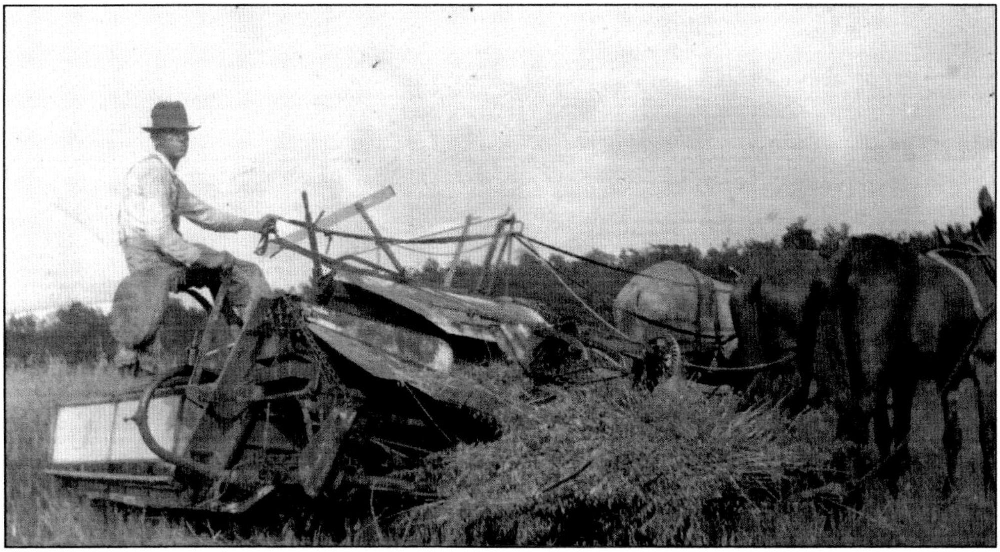

Mules were the standard on farms in rural areas until the mid-1900s. This man is cutting grain with a team of three. (Jeanne McCain Duke.)

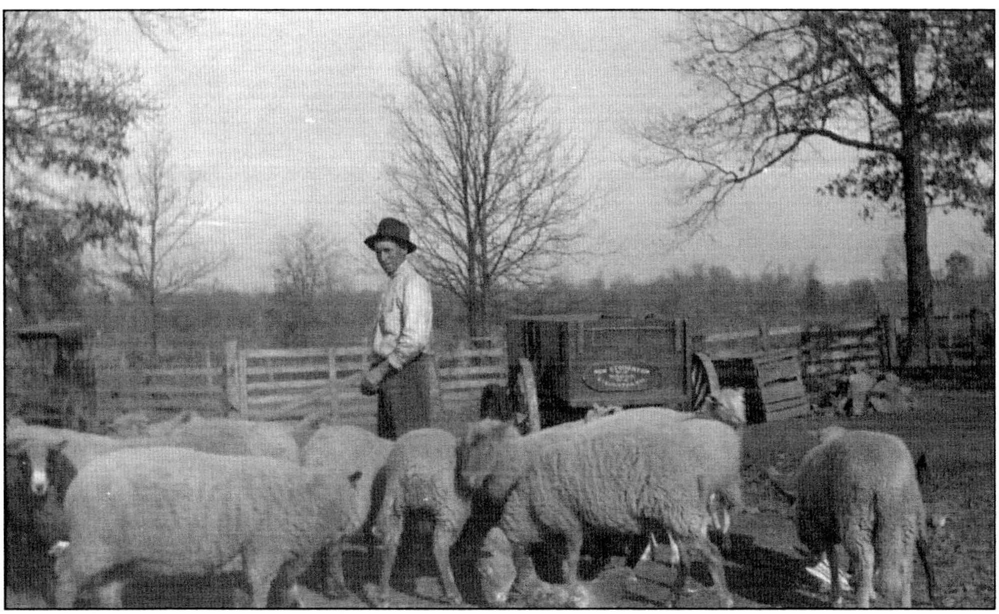

Keeping livestock was just part of the farming experience. This man has a flock of sheep that would be used for both wool and mutton. (Jeanne McCain Duke.)

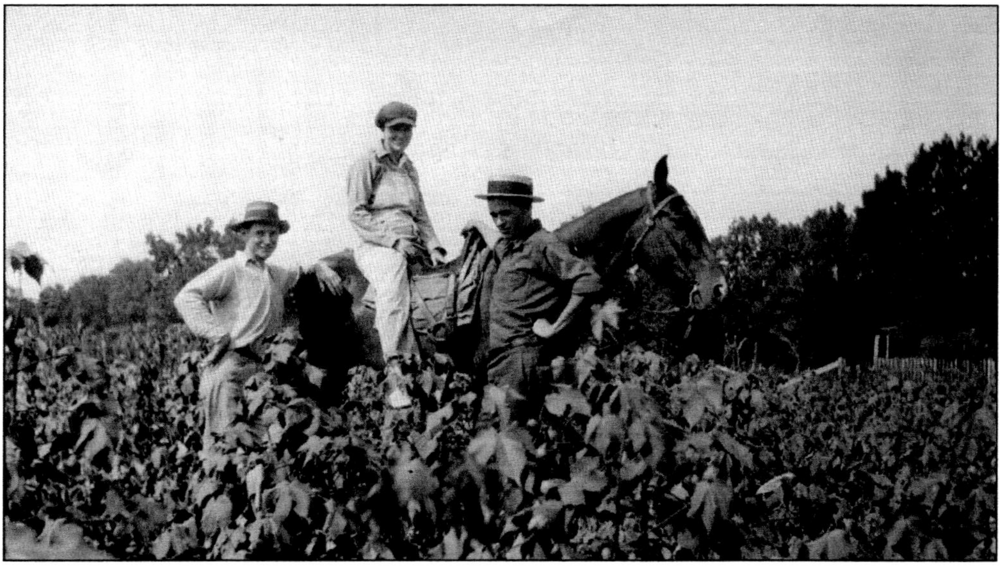

Arkansas provided good growing conditions for the king of southern crops. "Being in high cotton" was a saying that meant harvesting would be easier if you didn't have to bend over to pick, or that things were really going well. (Jeanne McCain Duke.)

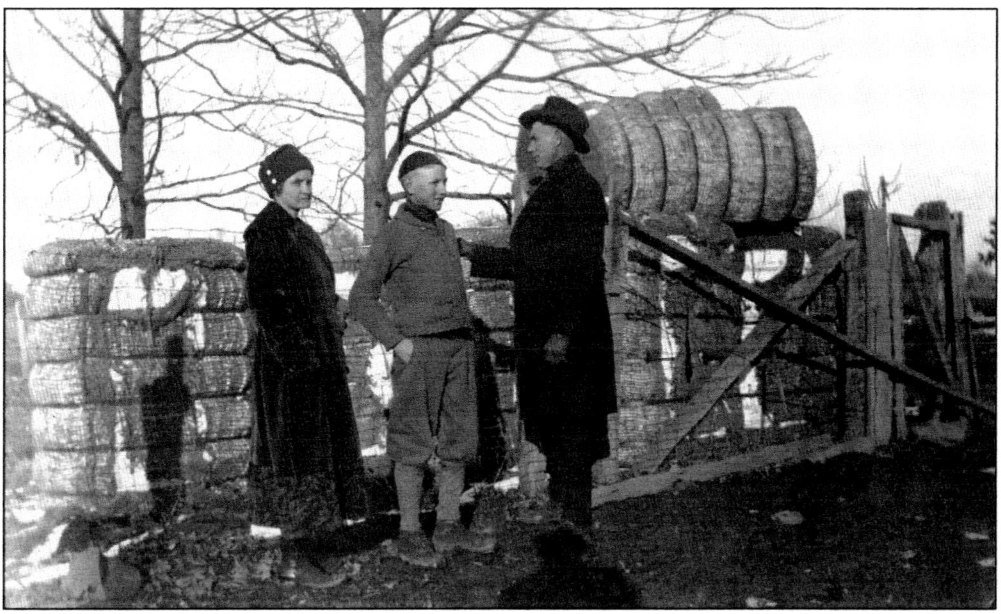

It was a satisfying time when the cotton was baled and ready for sale. This family was rightly proud of their crop. (Jeanne McCain Duke.)

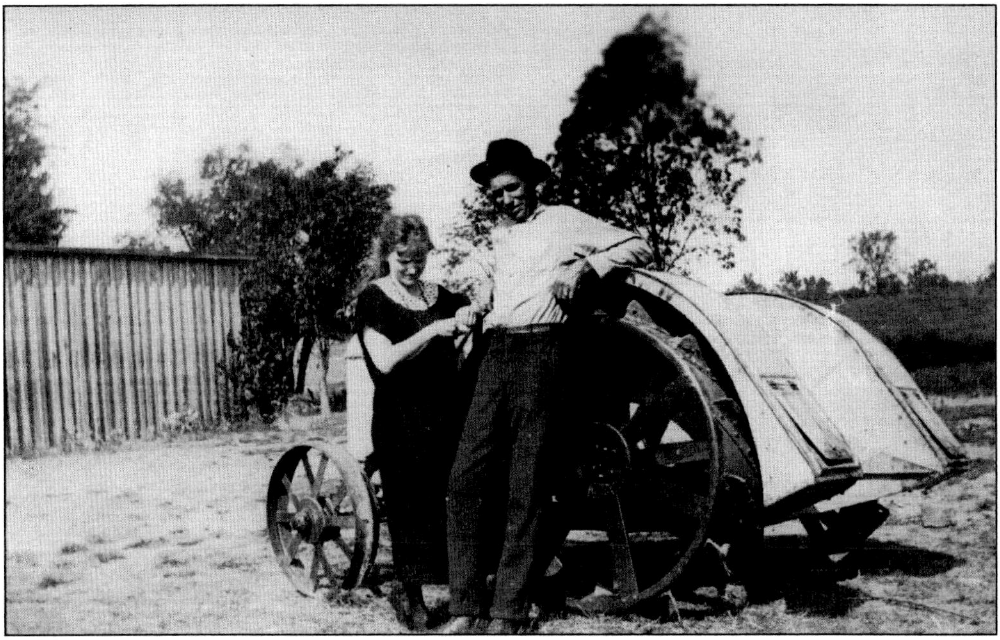

George McCain is pictured here. (Jeanne McCain Duke.)

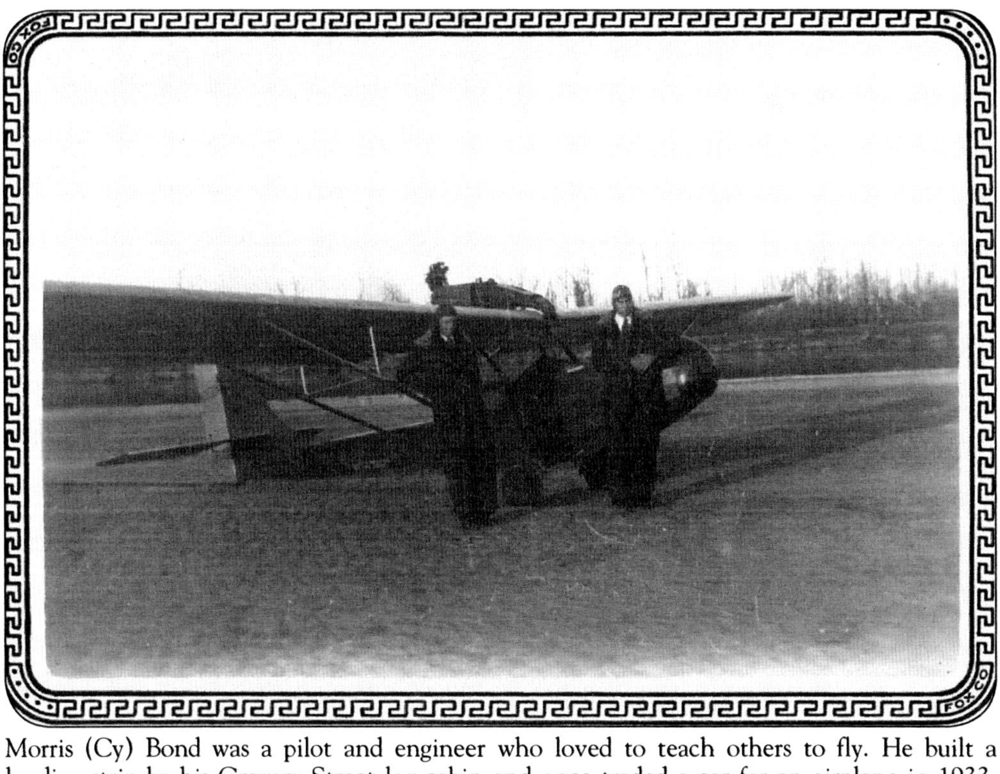

Morris (Cy) Bond was a pilot and engineer who loved to teach others to fly. He built a landing strip by his Gregory Street log cabin and once traded a car for an airplane in 1933. (Tommy Bond.)

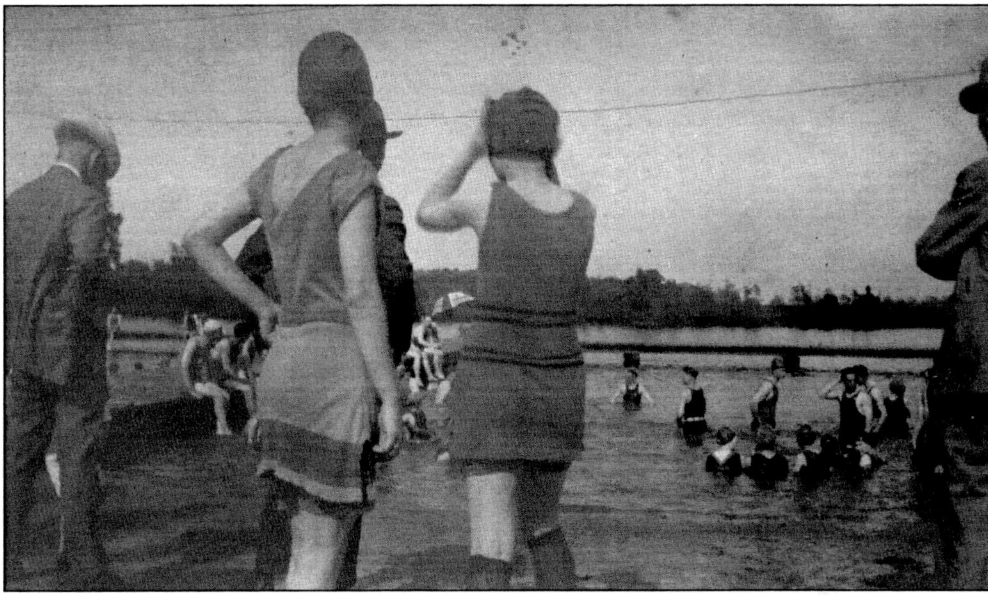

Things were not going so well with the economy in the early 1930s, but people still had fun. This group headed for the nearest lake to enjoy themselves. (Jeanne McCain Duke.)

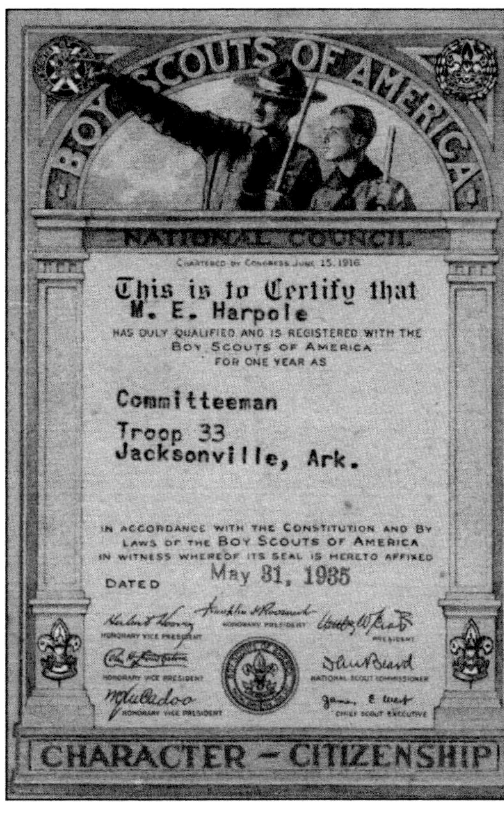

The Boy Scout program was active in Jacksonville. This card was issued to M.E. Harpole in 1935. (Marie Harpole Hackett.)

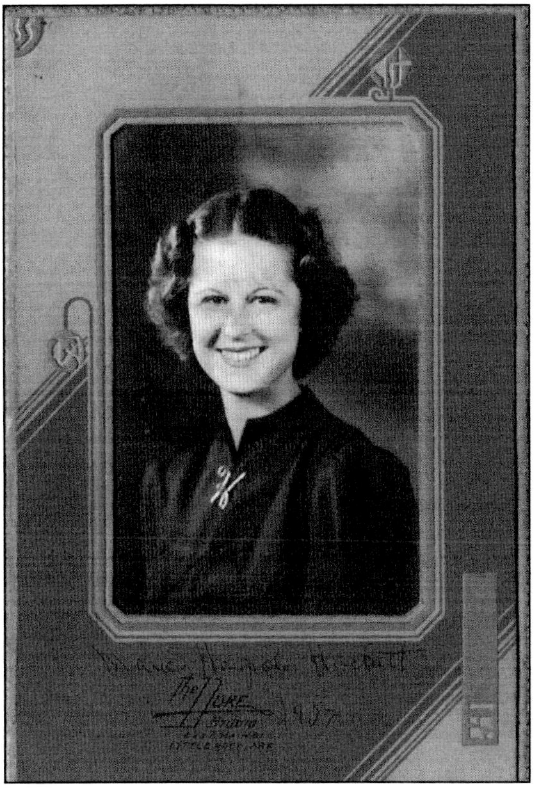

Here is Marie Hackett in 1937. (Marie Harpole Hackett)

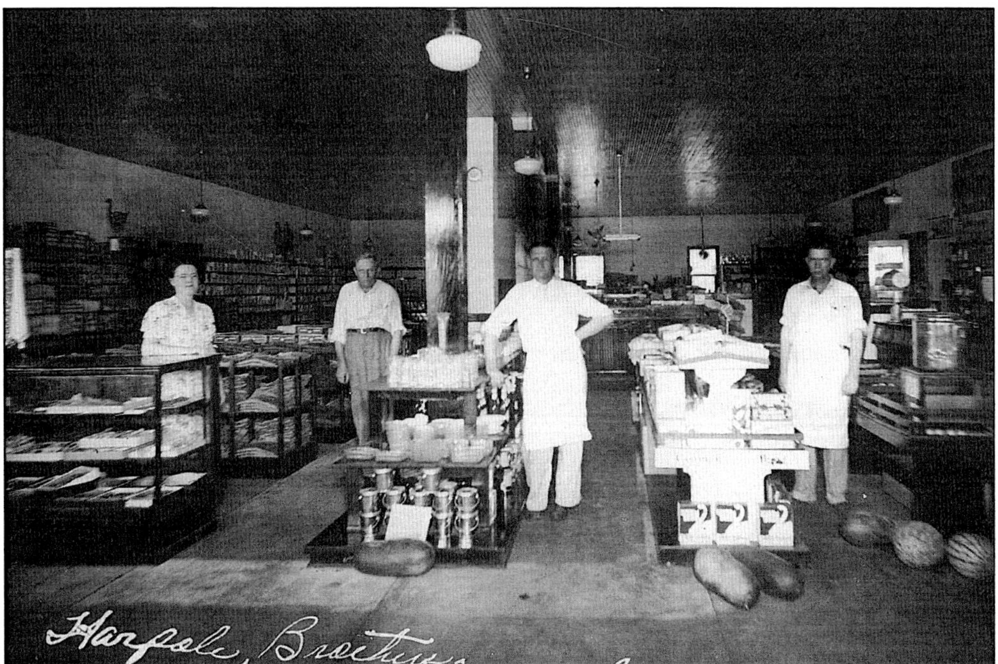

This photograph of the Harpole Brothers' store was taken in 1939. (Opal Harpole Mallett.)

Street photographers would take pictures in the hopes of a random sale. Here is the Caddo Studio in 1937. (Jacksonville Historical Society.)

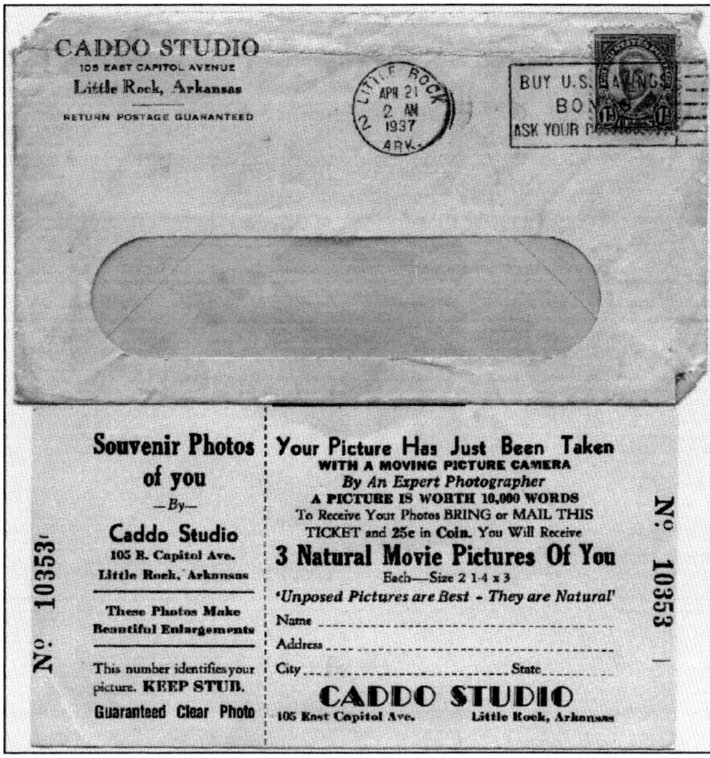

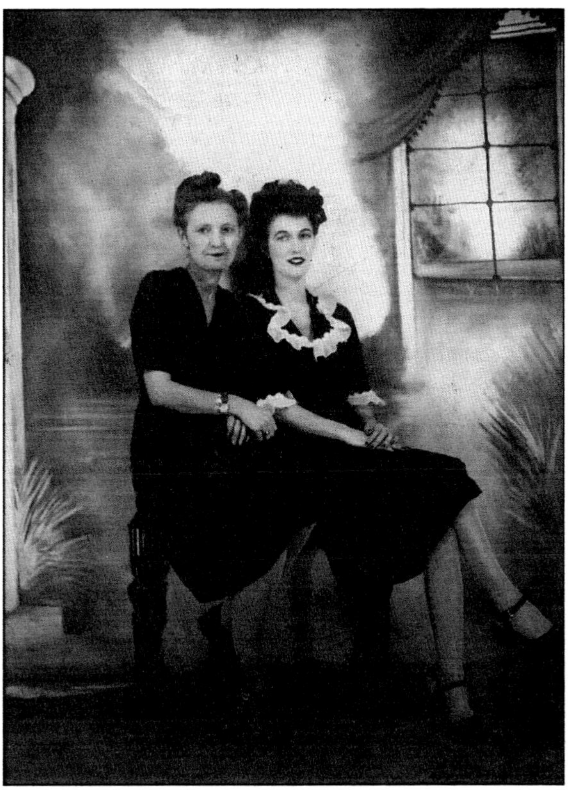

It must have been a special occasion when this mother and daughter sat for a studio portrait in the late 1930s. (John Vanderhoof.)

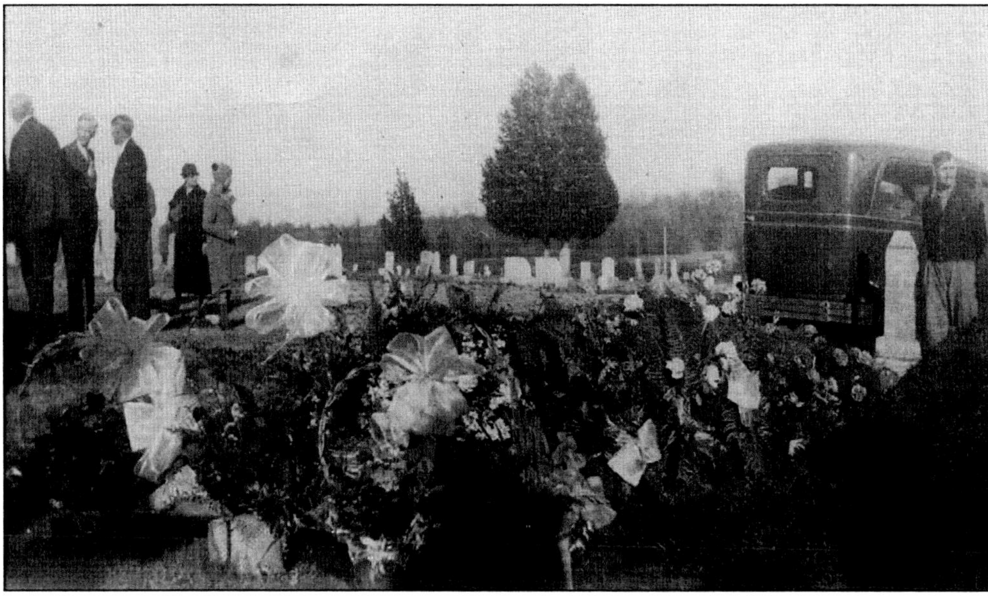

This funeral took place in the Bayou Meto Cemetery about 1936. The old oak tree in the background was estimated to be around 275 years old when lightning struck it in 1999, and it had to be cut down. (Pat Boyd.)

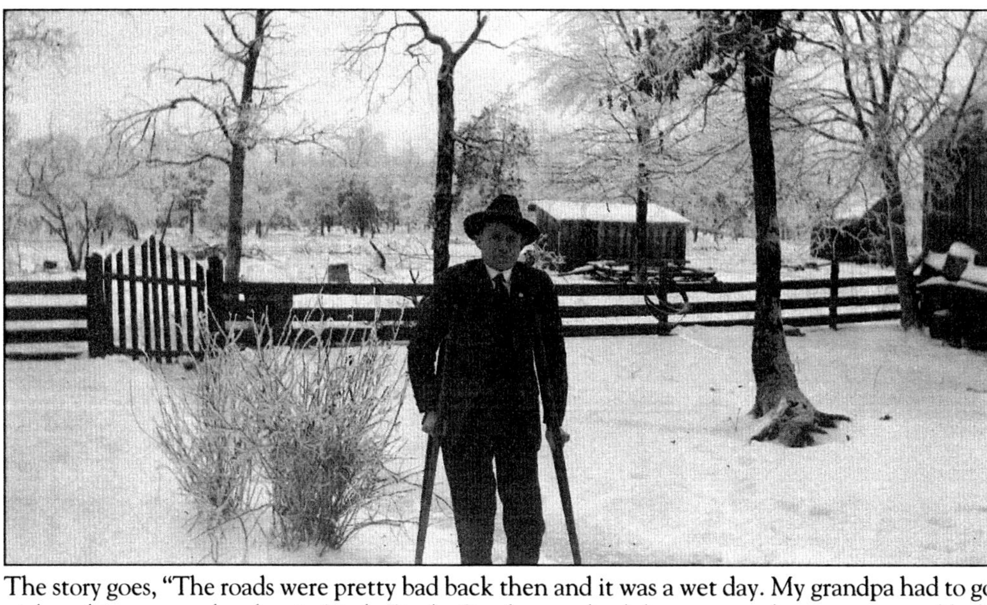

The story goes, "The roads were pretty bad back then and it was a wet day. My grandpa had to go pick up his younger brother in Little Rock. On the way back he met another car at a mud hole on a two-rut road. Neither driver would give way and they hit head on—Grandpa's passenger, Uncle Sam, broke his leg and was on crutches for weeks. Grandma was really mad." (Jeanne McCain Duke.)

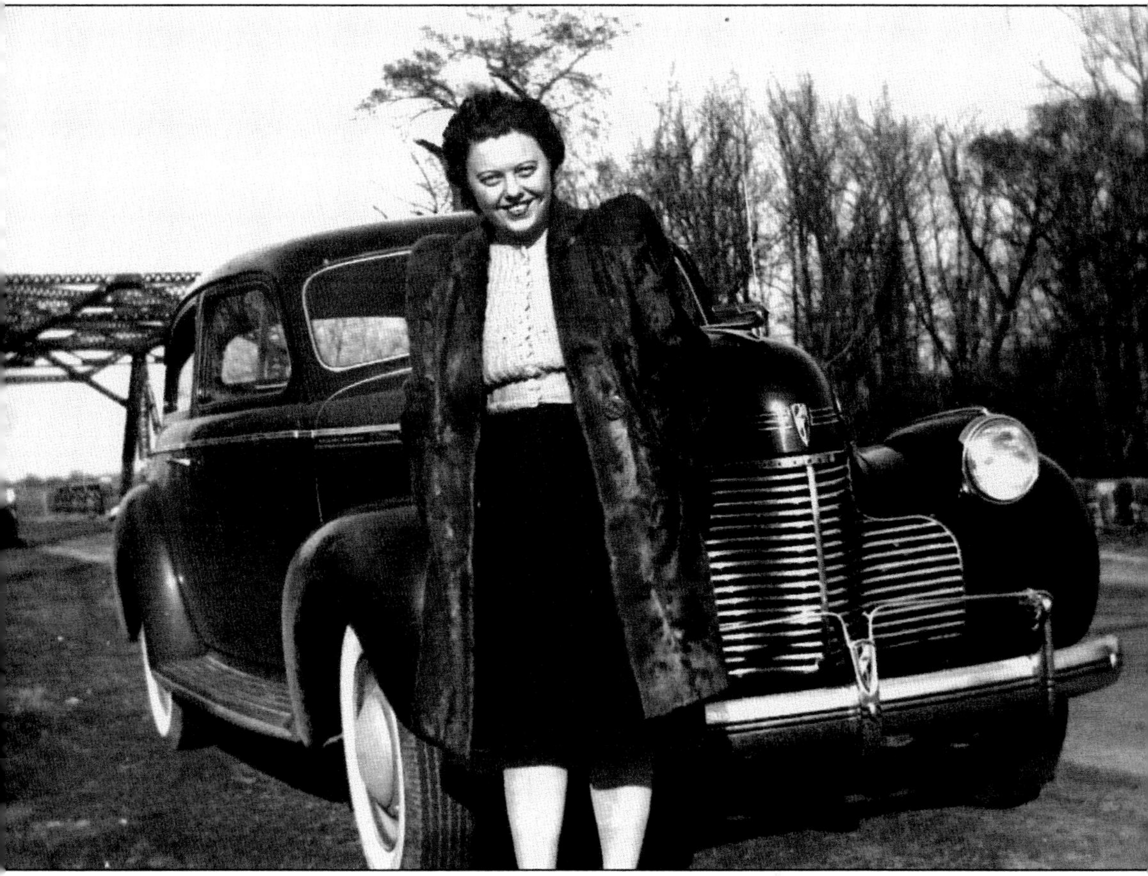

Margie Walker McCain is pictured at the old iron bridge at the site of the present Reed's Bridge Civil War Battlefield site on Highway 161. (Jean McCain Duke.)

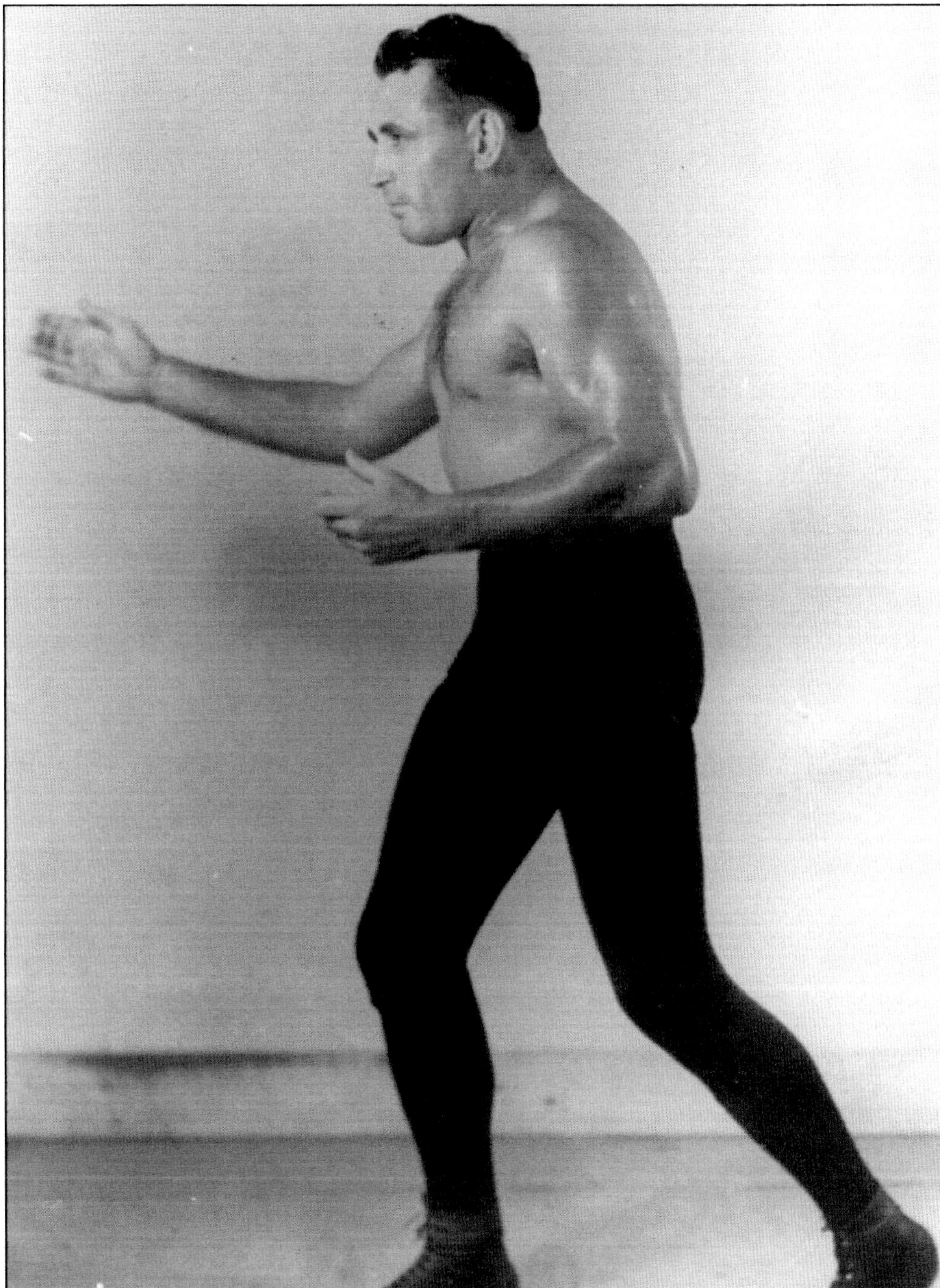

Lefty Williams, a light heavyweight wrestler, was a contender for the championship of the world three different times at the end of the '30s. His last championship fight went three hours and was declared a draw. He rode the wrestling circuit until WW II, when gas and rubber rationing made travel prohibitive. Williams came home and went into law enforcement, working as an Arkansas State Police officer, Lonoke County Warden, and Jacksonville City Marshal. (Doyle Webb.)

Four

The 1940s

In response to WW II, the Jacksonville Ordnance Plant was built and began production of fuse and detonator units for the war effort and the town changed forever. The plant employed thousands of persons, and most of the assembly line labor were women. Lack of housing was a huge problem, and many families lived in tents or makeshift shelter for months and years. Five hundred prefabricated housing units were built to ease the shortage, and the Sunnyside subdivision still stands today in modern Jacksonville. When the plant closed its doors in December 1945, it left an employment vacuum for the 5,000 residents. The Jacksonville Chamber of Commerce was organized in 1947, and worked to fill the needs in industry, business, and community areas.

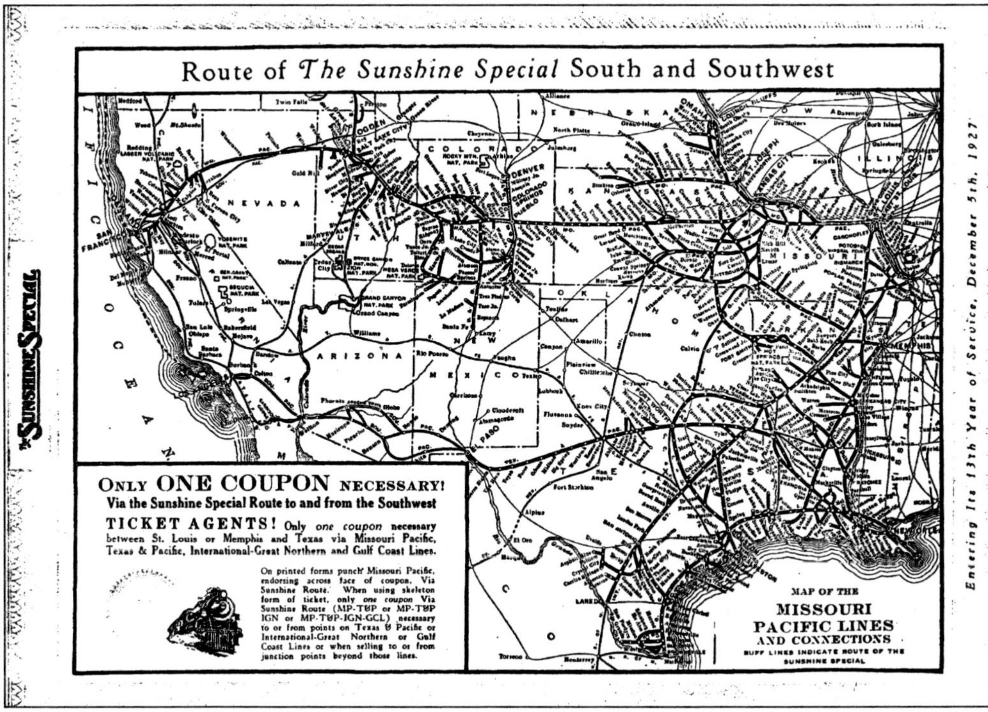

Jacksonville owed its beginnings to the railroad, and it was an important link well into the 20th century. The Missouri Pacific's *Sunshine Special* came through on a regular basis. (Nixon Library, Jacksonville.)

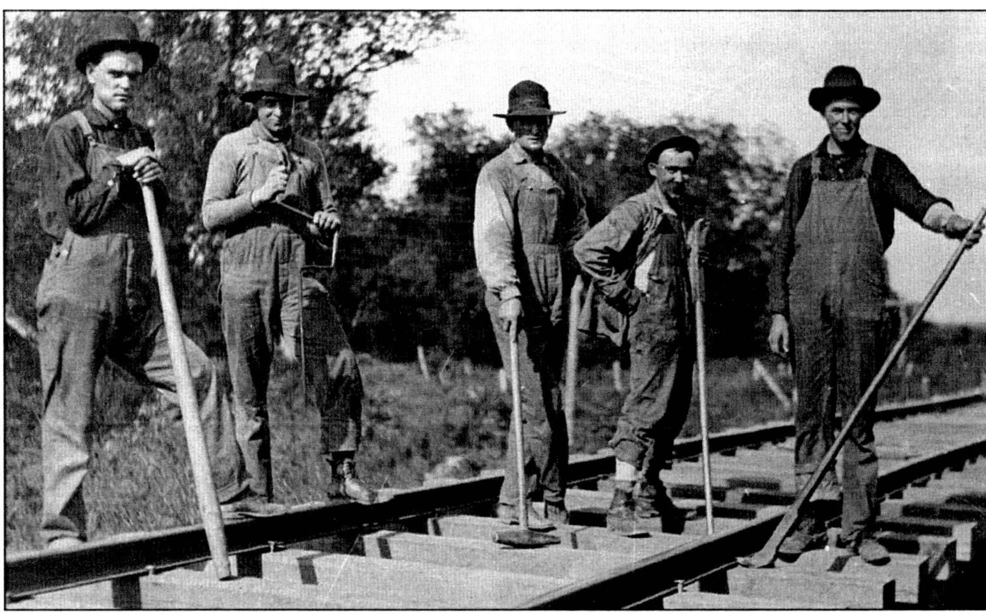

These Gandy Dancers are shown in the 1940s. Railroad crews were required to constantly keep up the roadbeds for train safety, and it was hot and dangerous work. The men used tools from the Gandy Mfg. Company in Chicago, and the crews often kept in rhythmic movements by singing—thus they were called Gandy Dancers. (Gary Laney.)

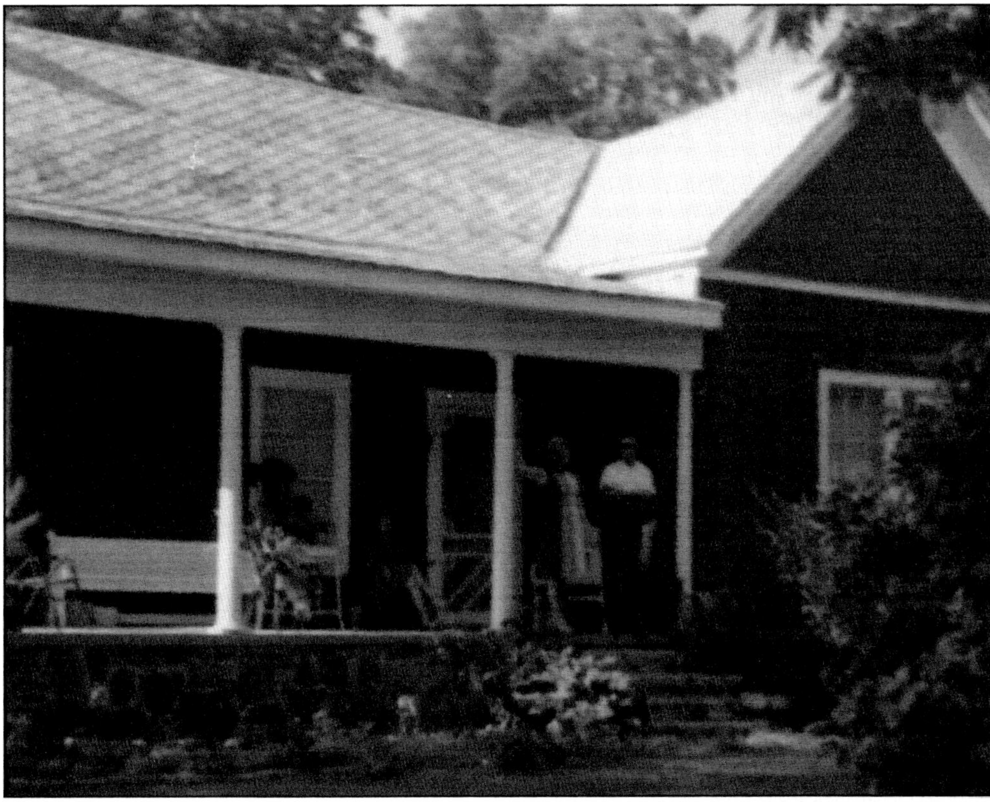

The Nixon homestead on Graham Road still stands. (Esther Nixon.)

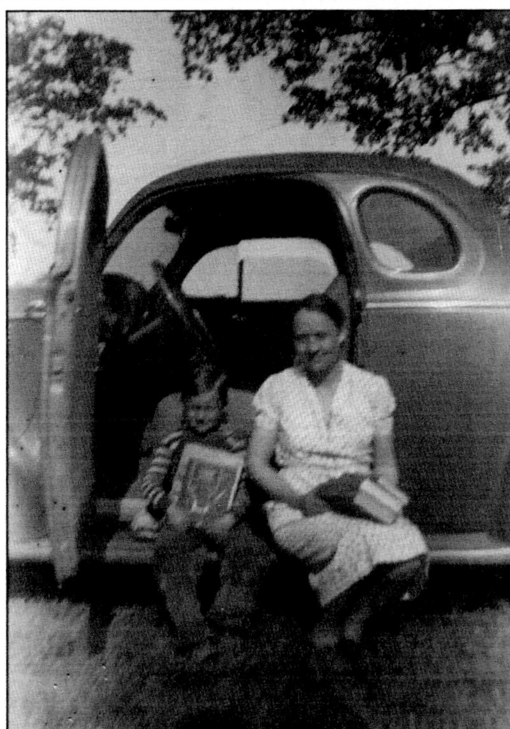

Lorene and seven-year-old Pete Dupree had just been to the bookmobile in this 1942 photograph. (Tommy Dupree.)

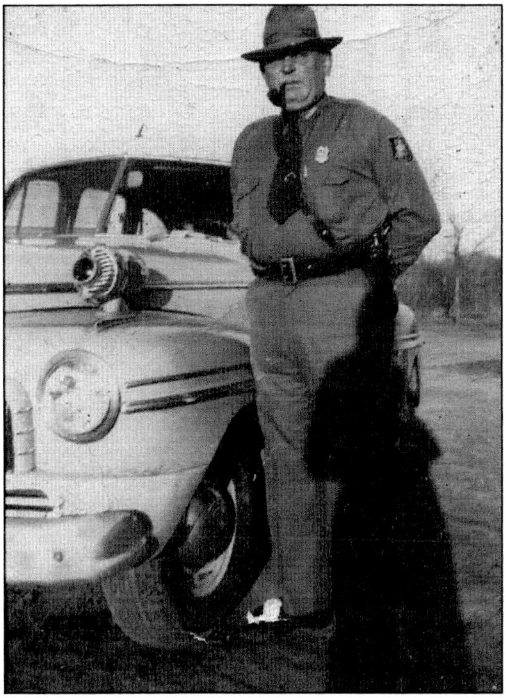

Lefty Williams, Jacksonville City Marshal, is shown here in 1943. (Doyle Webb.)

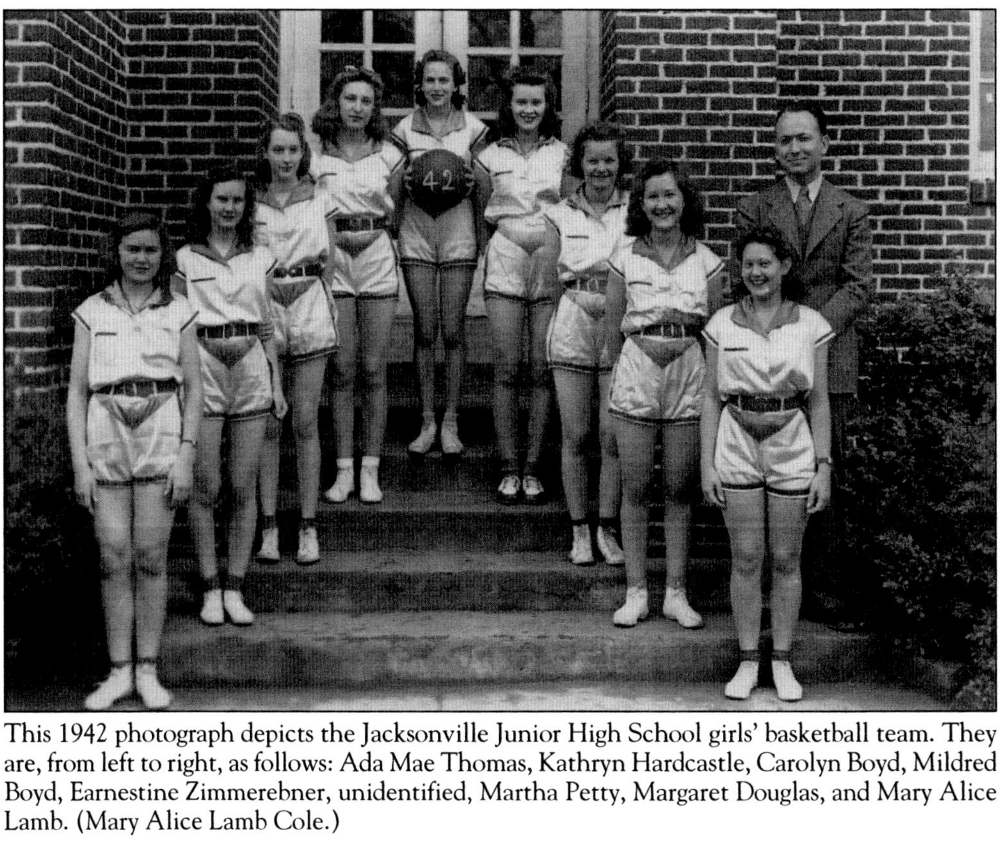

This 1942 photograph depicts the Jacksonville Junior High School girls' basketball team. They are, from left to right, as follows: Ada Mae Thomas, Kathryn Hardcastle, Carolyn Boyd, Mildred Boyd, Earnestine Zimmerebner, unidentified, Martha Petty, Margaret Douglas, and Mary Alice Lamb. (Mary Alice Lamb Cole.)

P.W. Dupree III had many tenant farmers, and visited the different properties on horse-back as shown in this 1941 photograph. (Tommy Dupree.)

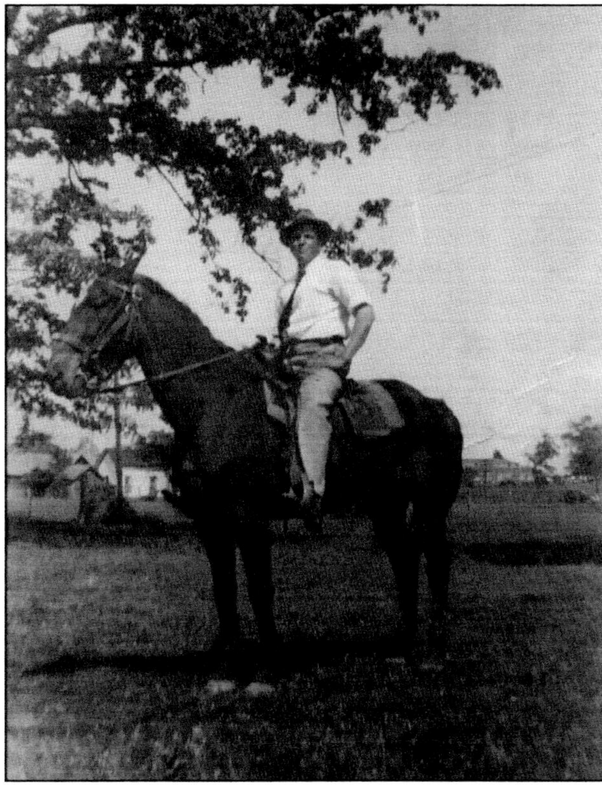

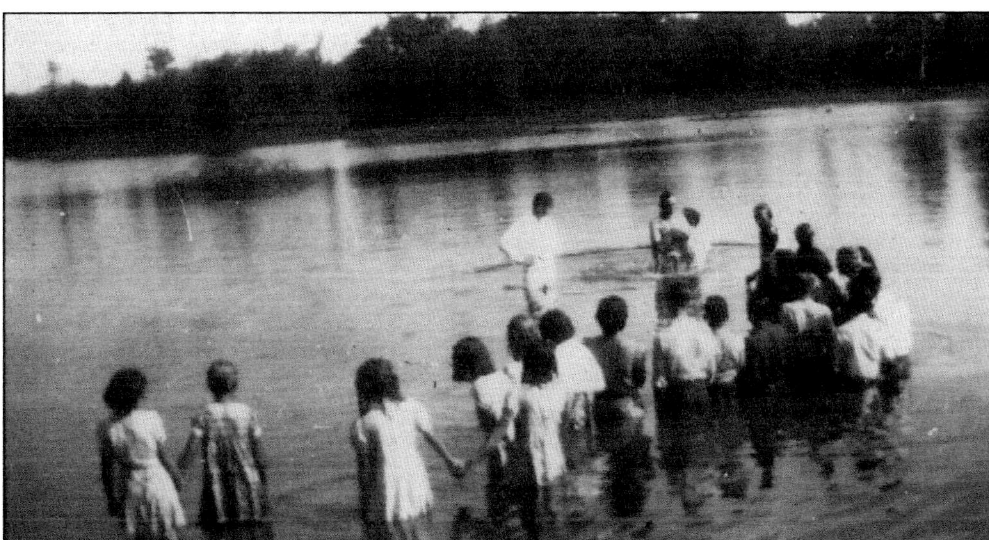

This 1941 photograph shows Robert Cole's baptism at Sadler Pond. (Mary Alice Lamb Cole.)

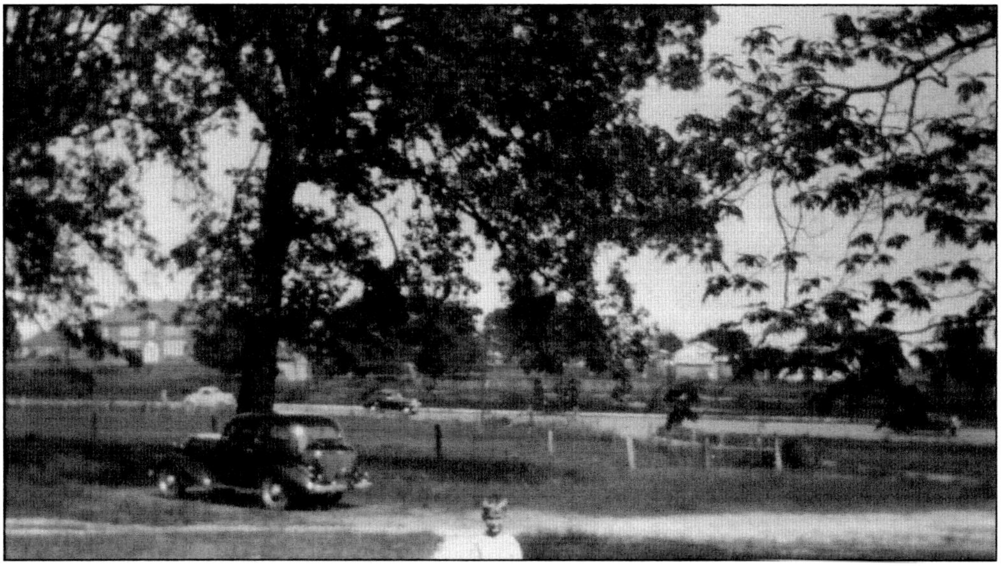

Here, Tommy Dupree is shown at his granddad's house looking east to First Street and the railroad track. The old Jacksonville School is in the background. The photograph dates to 1942. (Tommy Dupree.)

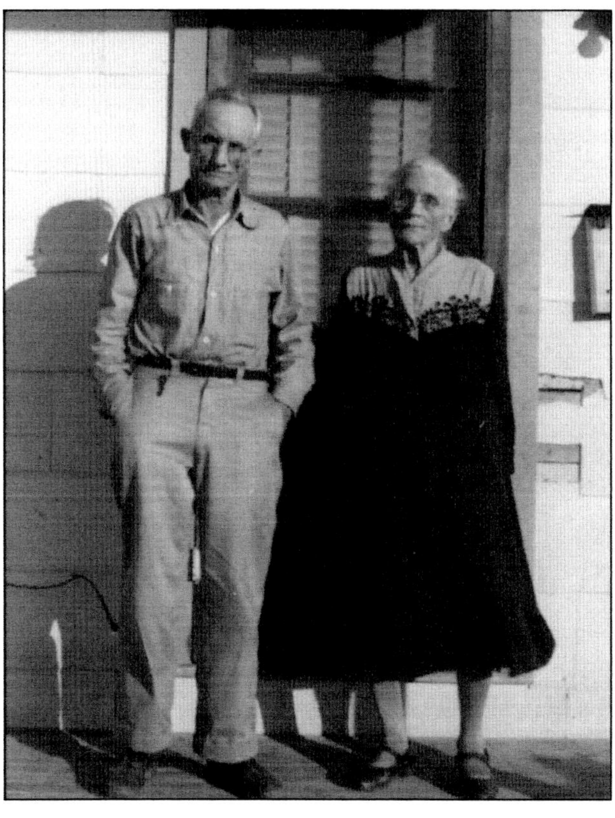

C.F. Neal and his mother, Cornelia Baggett, moved to Jacksonville, where he worked for the Ordnance Plant in the 1940s. (Stephen Eudy.)

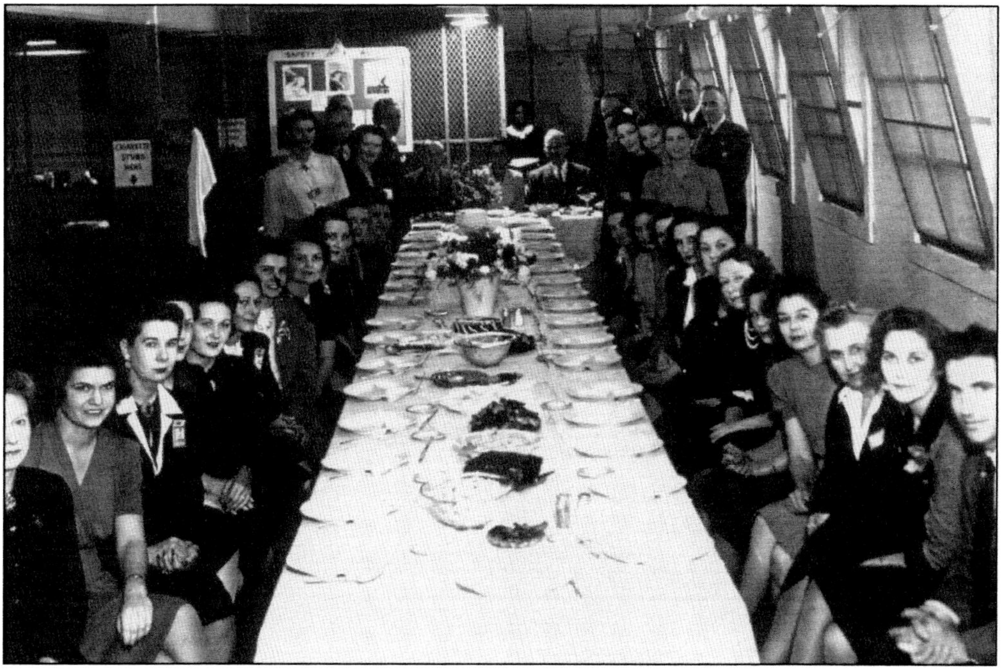

This Ordnance Plant workers' dinner was held in the 1940s. (Jacksonville Historical Society.)

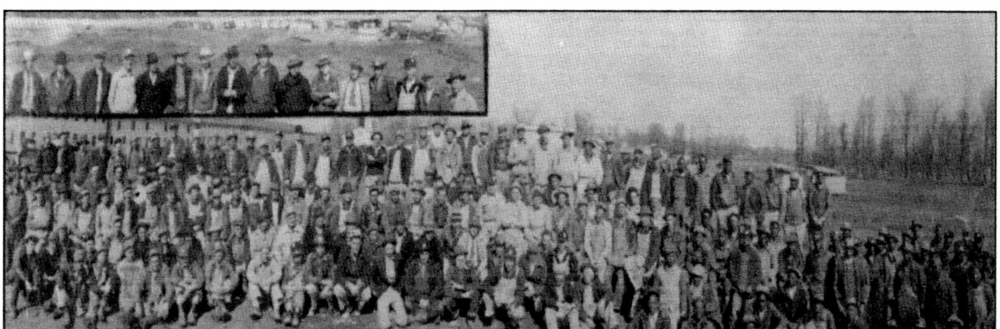

Pictured are Ordnance Plant workers. The Ordnance Plant was an employment opportunity for many. The plant started a production line in March 1942, making fuses and detonators for the war effort. Hiring women and blacks in mass for the first time, it changed the social life of the community and began an era of economic growth. At its peak production, the plant consisted of 476 buildings and employed 13,500 workers. Females earned $60 to $90 a month, while men earned $90 to $250 a month. The plant had its own library, hospital, fire department, recreation hall, cafeteria, coffee shop, dining room, athletic field, auditorium, barber and beauty shop, and weekly newspaper. (Jacksonville Historical Society.)

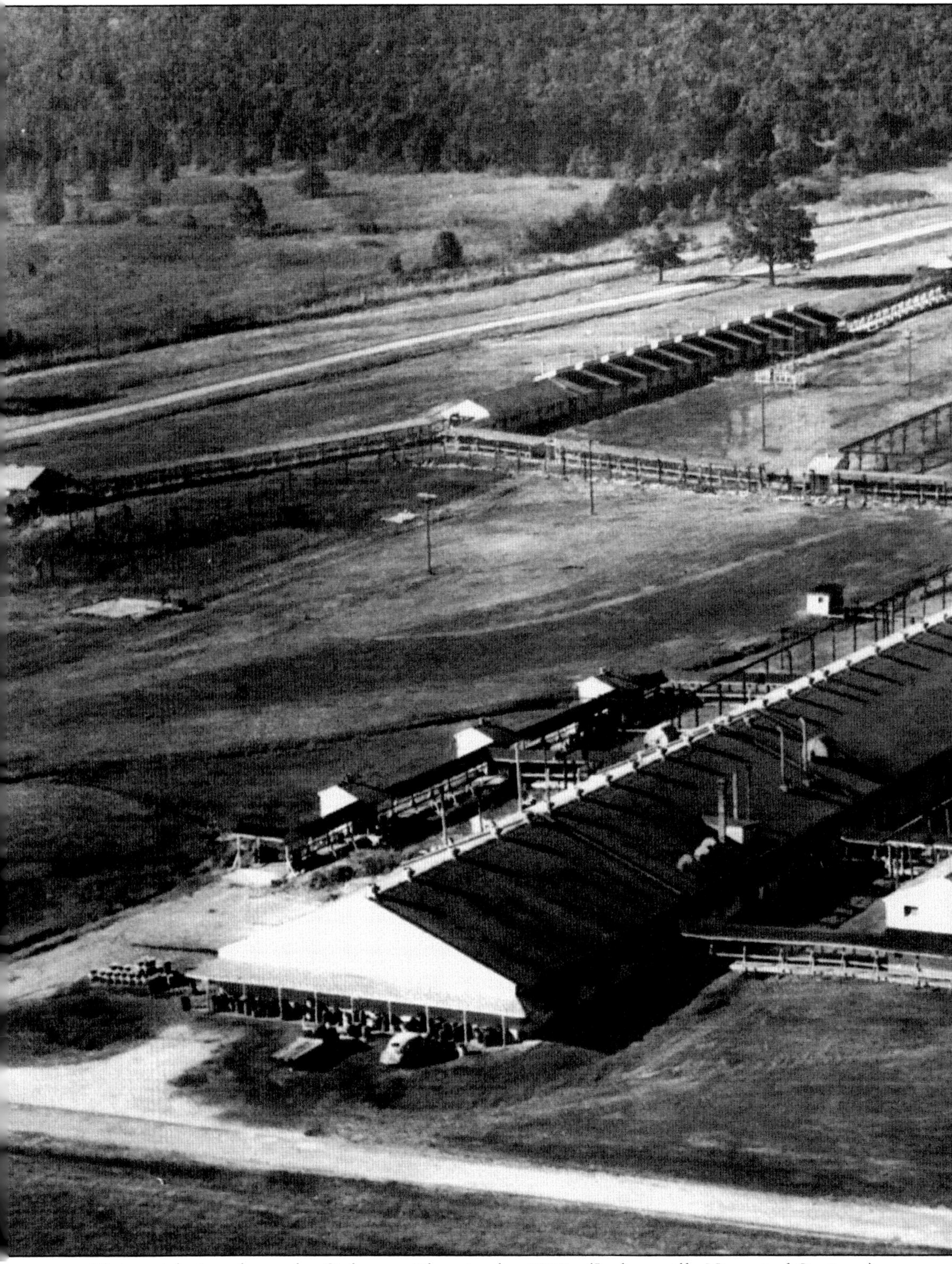

This aerial view shows the Ordnance Plant in the 1940s. (Jacksonville Historical Society.)

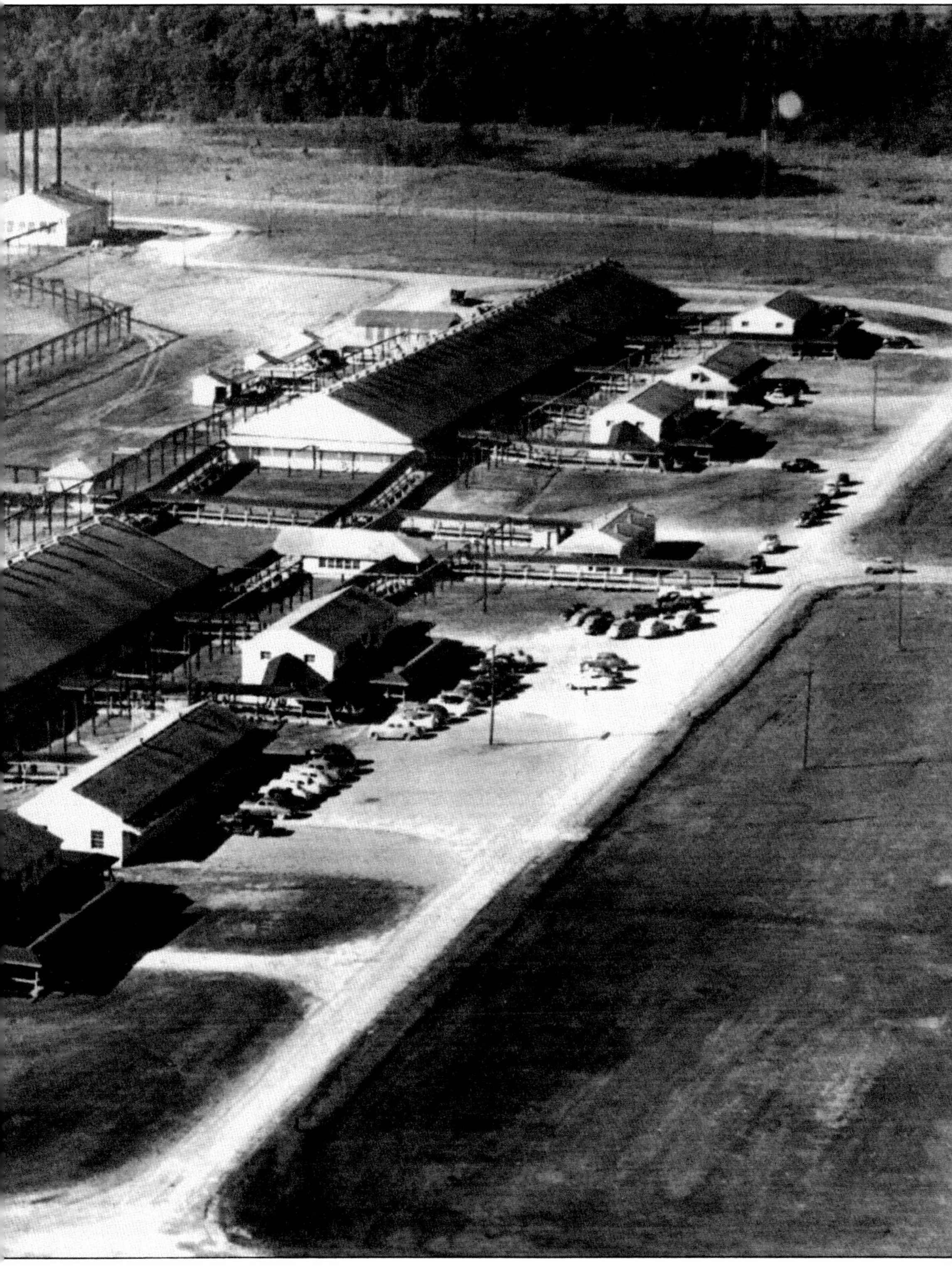

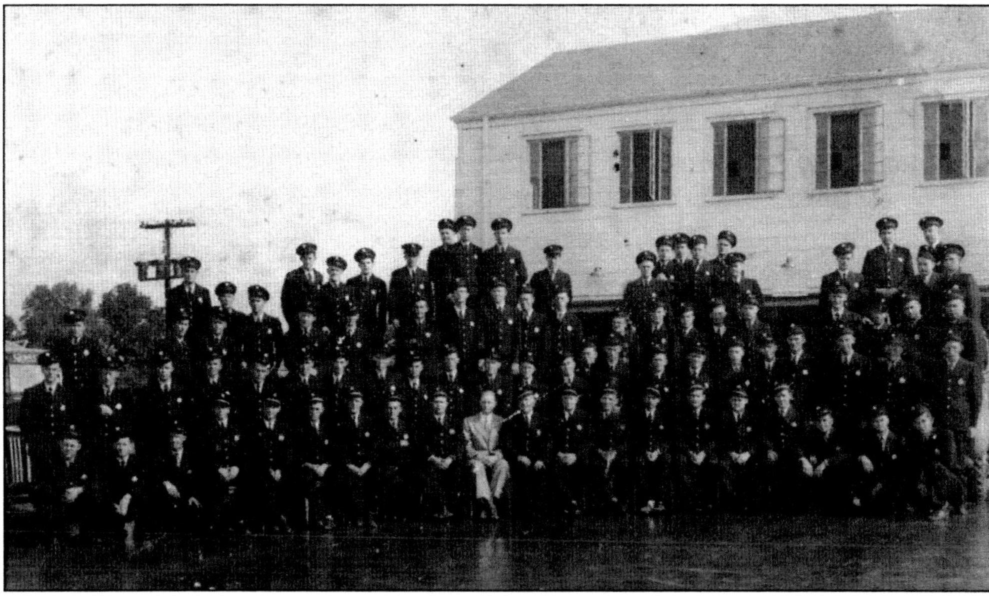

This 1942 photograph shows the Ordnance Fire Department. Because the Ordnance Plant was nearly self sufficient, it had one of the largest fire departments in the state. (John Vanderhoof.)

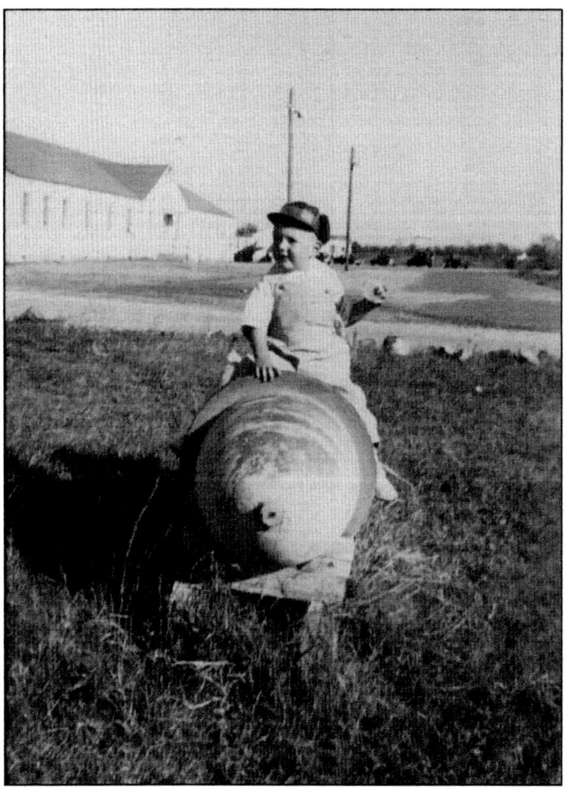

This bomb sat in front of the Ordnance Fire Station, and young John Vanderhoof got to ride on it because his father was a fireman. (John Vanderhoof.)

Rationing was a way of life for a few years during WW II. People were notified when and where they could obtain goods if they had the right ration stamps. (Jacksonville Historical Society.)

Ration Dates

(Clip Out and Save)

COFFEE—Coupon No. 25 became valid Monday, February 8. Good for one pound of coffee until March 22.

SUGAR—Coupon No. 11 now valid, good for three pounds, and is good until March 15.

MILEAGE GASOLINE and TIRES—No. 4 coupon in A books good for four gallons each through March 21st. February 28—Deadline for holders of B and C cards to have their tires inspected. This is also the last day for tire inspection on trucks. March 31—Deadline for holders of A cards to have their tires inspected.

SHOES—No. 17 coupon, Ration Book 1, good for one pair of shoes, until June 15.

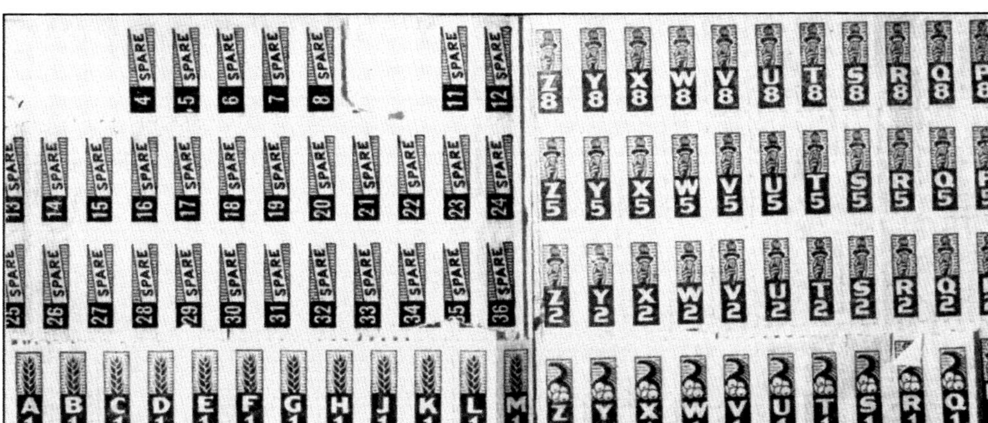

Here are ration stamps that were used locally. (Jacksonville Historical Society.)

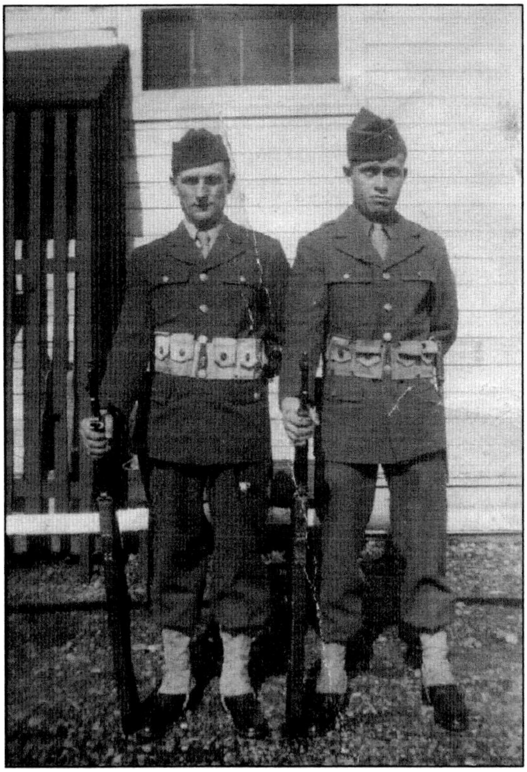

Pick Boyd, pictured, was a WW II soldier. (Pat Boyd.)

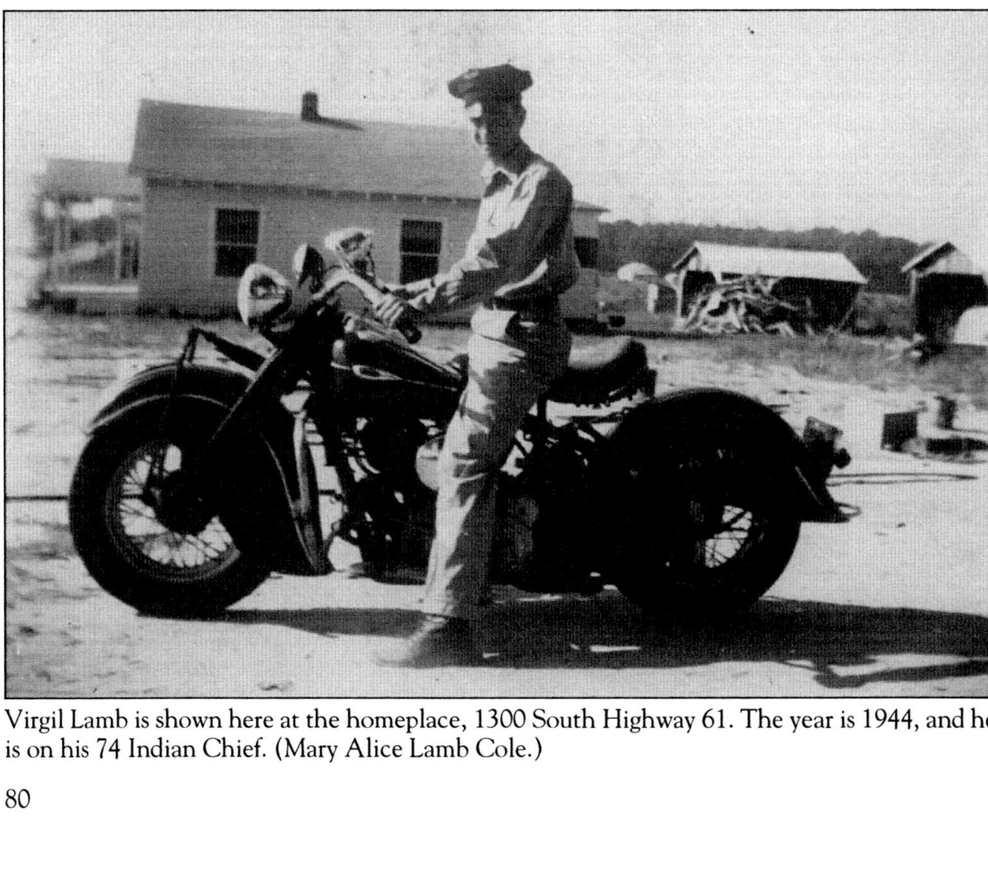

Virgil Lamb is shown here at the homeplace, 1300 South Highway 61. The year is 1944, and he is on his 74 Indian Chief. (Mary Alice Lamb Cole.)

Patricia and Stephen Eudy are at home here in Sunnyside at 127 Wilson. The property had a storm cellar for protection from tornados, which frequented the area in the 1940s. (Stephen Eudy.)

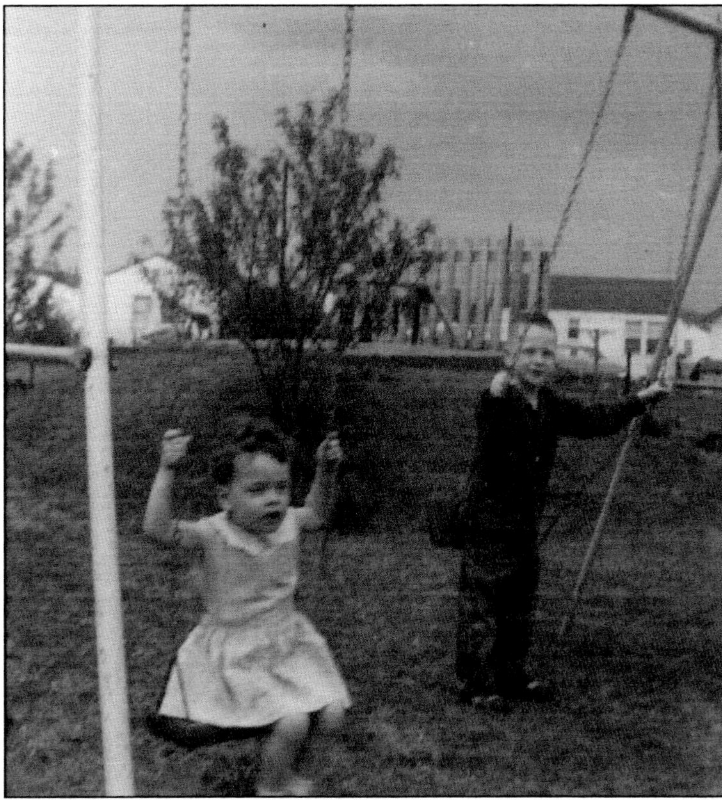

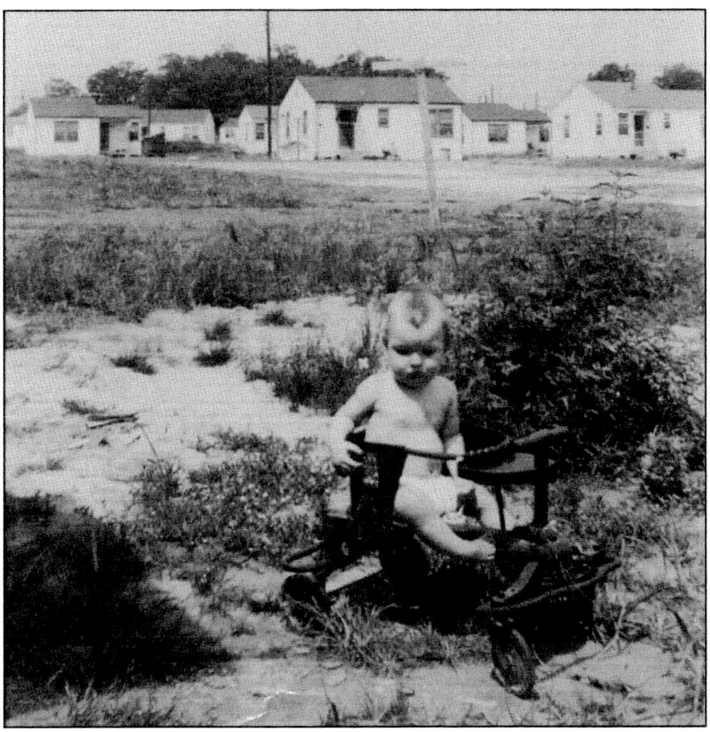

In this early 1940s photograph, Sunnyside was new and the lawns were not even in, but the families were growing. (John Vanderhoof.)

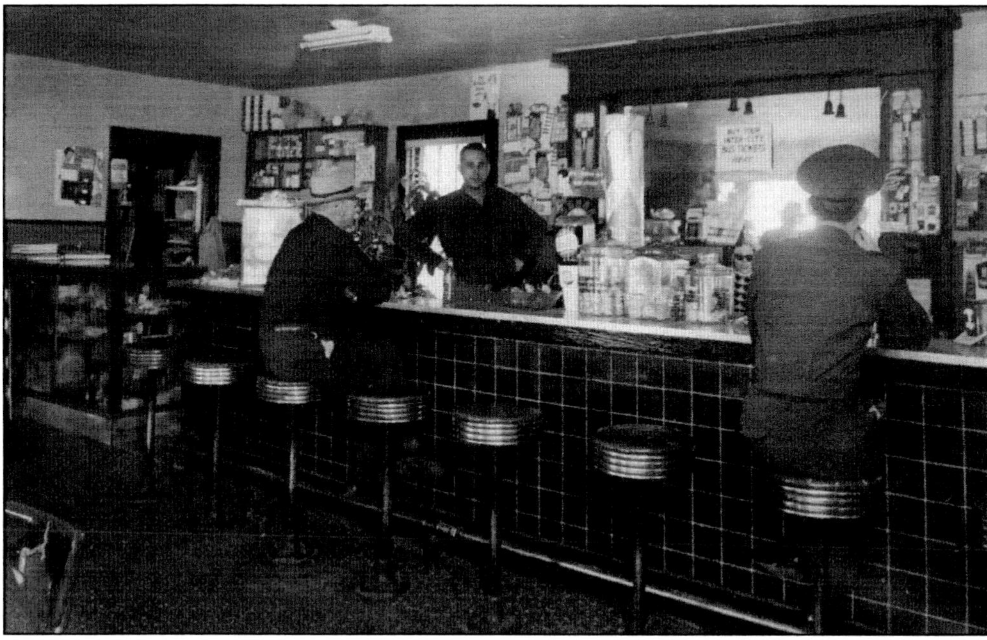

Harpole's operated the Confectionery and Bus Station from 1947 to 1967. It was a Jacksonville institution, and most of the town passed through the doors at one time or another. (Opal Harpole Mallett.)

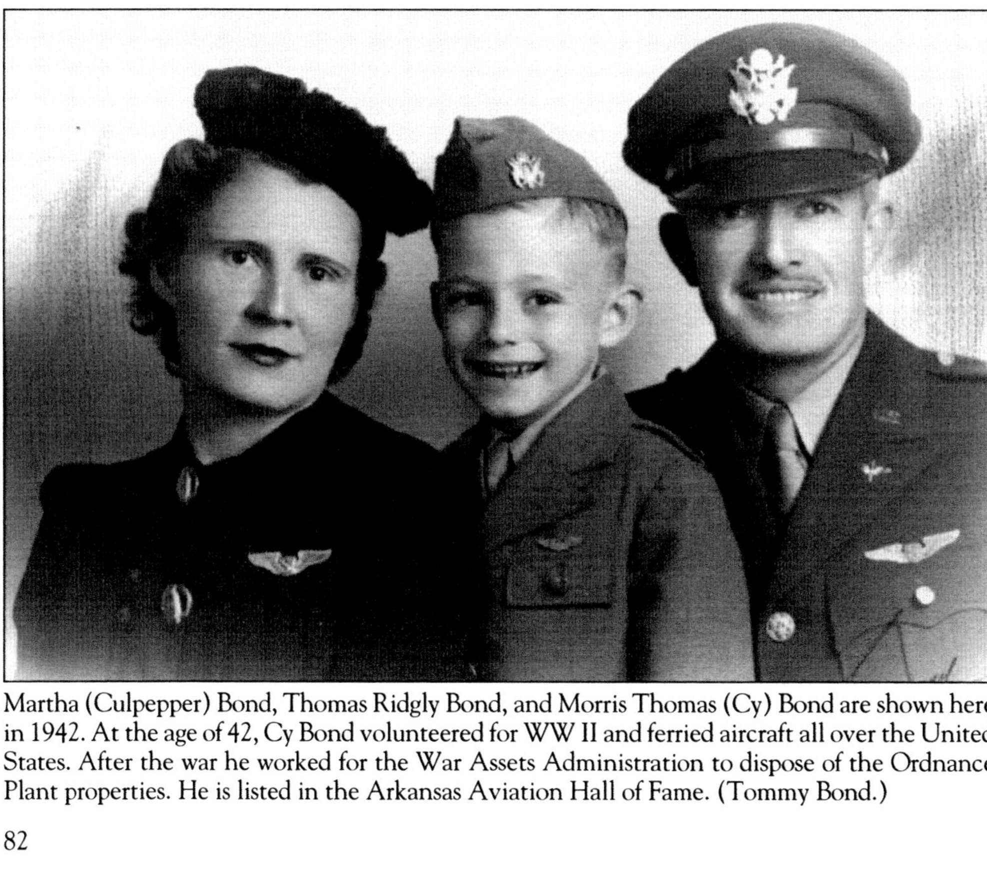

Martha (Culpepper) Bond, Thomas Ridgly Bond, and Morris Thomas (Cy) Bond are shown here in 1942. At the age of 42, Cy Bond volunteered for WW II and ferried aircraft all over the United States. After the war he worked for the War Assets Administration to dispose of the Ordnance Plant properties. He is listed in the Arkansas Aviation Hall of Fame. (Tommy Bond.)

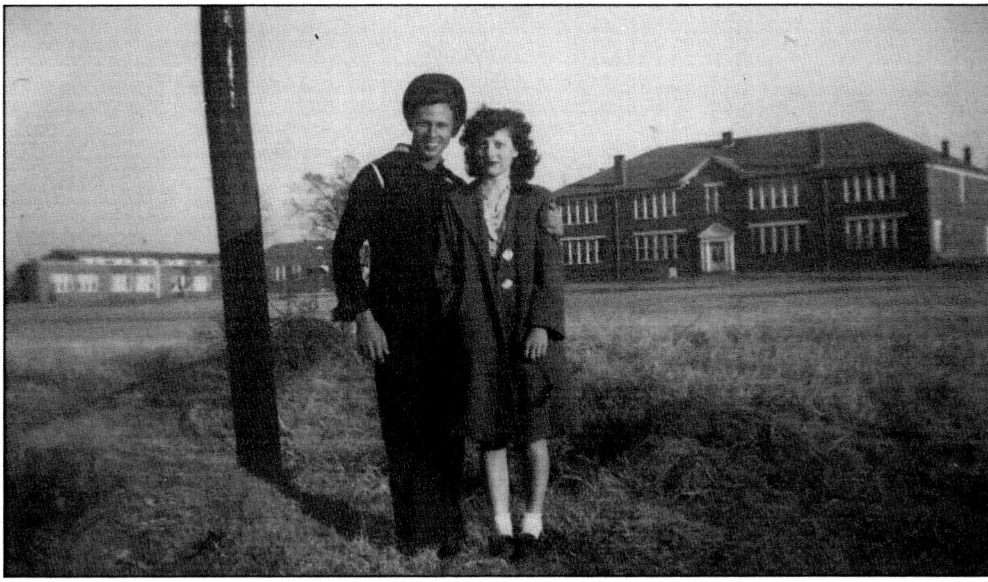

Shelly Lamb and Christine Cole paused for a picture in 1943. The old Jacksonville School is in the background. (Mary Alice Lamb Cole.)

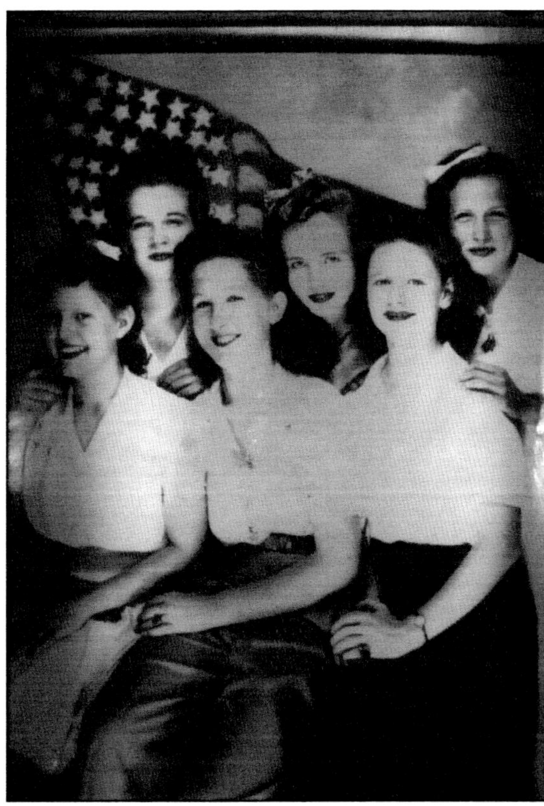

According to a student, during the war, the school was always losing teachers at the school because they could make so much more money at the Ordnance Plant. On this day the teacher didn't show up, so the girls went to Little Rock and had their picture made. From left to right, they are as follows: Mary Alice Lamb, Thelma Hammons, Margaret Ann Douglas, June Pickard, Jeanne McCain, and Earnestine Zimmerebner. (Jeanne McCain Duke.)

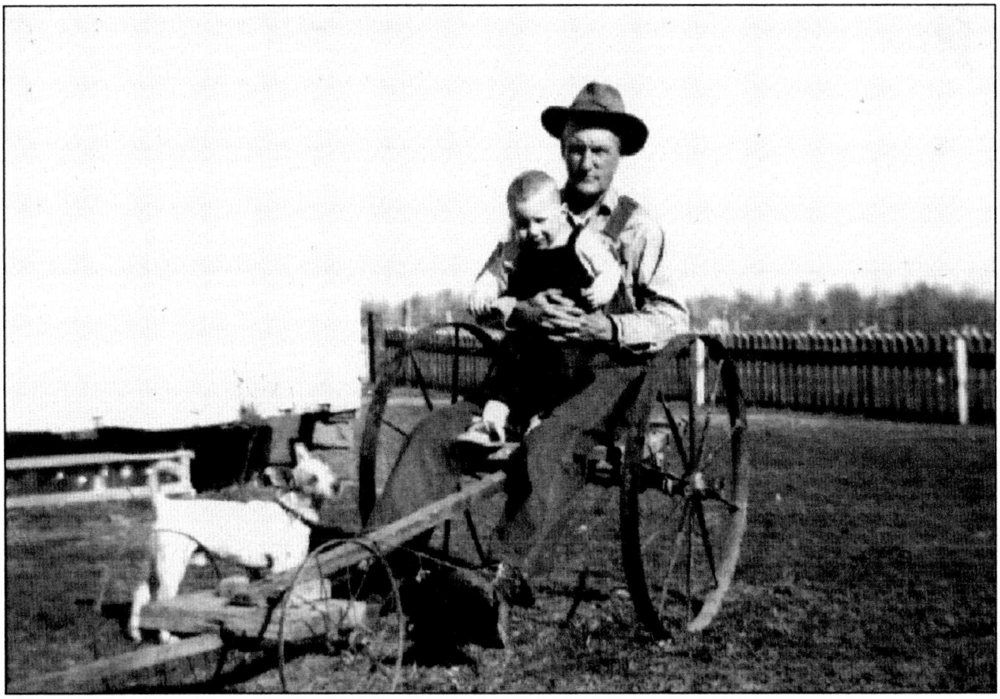

R.D. Boyd is shown here with one of his grandchildren. (Pat Boyd.)

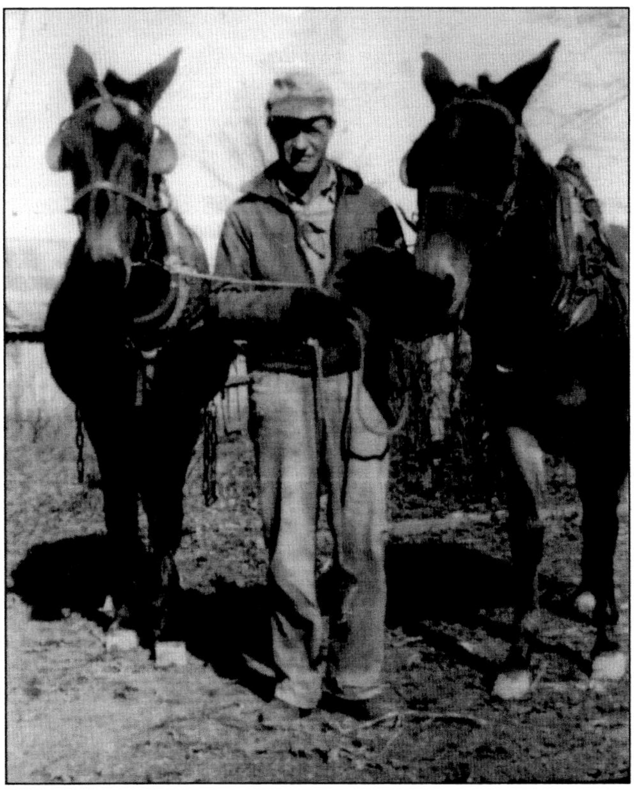

Edgar Green sharecropped cotton near South Bend working with his two mules, Red and Bell, in 1945. (William A. Carr.)

Robert Cole is shown here with his sister Christine in 1943. (Mary Alice Lamb Cole.)

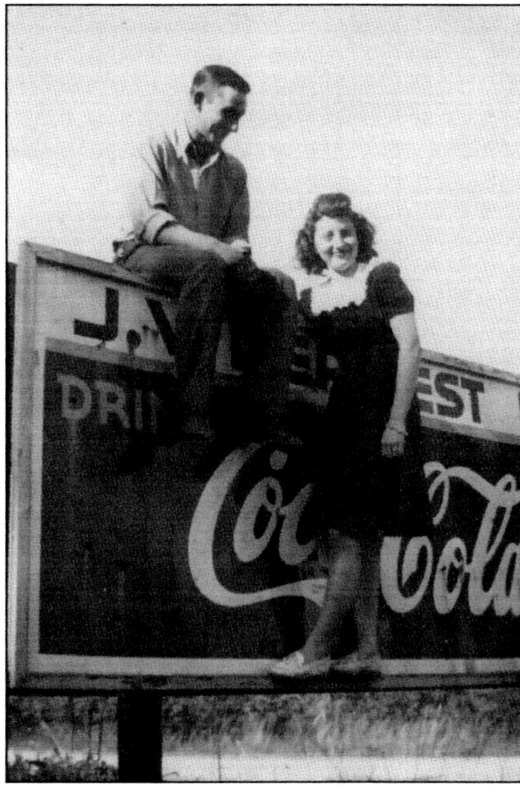

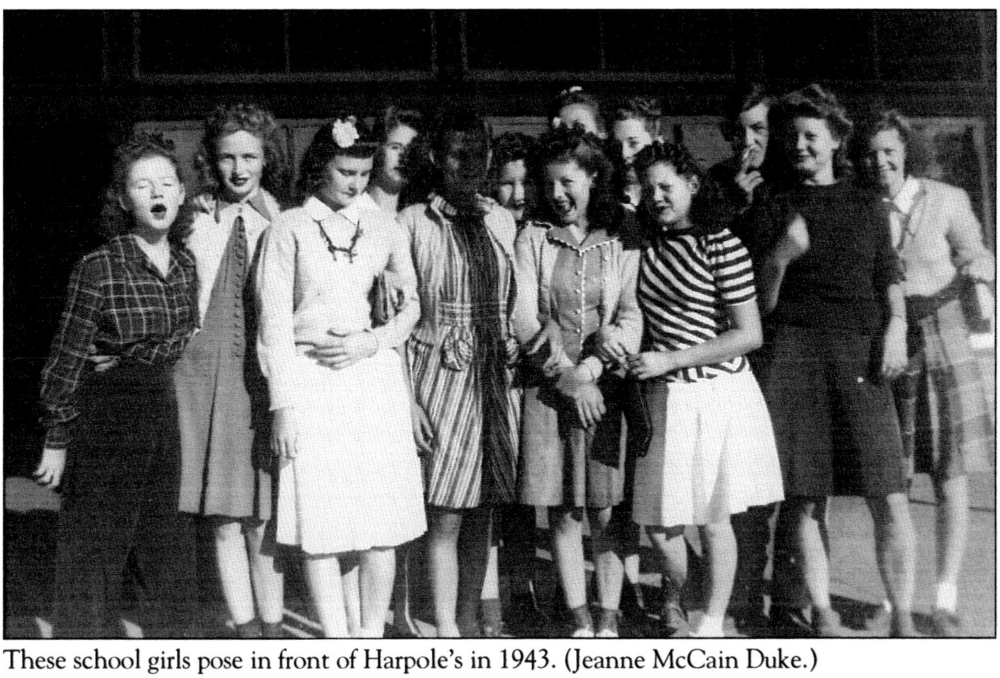

These school girls pose in front of Harpole's in 1943. (Jeanne McCain Duke.)

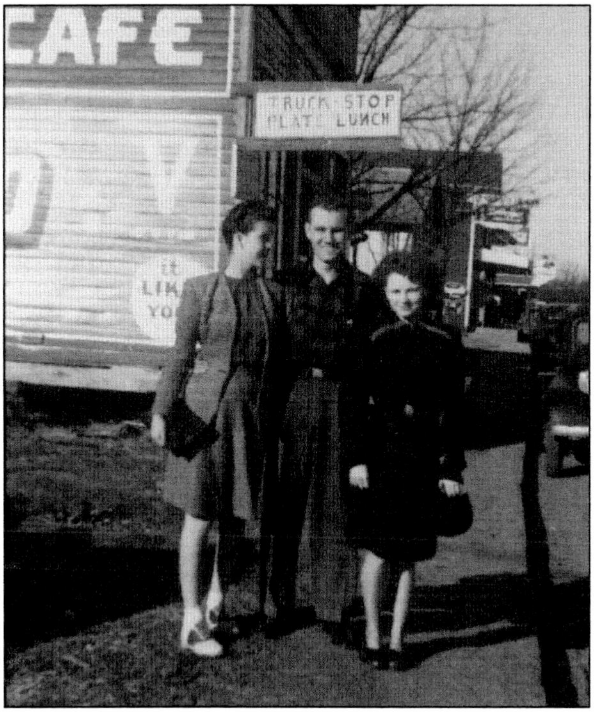

This 1942 photograph shows Pearcey's Café on First Street. The restaurant was open 24-hours to serve Ordnance Plant shift workers. (Jeanne McCain Duke.)

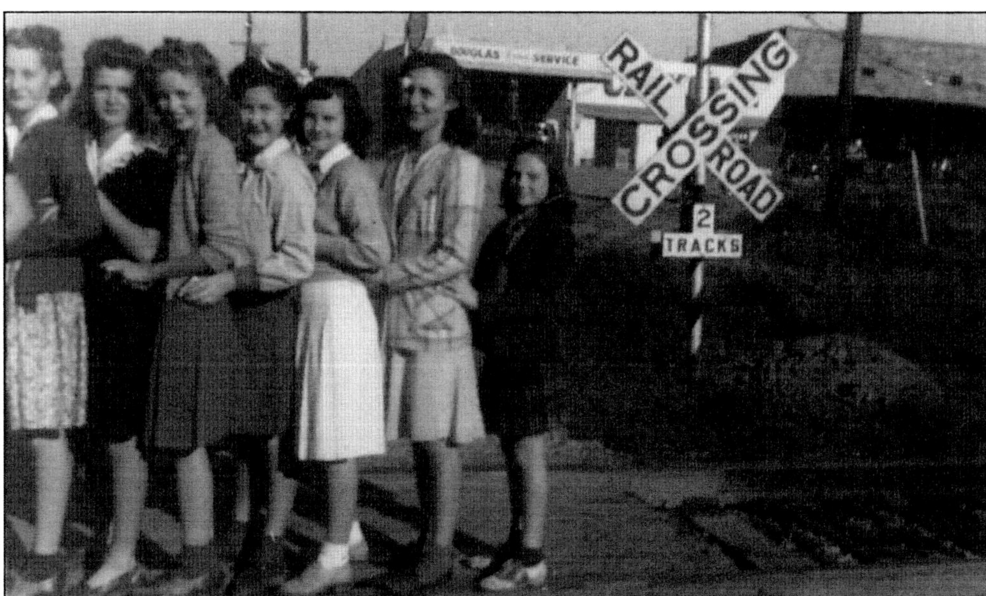

Pictured in 1943 are schoolgirls on the railroad track. First Street is in the background with Douglas' Station, the City Café, and Harpole's. (Jeanne McCain Duke.)

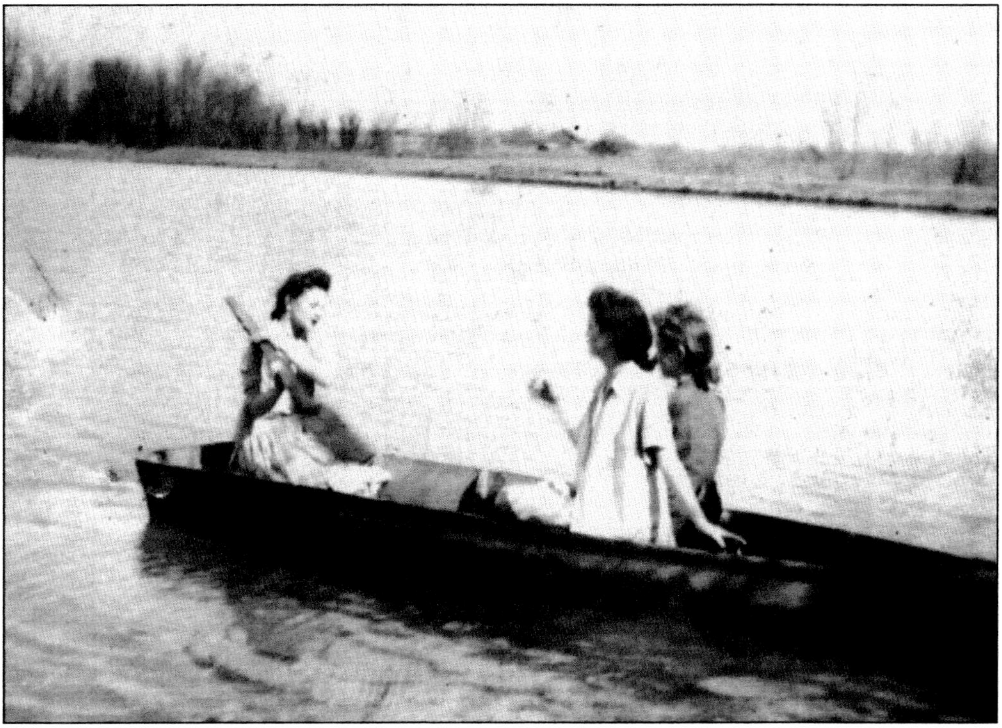

These girls are boating on nearby Lake Nixon. (Jeanne McCain Duke.)

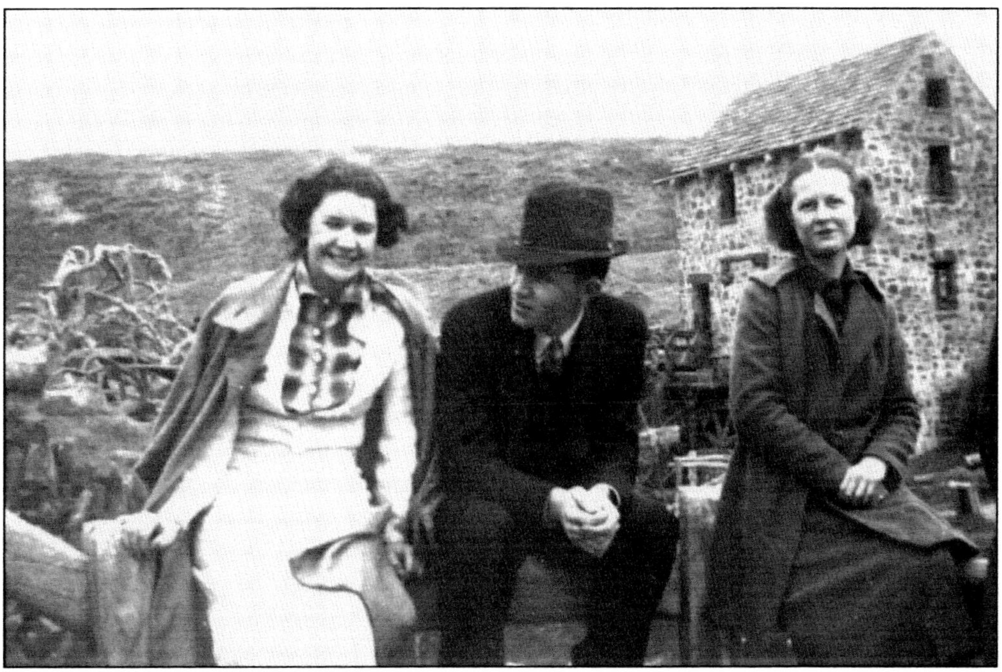

Marie Harpole (at right) and college friends visit the Old Mill in North Little Rock in the 1940s. (Marie Hackett.)

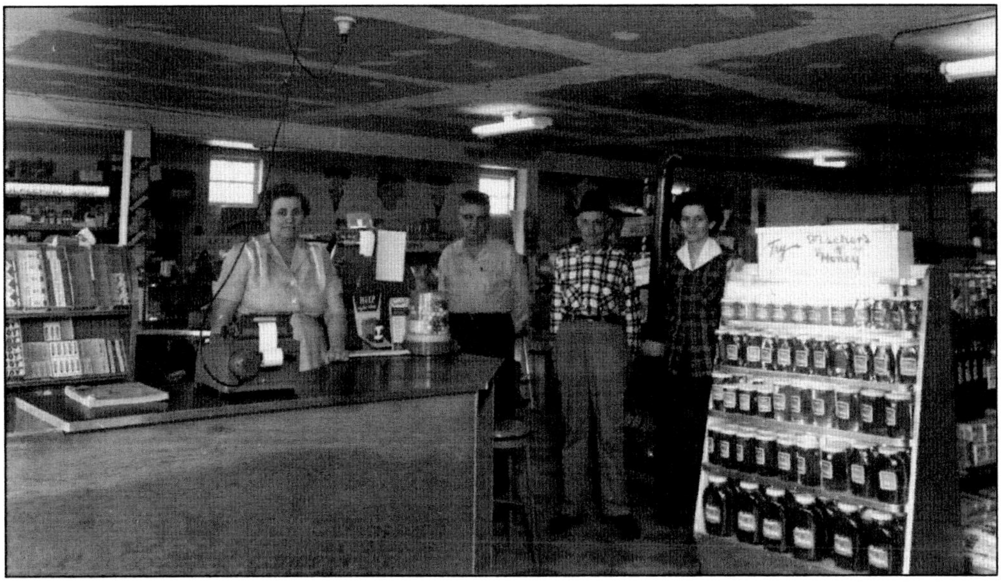

Noel Webb bought his grocery store in 1945, and by the next year, he had remodeled the building. Pictured, from left to right, are: Elia and Noel Webb, Tom LaForce, and Lu Trotter. (Doyle Webb.)

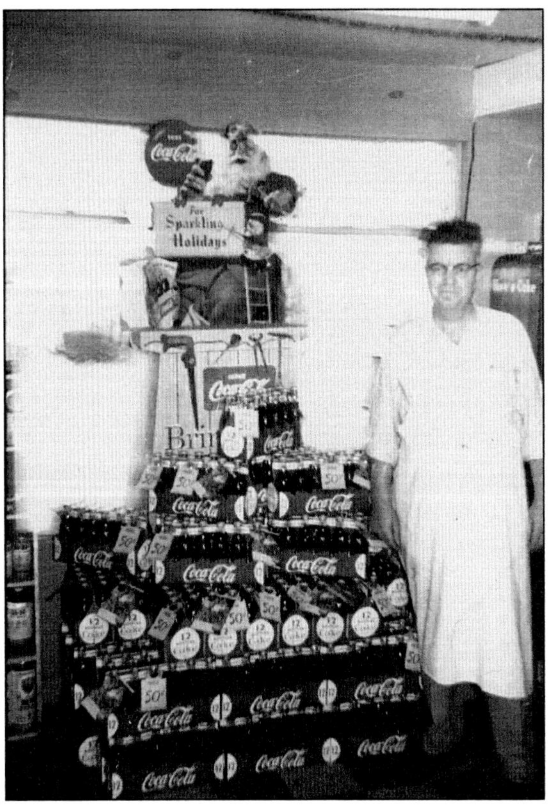

Noel Webb's grocery store operated in Jacksonville from 1945 to 1963, and he was very proud of his Coke display. A meat cutter by trade, he also opened Webb's Dairy Diner on Main Street where he made his own BBQ, lunch meats, and chili. (Doyle Webb.)

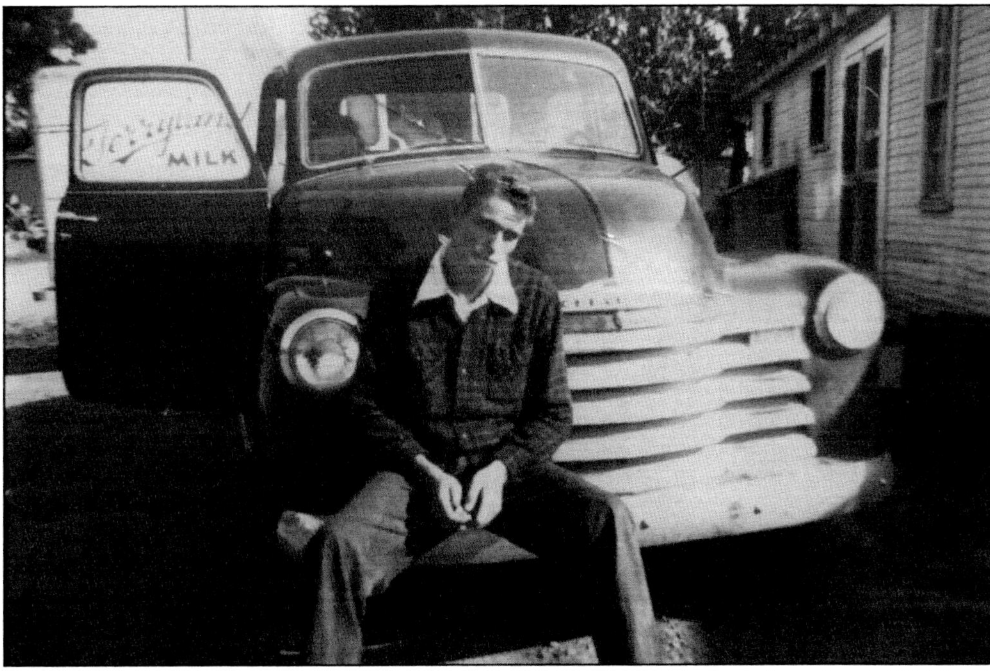

Here is the Webb's Grocery delivery boy. The grocery was a full-time job for Doyle Webb. He was at the store early to sweep out before business opened and returned after school until closing time. He delivered groceries and animal feed in the 1946 pickup truck. After graduation, he worked for the railroad for the next 41 years. (Doyle Webb.)

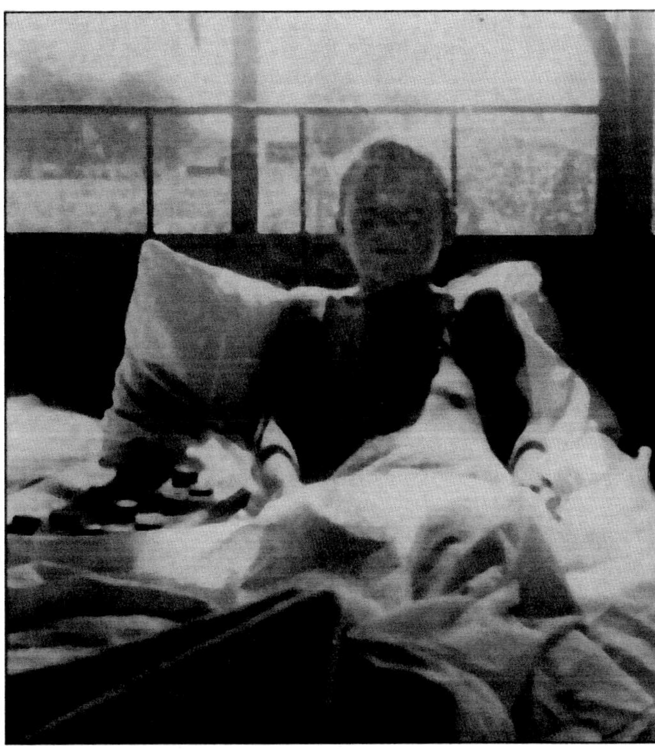

Jack Boyd fell off a horse and was recuperating at home from a broken hip. His mother made him up a bed on the screened porch for his convalescence in 1945. (Pat Boyd.)

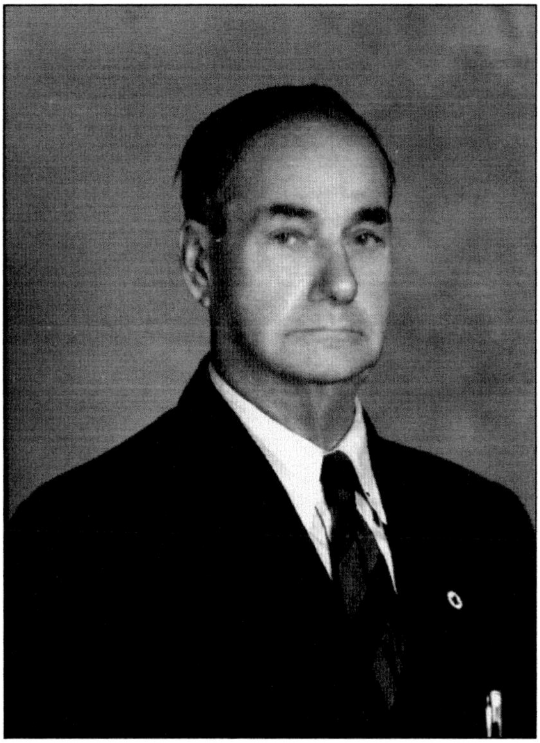

Dr. J.W. Evatt was a doctor in the Jacksonville area for over 50 years. He often said he wore out several horses, and then cars, over the red clay roads. Often with the help of his wife, Rose Brewer Evatt, he delivered babies for his patients, sometimes naming the newborns when the parents couldn't think of a name. The doctor was often paid in produce, canned goods, chickens, and firewood when money was scarce. (Otis Stewart.)

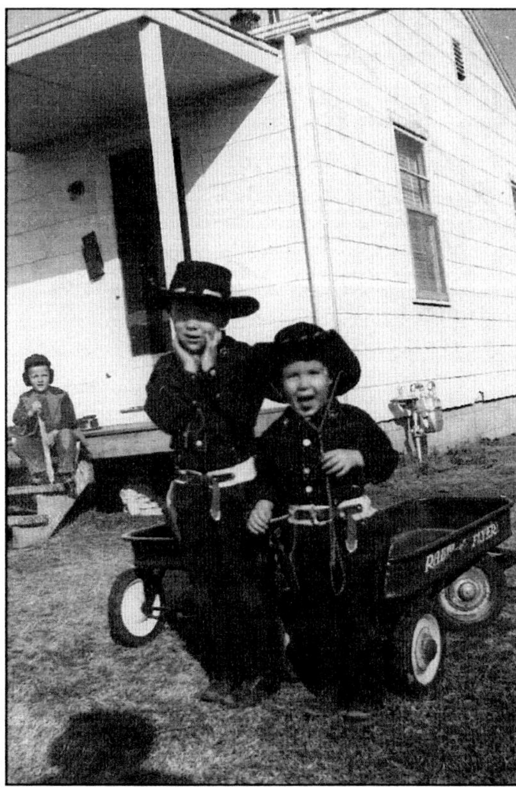

Cowboys Wally and DeWitt Nixon are pictured here with their red wagons in the Sunnyside subdivision in 1946. (Esther Nixon.)

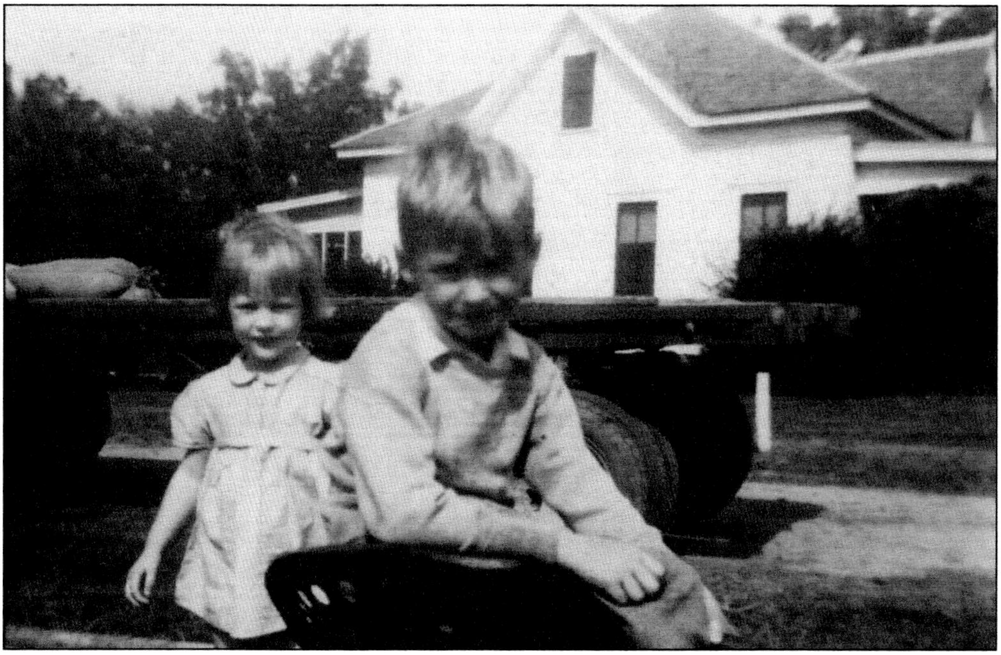

This is Tommy Dupree and his cousin Sue in 1945. The Dupree house is in the background. (Tommy Dupree.)

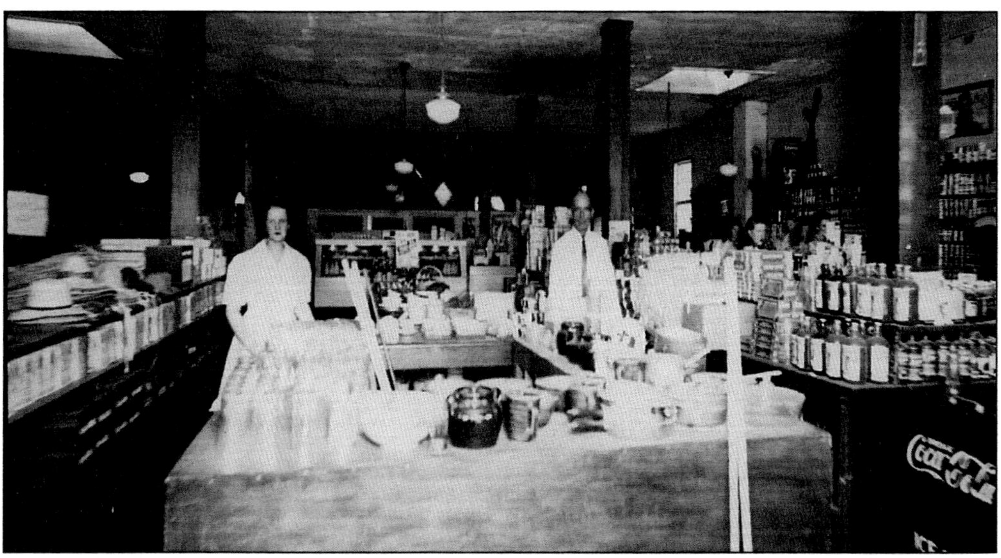

This 1945 photograph shows the Henry Brothers' Store. (Mary Alice Lamb Cole.)

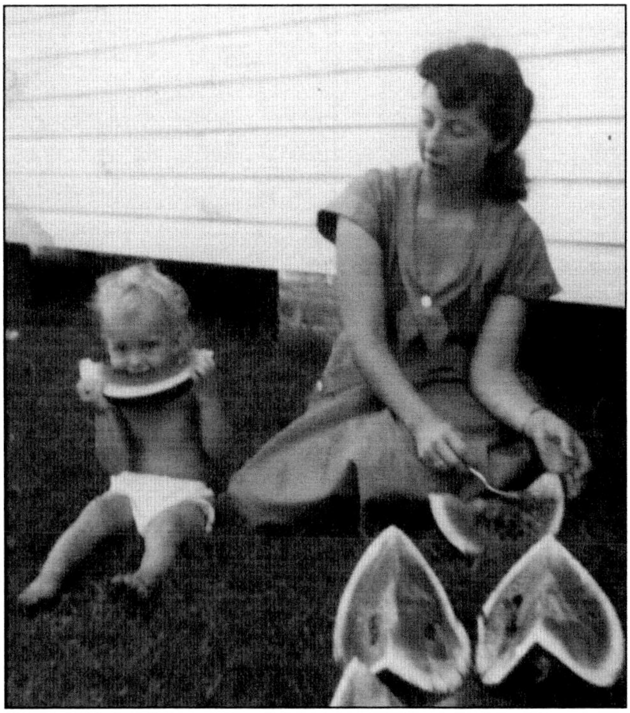

Christine Cole and her child were cooling off on a warm day with cool watermelon in 1949. (Mary Alice Lamb Cole.)

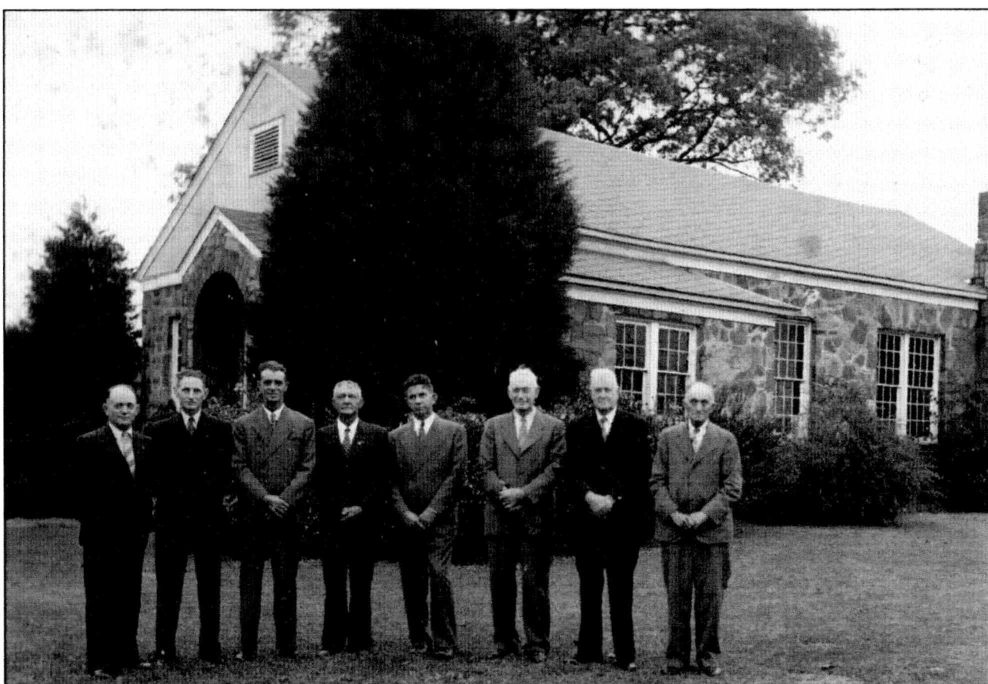

Here is the First Presbyterian Church on Oak Street in 1943. Pictured, from left to right, are as follows: Elders Ed Boyd, George E. McCain, John Jenkins, Dave Edwards, Lanny Parnell (pastor), Mr. Reeser, Mr. Blodgett, and R.D. Boyd. (Jeanne McCain Duke.)

This 1949 photograph shows four boys, the sons of C.B. Carr. They are, from left to right: Charles, William, Kenneth, and James. (William A. Carr.)

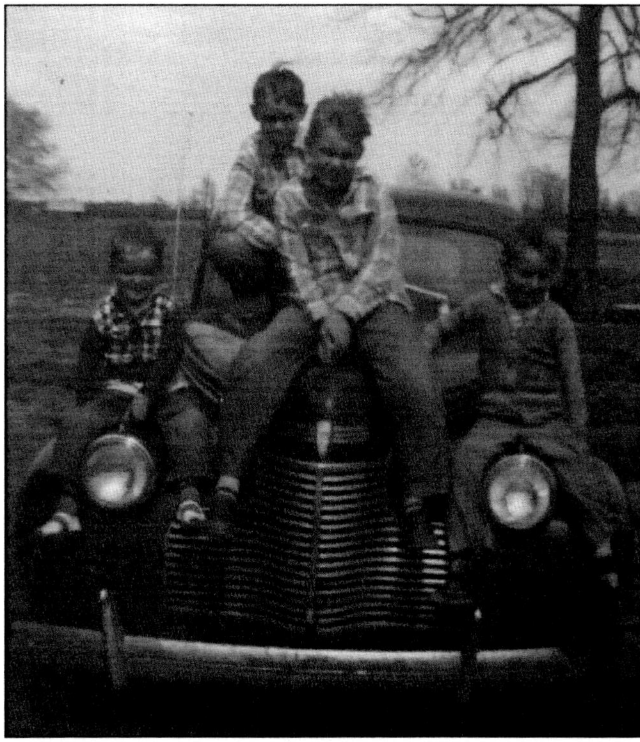

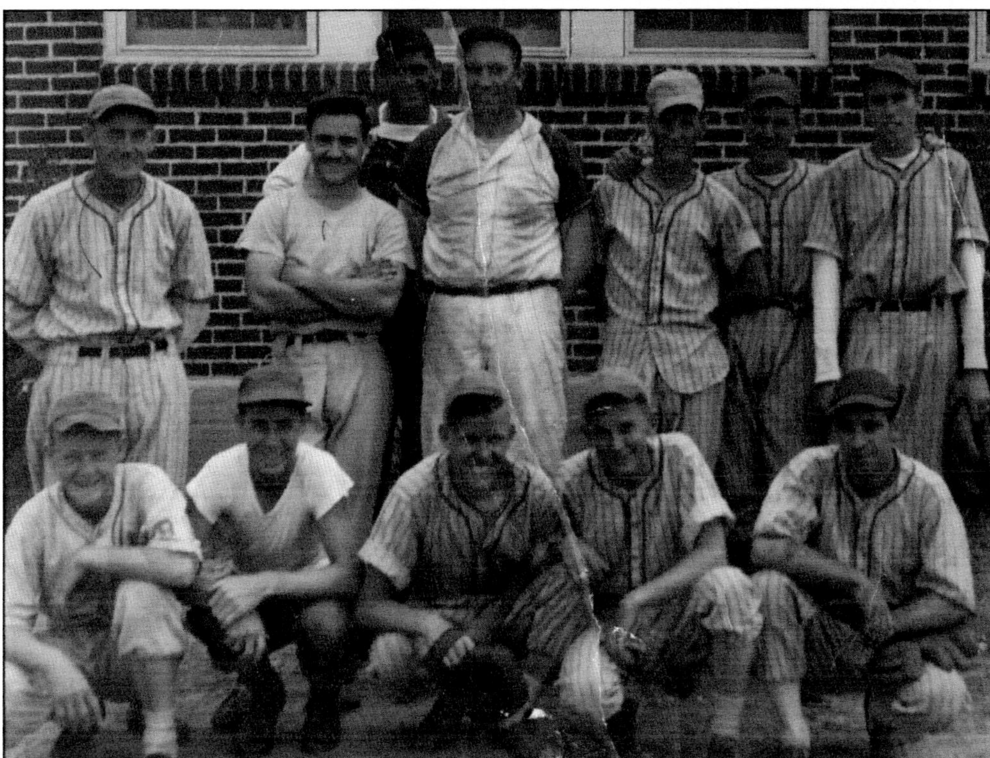

This is a 1947 volunteer baseball club. (Doyle Webb.)

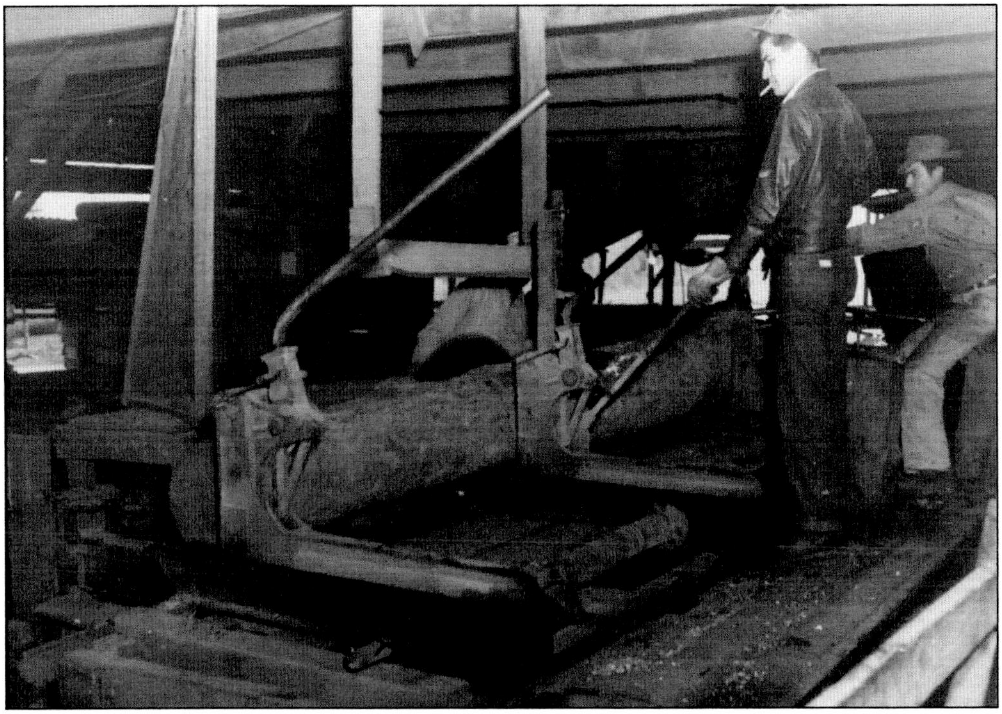

The Williams-Brown Lumber Company is shown here in the late 1940s. Located on Graham Road by the railroad tracks, the operation made railroad ties. A fourth-generation lumberman, James (Trix) Williams, bought the company in 1946. It burned in 1961 and was rebuilt, but burned again 10 years later and the business was closed. (Kathryn Williams.)

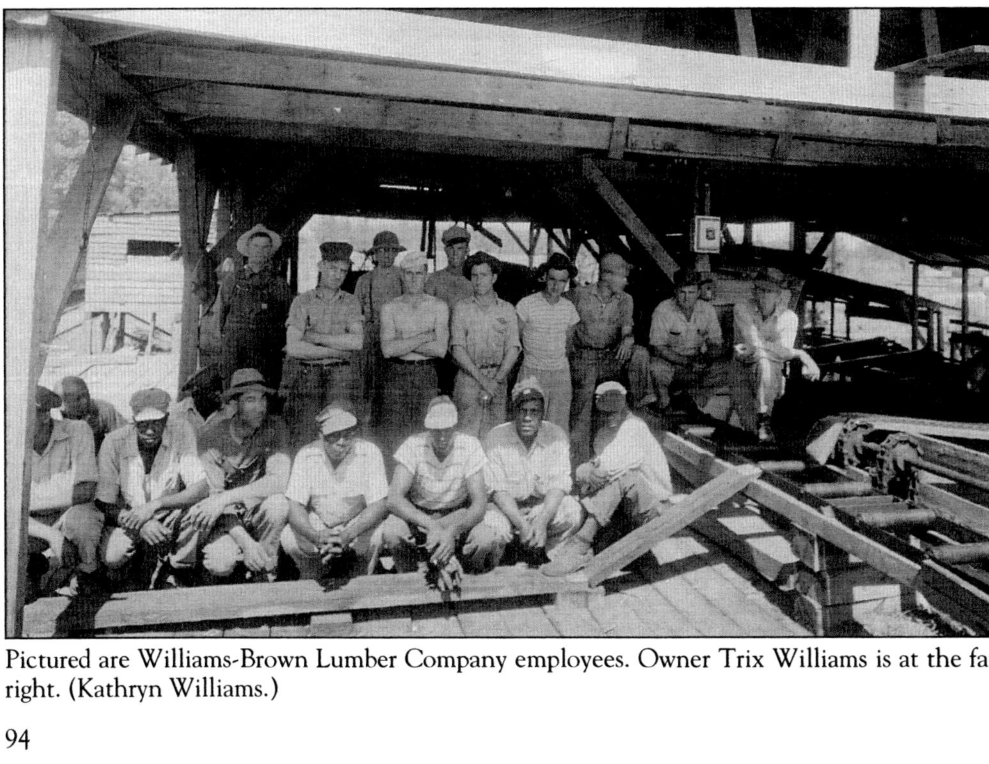

Pictured are Williams-Brown Lumber Company employees. Owner Trix Williams is at the far right. (Kathryn Williams.)

Five

THE 1950S AND BEYOND

In the years following the closing of the Ordnance Plant, the newly formed Jacksonville Chamber of Commerce attempted to attract business and industry into the town. The group also set their sights on securing another federal installation—a proposed Air Force base. In an extraordinary effort with several area organizations and individuals cooperating over the ensuing years, the local group managed to raise money to purchase the land for the facility, offering to give it to the military. In December 1952, the military announced its selection, and the Little Rock Air Force Base found a home at Jacksonville. It broke ground in December 1953 and opened in 1955. A four-lane highway was completed, connecting the town to other major areas of the state.

The Air Base brought both economic and population growth to Jacksonville, and the area expanded to 15,000 people in the early '60s, and to nearly 30,000 at the end of the century.

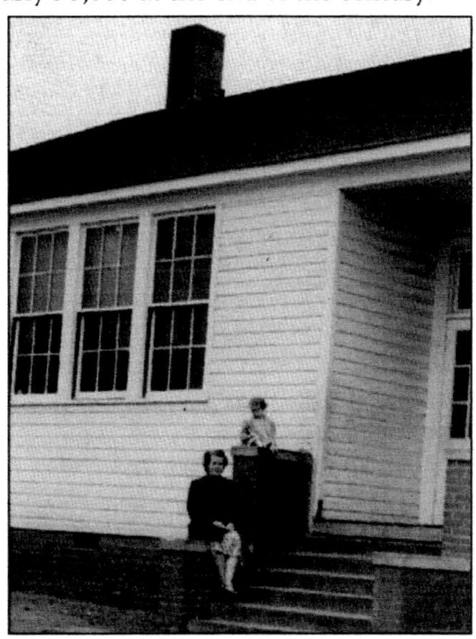

Mrs. Hibbs sits with a child in front of the Federal Building in 1952. This structure was built by the Federal Government for school children when the Ordnance Plant was created. It is still in service in the present-day elementary school complex. (Richard Hibbs.)

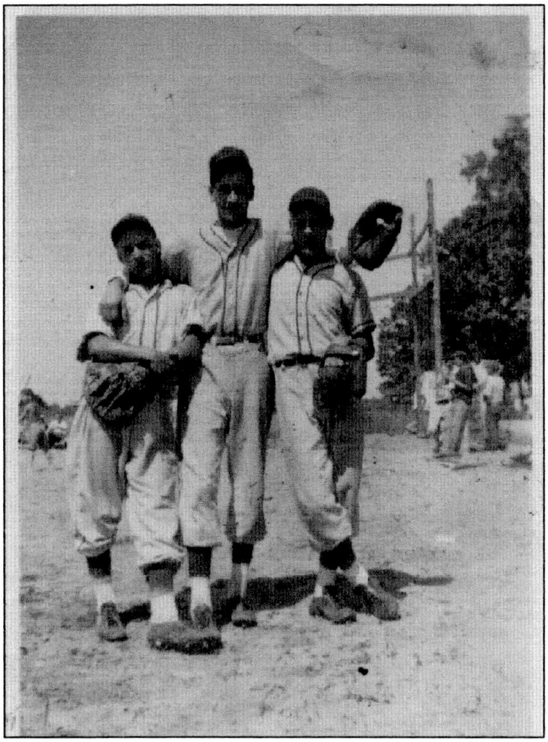

Jack Boyd and his baseball pals are pictured here in 1950. (Pat Boyd.)

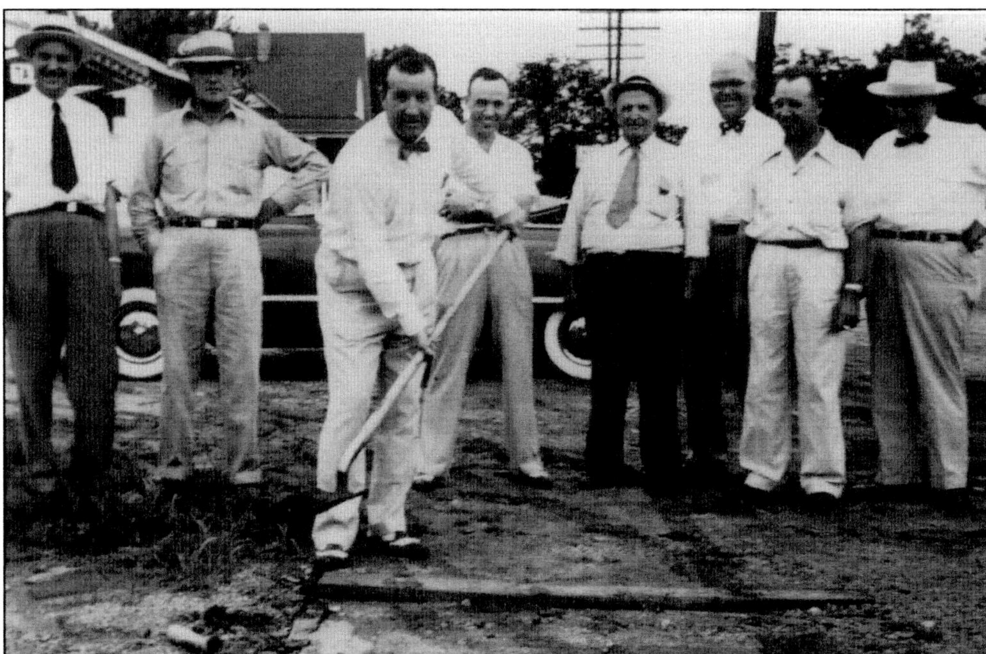

Raymond Rebsamen is shown here breaking ground for the Jacksonville State Bank in 1950. Standing behind, with his arms crossed, is Pat Wilson. Believing in the potential growth of Jacksonville, Wilson managed to organize backing to start the first financial institution in the town. (Jacksonville Historical Society.)

Melda Rice and Robert Mallett were at the Jacksonville State Bank opening in 1951. (Opal Harpole Mallett.)

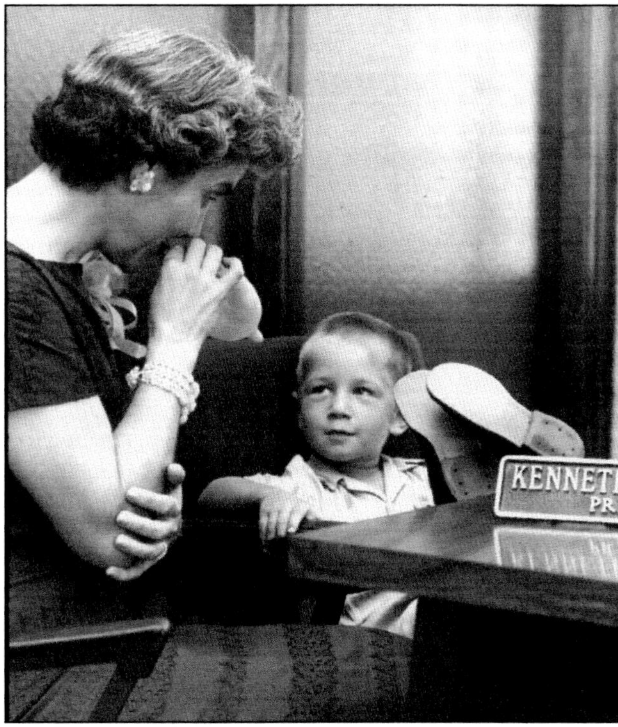

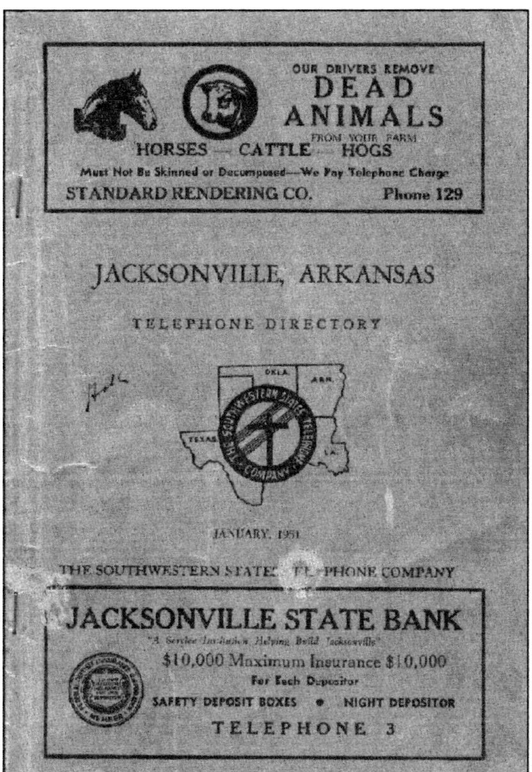

This is the Jacksonville Phone Directory from 1951. (Nixon Library, Jacksonville.)

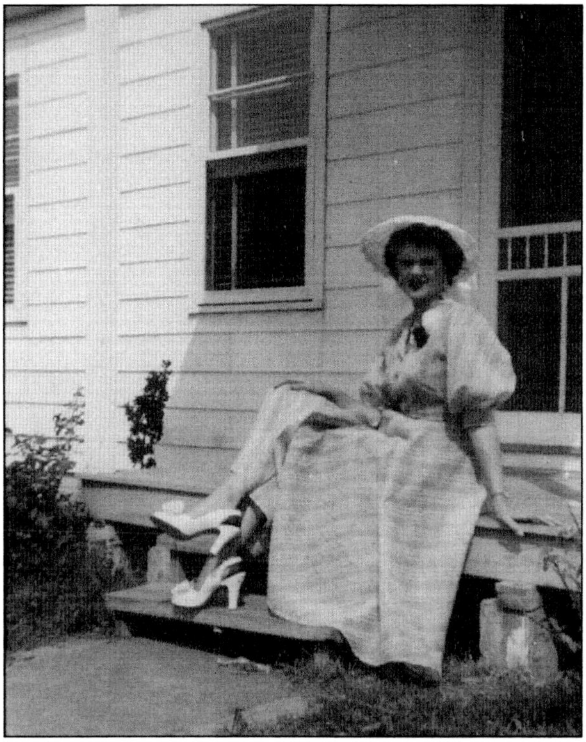

Fannie Neal is a picture of the '50s fashions in this 1952 photograph. (Stephen Eudy.)

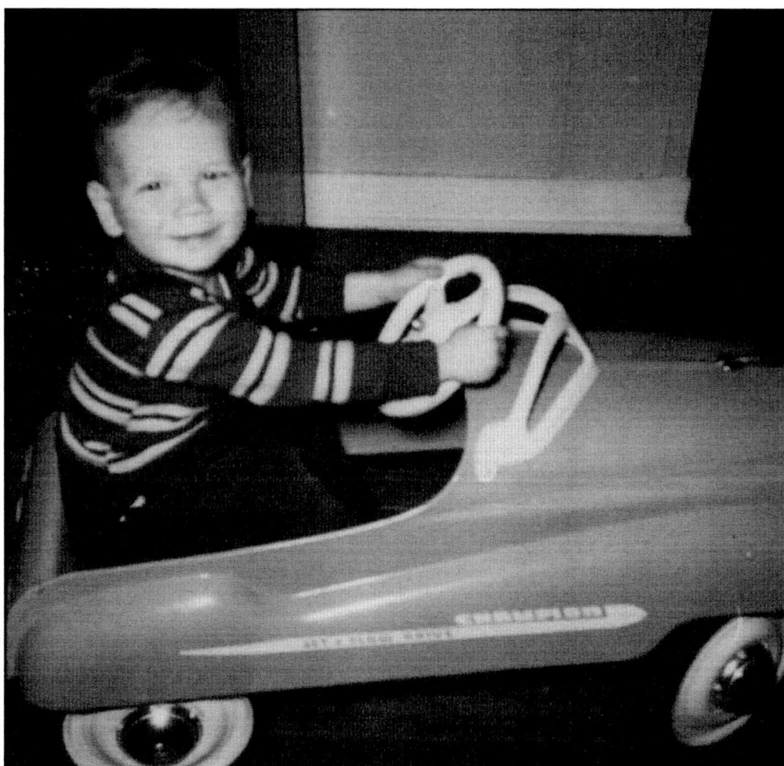

Stephen Eudy drives a popular model '50s car in this 1952 shot. (Stephen Eudy.)

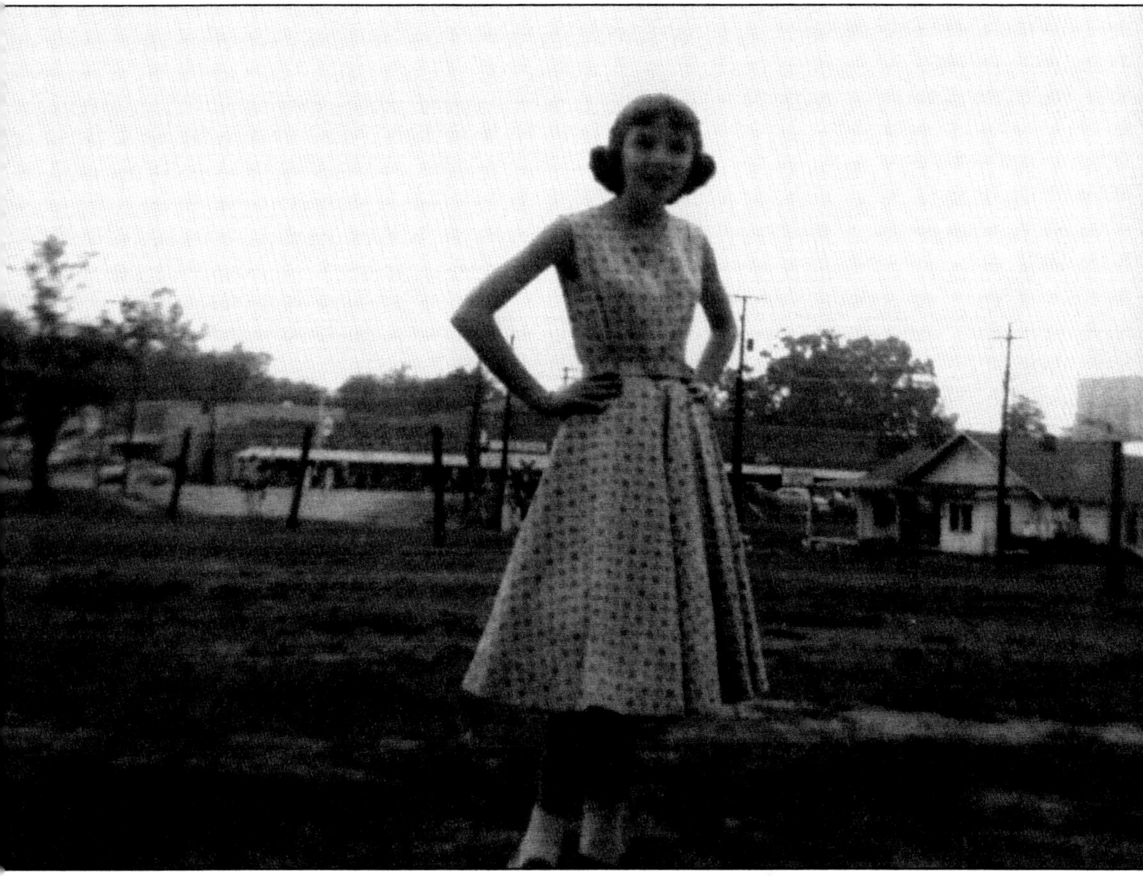

Jacksonville's Main Street is in the background with an unidentified young woman from the 1950s. (Richard Hibbs.)

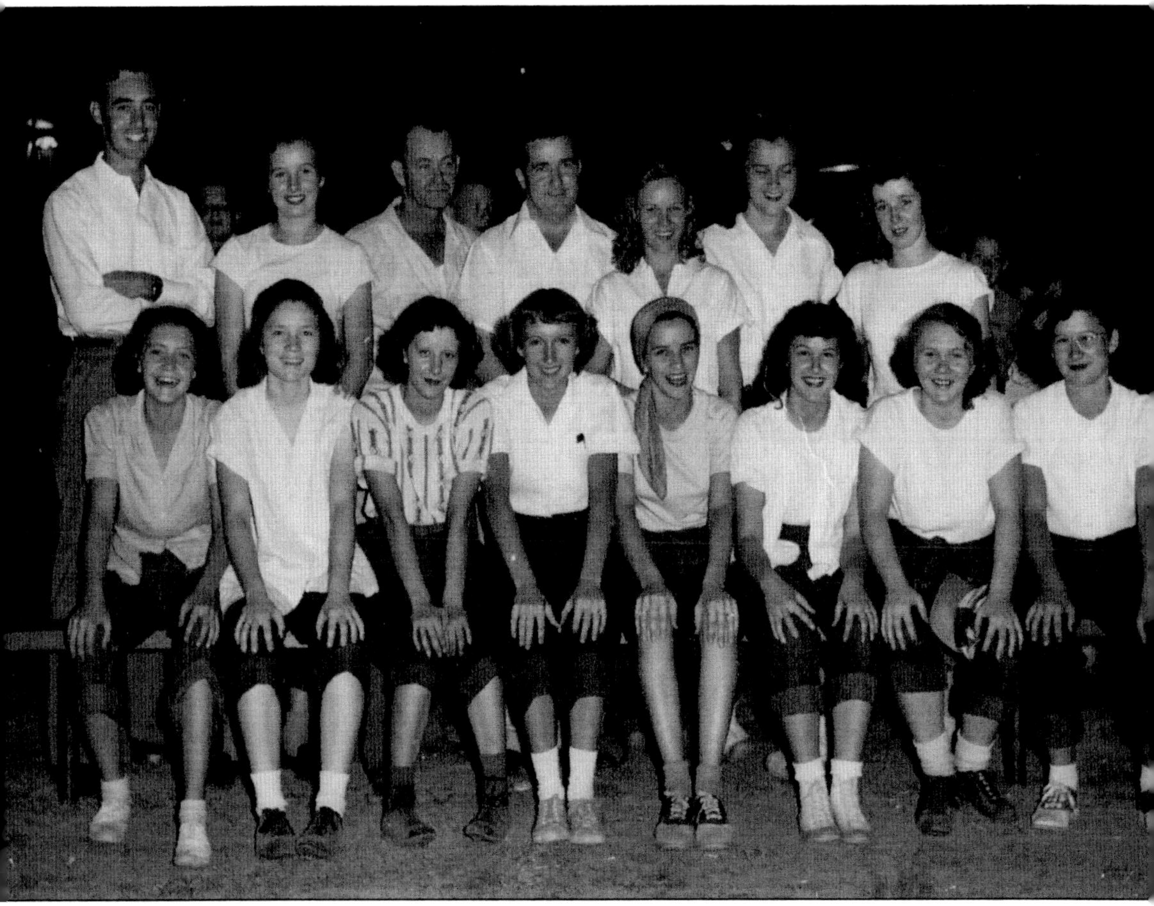

This is the Jacksonville Girls' Basketball Team. (Stephen Eudy.)

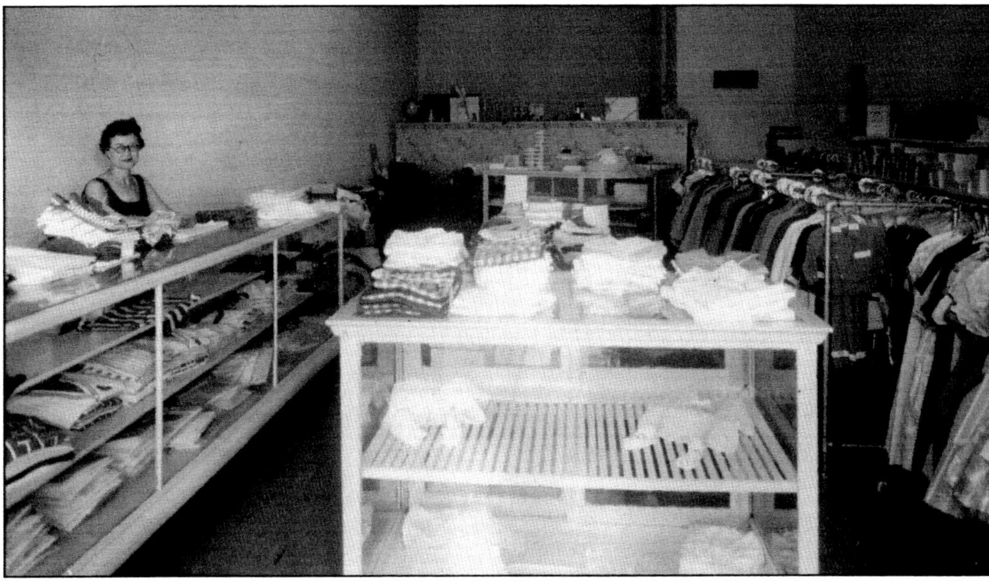

Marie Hackett followed her family tradition and opened Scamper Shop, a children's clothing store. (Marie Harpole Hackett.)

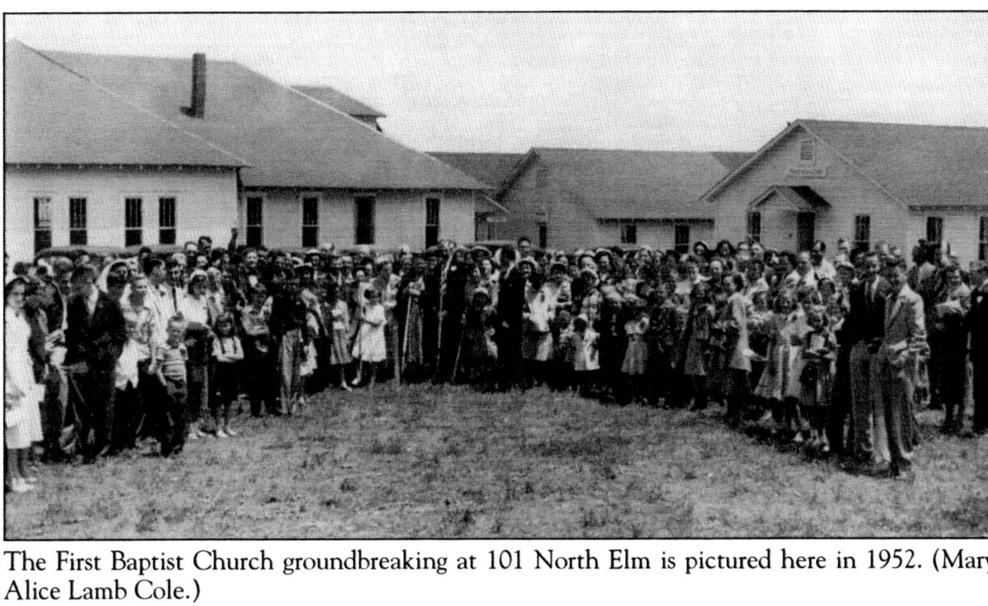

The First Baptist Church groundbreaking at 101 North Elm is pictured here in 1952. (Mary Alice Lamb Cole.)

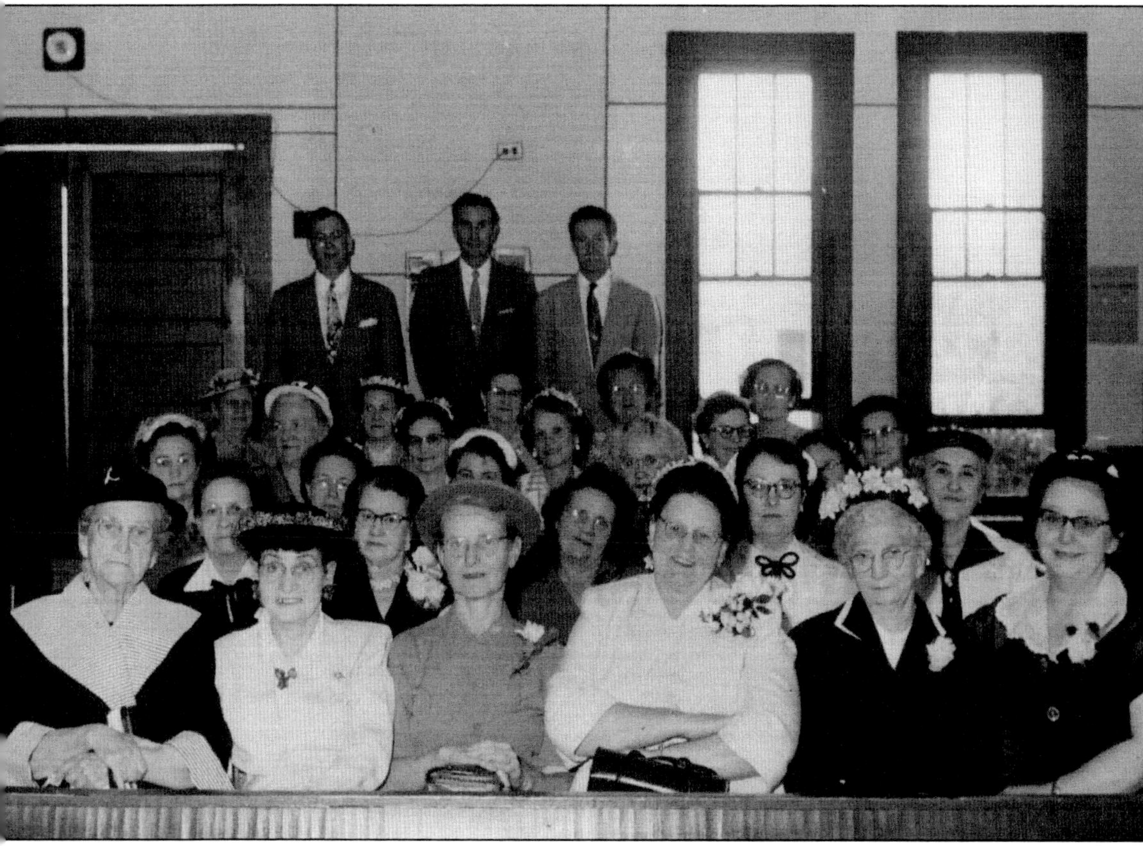
This 1952 photograph shows a First Baptist Church adult Sunday school class. (Mary Alice Lamb Cole.)

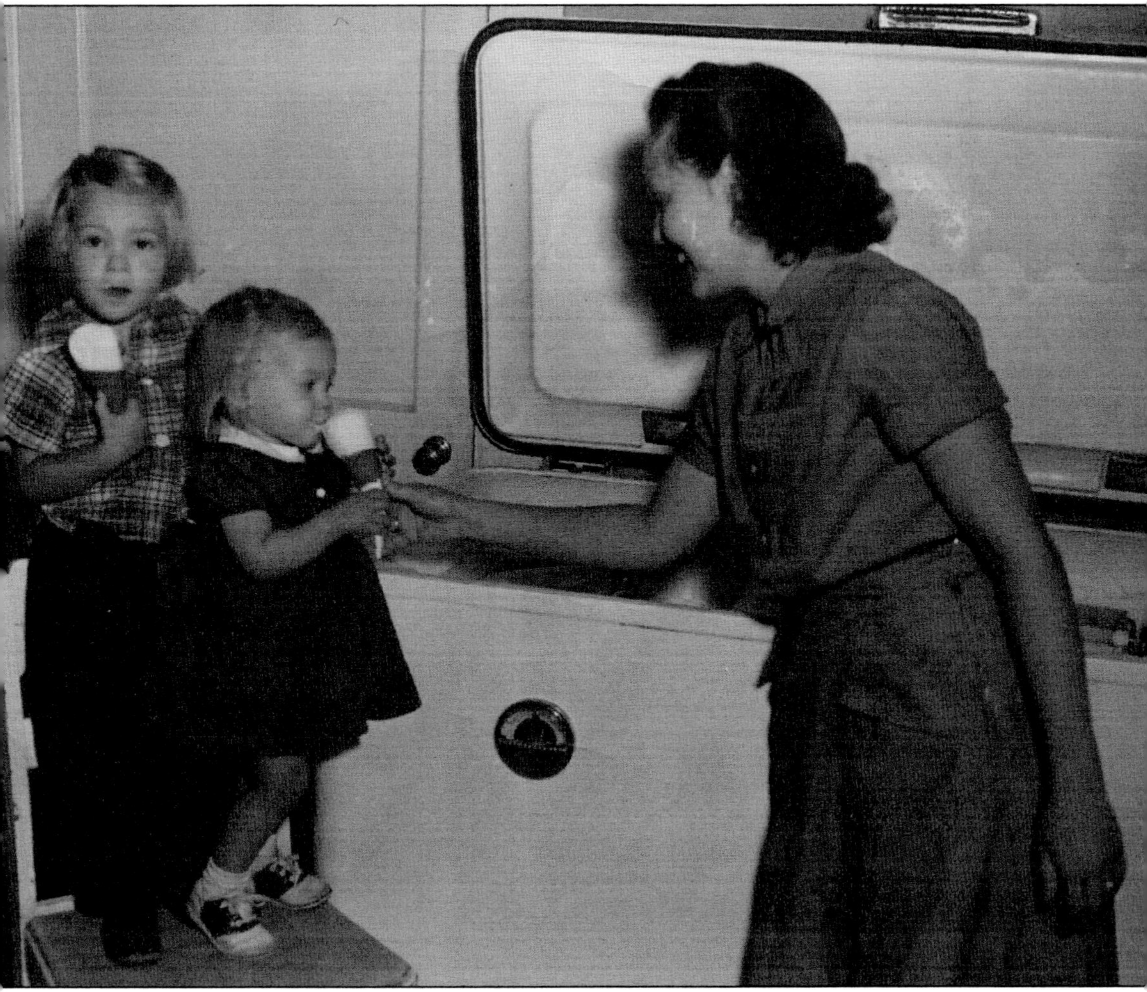

The '50s were times of many new discoveries and conveniences. Mary Alice Lamb Cole and her daughters were pictured with her new deep freezer, only the second one in the area. (Mary Alice Lamb Cole.)

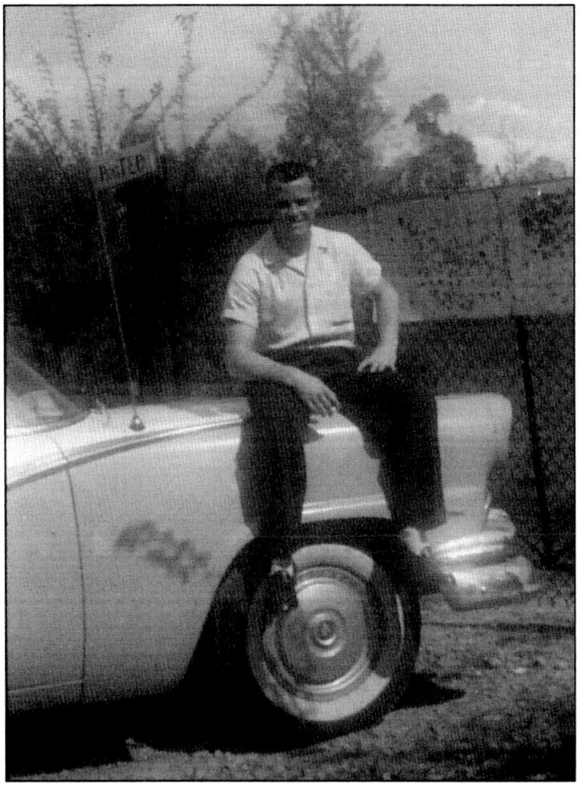

Jerry Boyd is shown here in 1957. Being a teenager in the '50s meant feeling pride of ownership in a car. (Pat Boyd.)

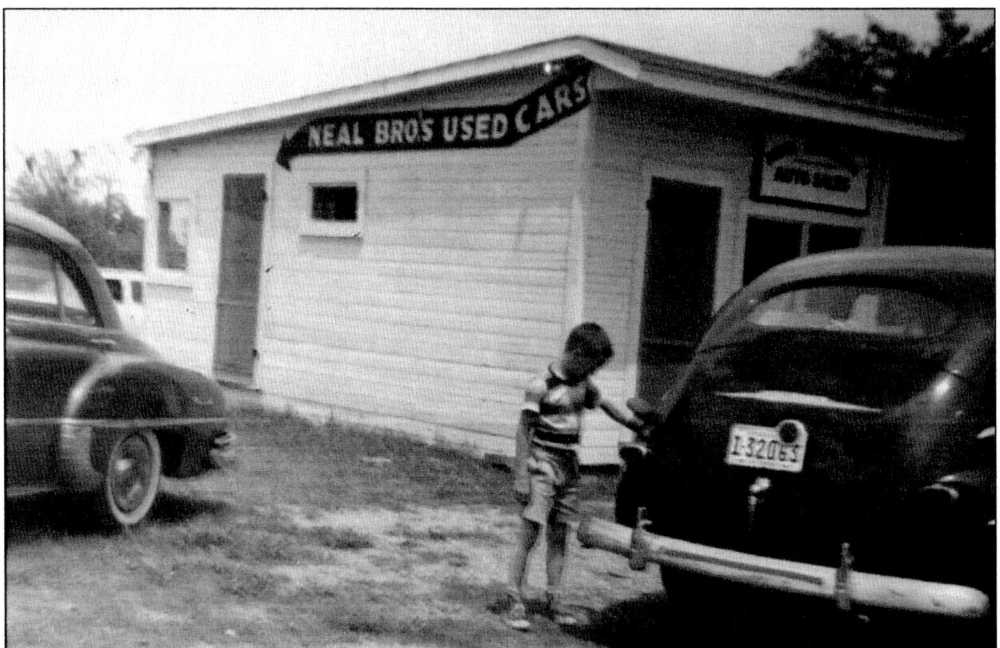

The late '50s proved to be a classic time for automobiles. The Neal brothers (Bill and Joe) opened a used car lot on the corner of South Elm and Victory Circle. (Stephen Eudy.)

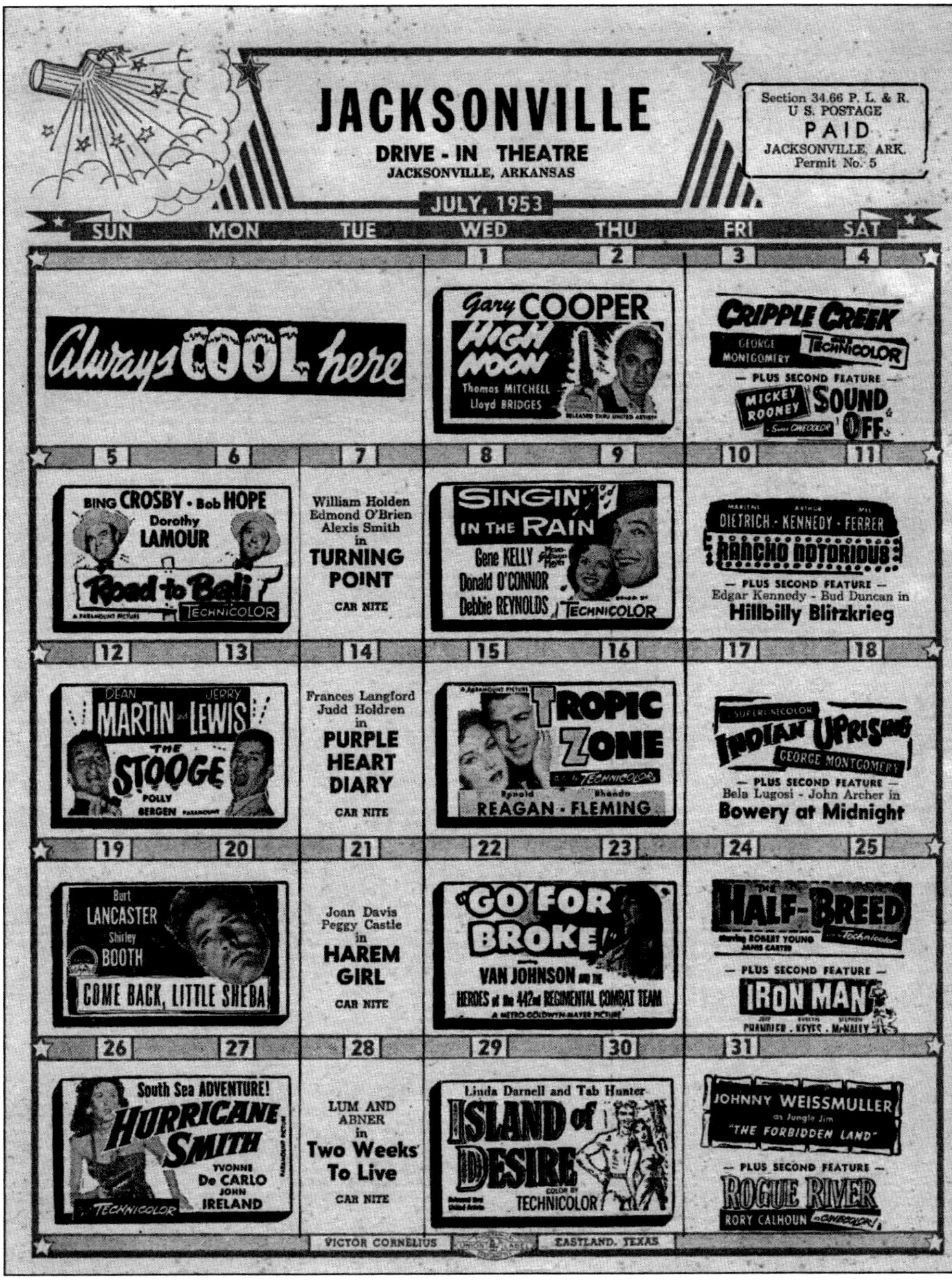

Prosperity bought cars, and cars spawned drive-in movies. The Jacksonville Drive-In Theater showed movies every night of the week. (Nixon Library, Jacksonville.)

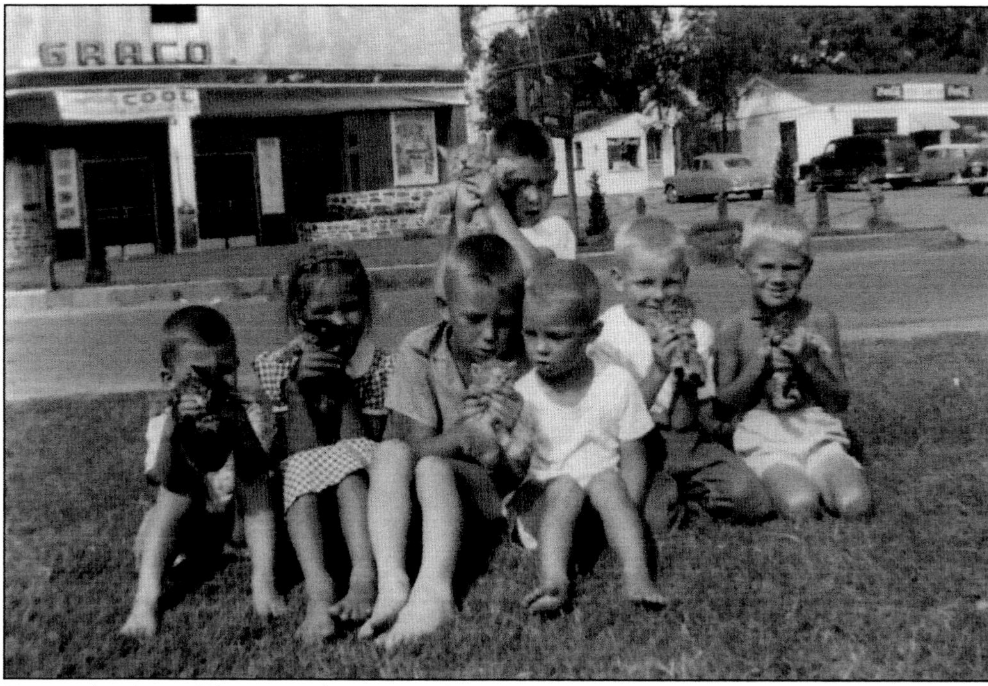

Here is the Graco Theater in the 1950s. These lucky kids lived right across the street from the movie theater. The theater was demolished in the 1990s to make way for the Senior Activity Center. (Esther Nixon.)

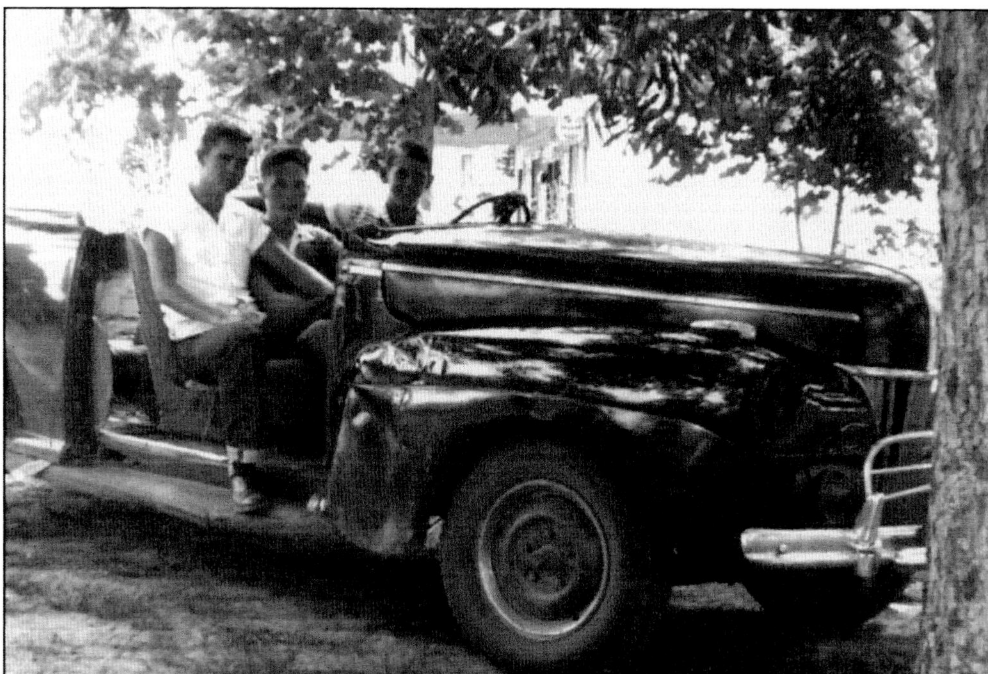

The Webb grocery in the background was a convenient meeting place for these teens in 1954. They are, from left to right: William Carr, Rayburn Lamb, and Roger Uric. (William A. Carr.)

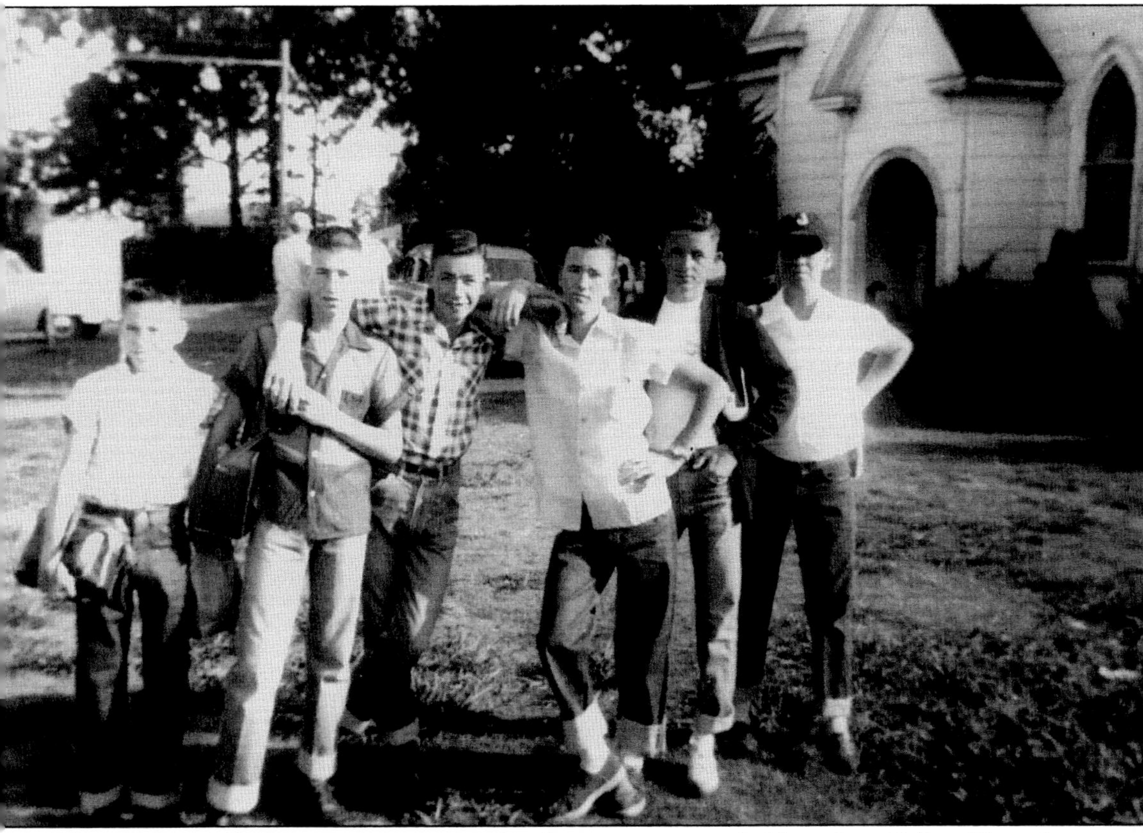

These Jacksonville boys were active in the Scouting program held at the old First United Methodist Church in 1954. Pictured second from right is Kenneth Griggs, and third from right is Charles Van Ostrum. (Richard Hibbs.)

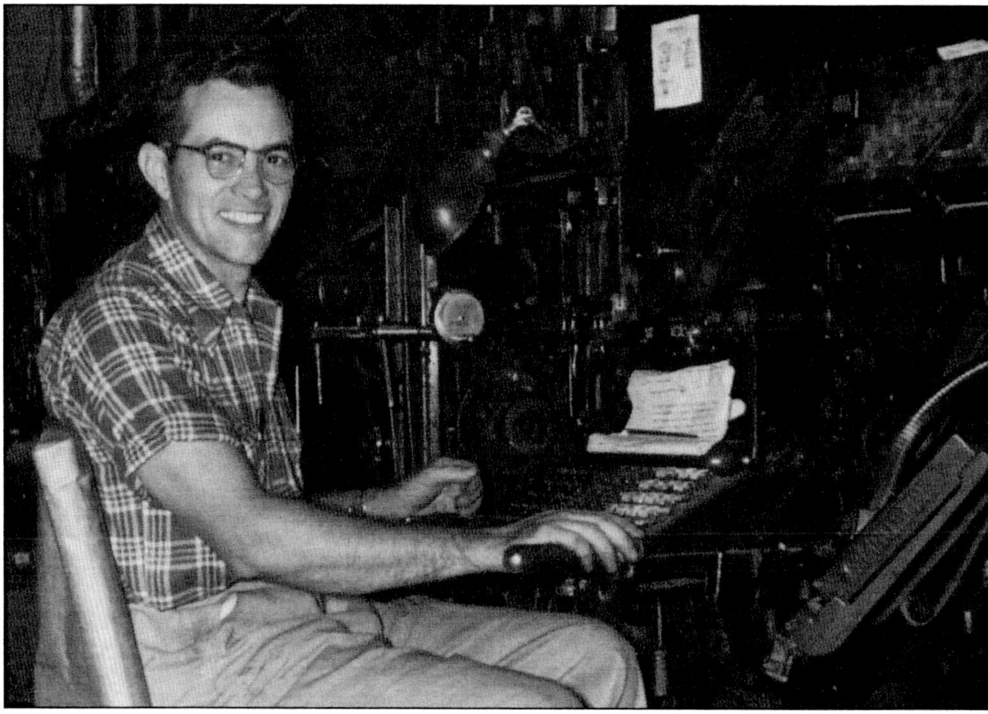

Marion Lamb, linotype operator for the *Arkansas Gazette* newspaper, is shown here in 1955. (Mary Alice Lamb Cole.)

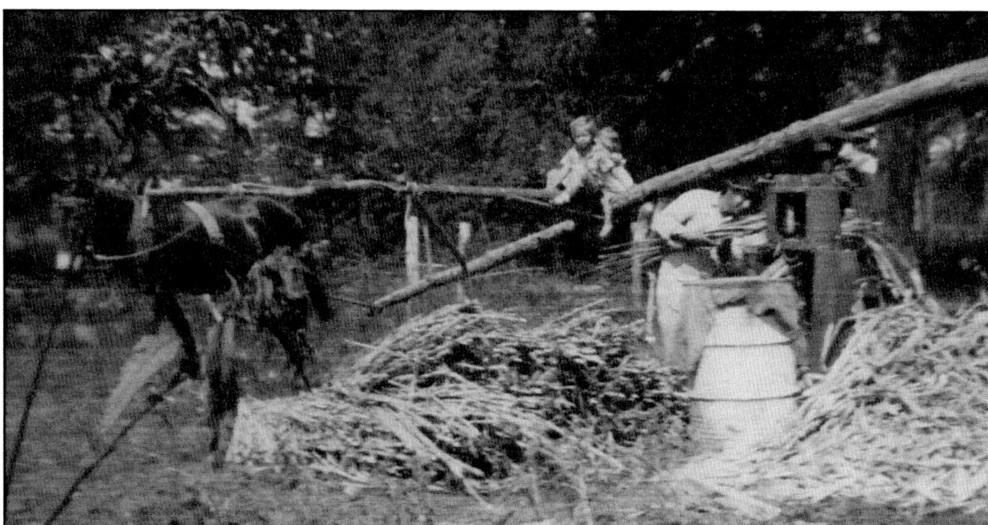

Robert Cole worked for First Electric, but he loved farming. Here he is pressing sorghum cane to make molasses, 1955. (Mary Alice Lamb Cole.)

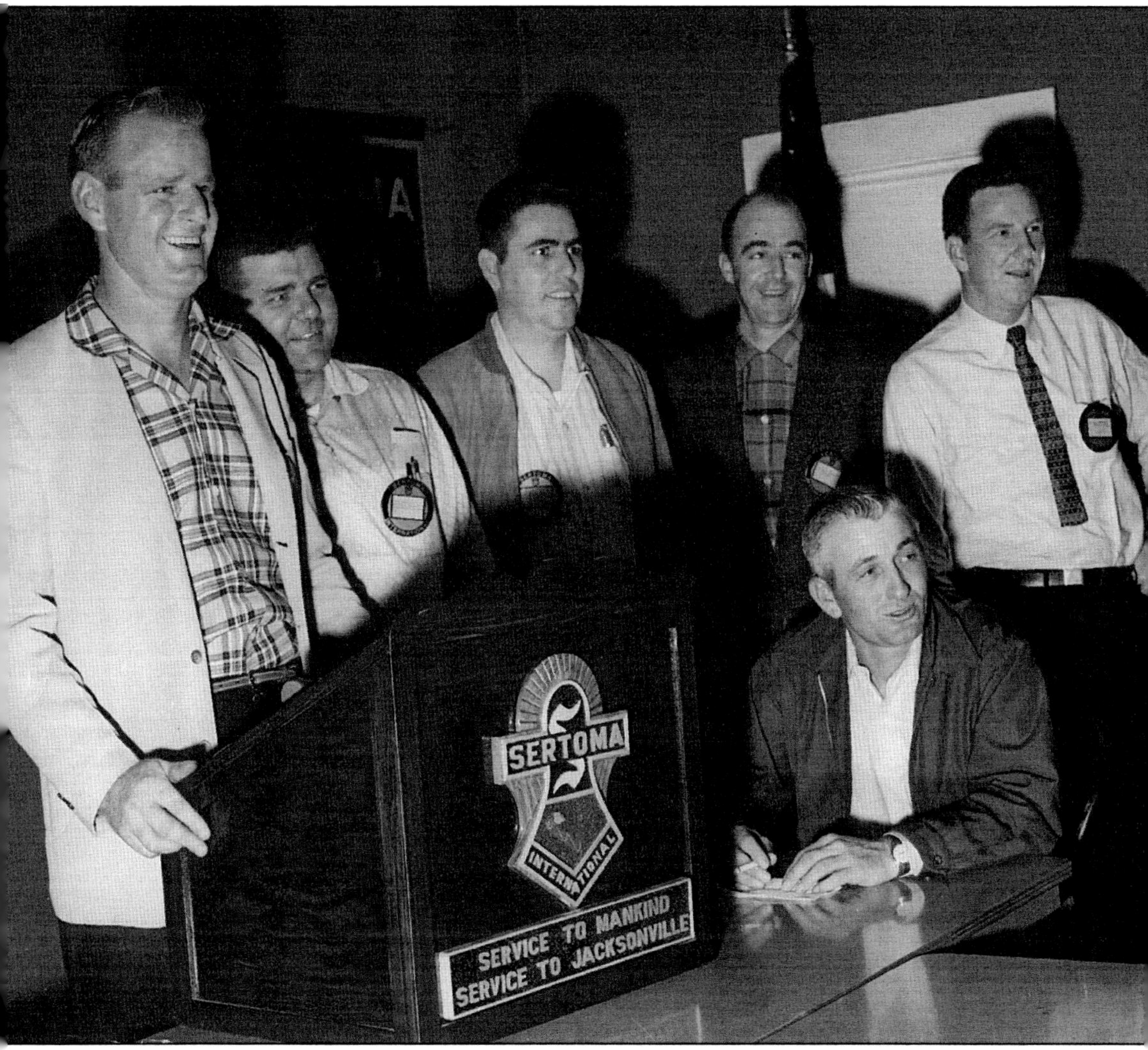

This is the Sertoma Club in 1954. Pictured, from left to right, are as follows: Johnny Wright, Bill Pearson, Doyle Webb, Eddie Thompkins, Bill Chambers, and John Harden (later mayor of Jacksonville). (Doyle Webb.)

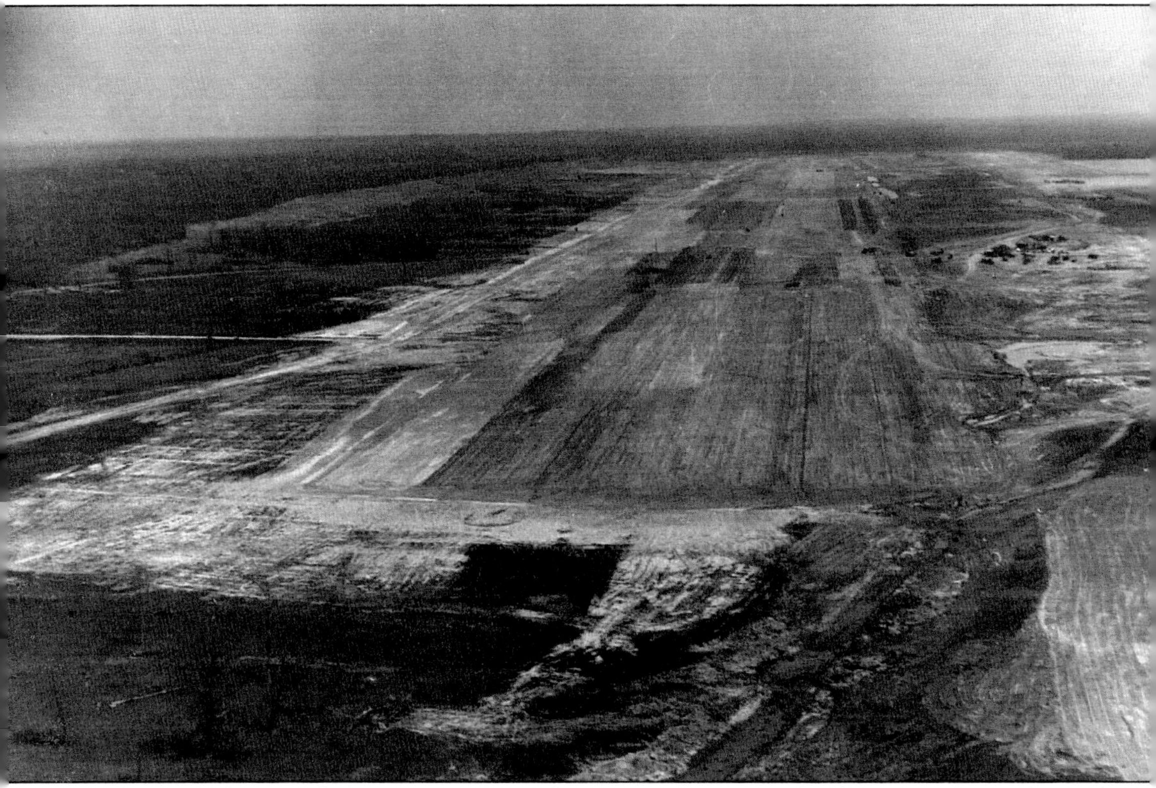

This 1953 photograph shows an airstrip under construction. Once the decision to locate the Air Base in Jacksonville had been made, land was purchased, and 150 local families were required to relocate. Construction on the base began in December 1953. (LRAFB Historian.)

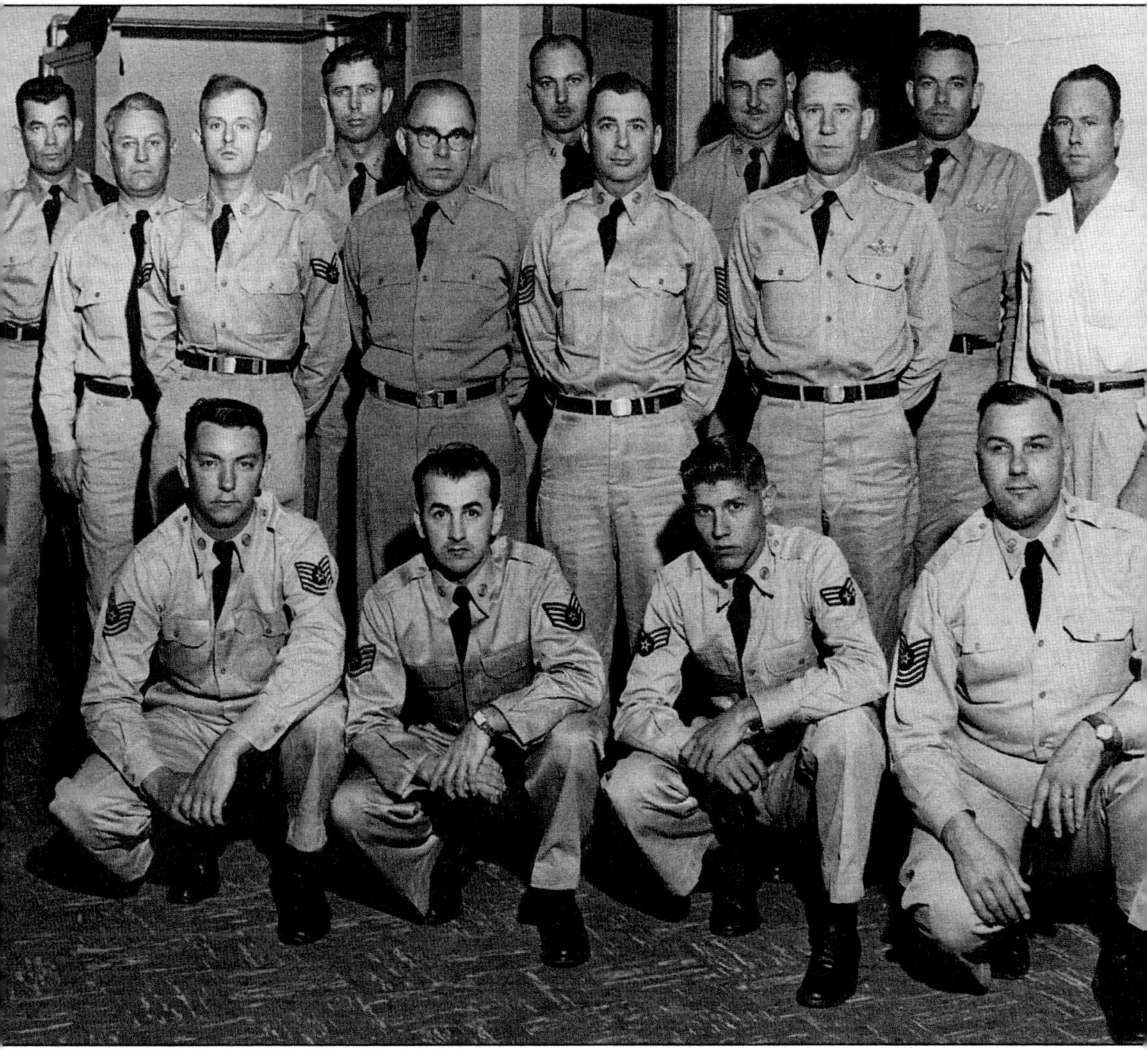

Here is the LRAFB First Command. (LRAFB Historian.)

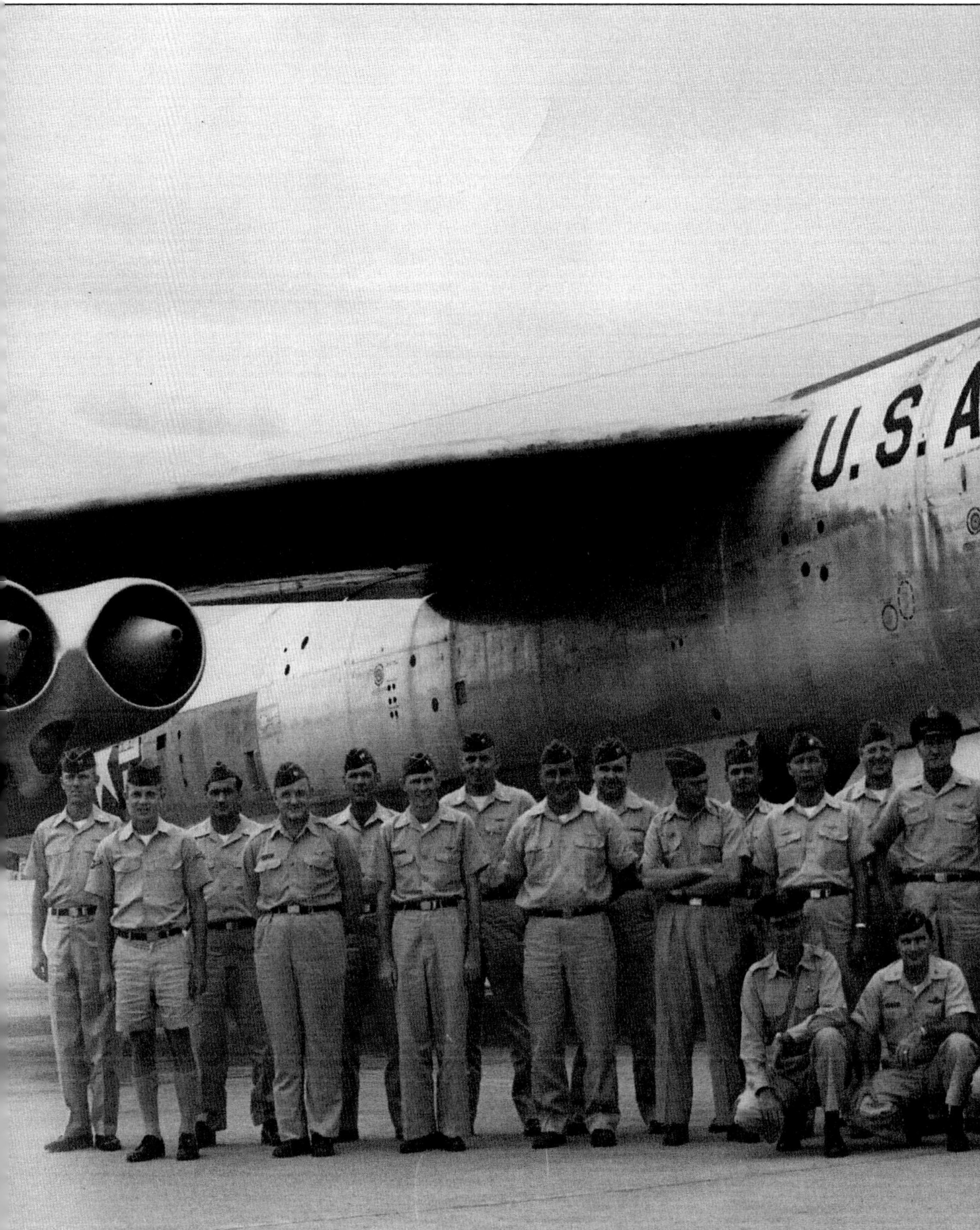

The 70th Strategic Reconnaissance Wing RB 47s, pictured here, served at the base from 1955

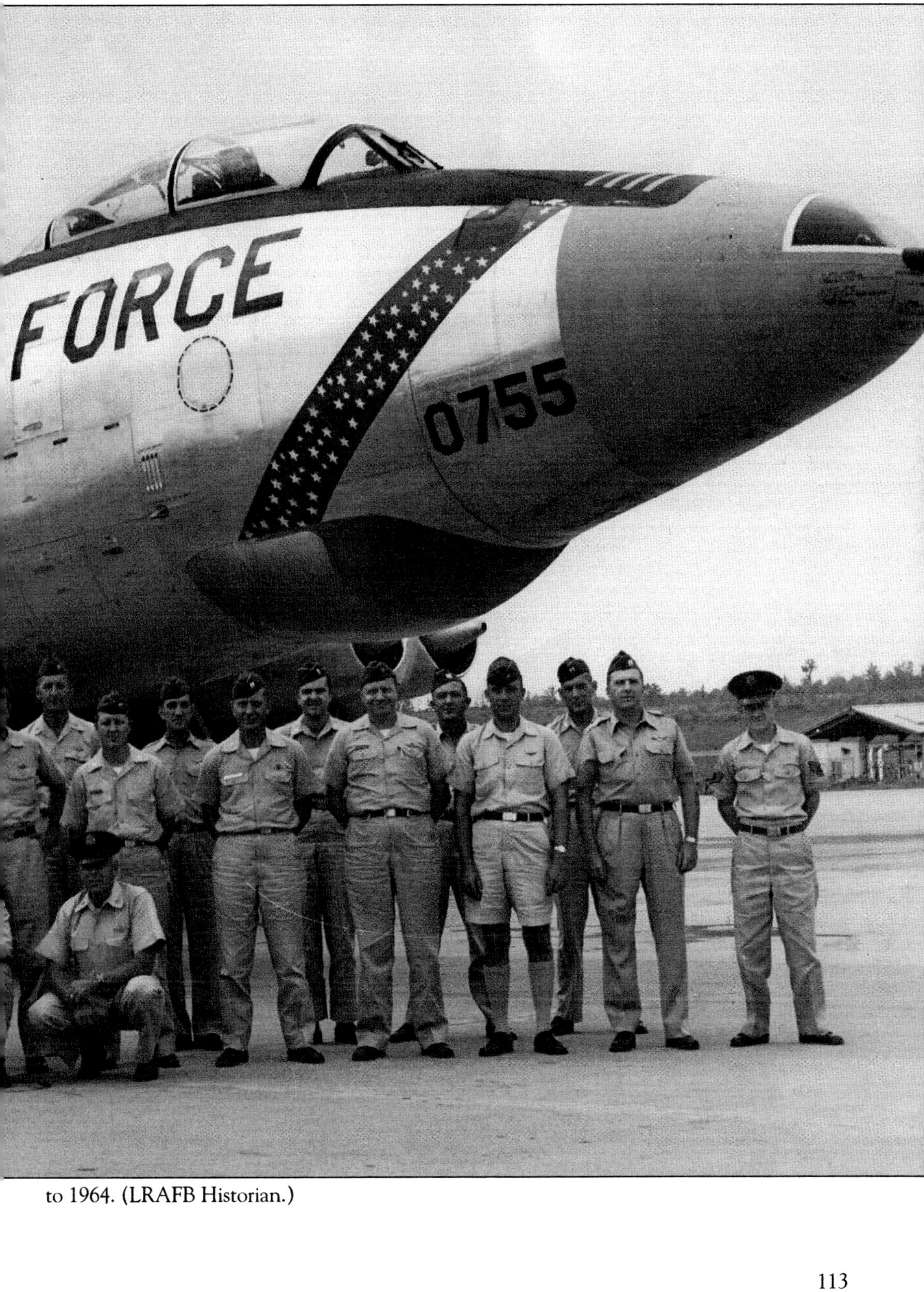

to 1964. (LRAFB Historian.)

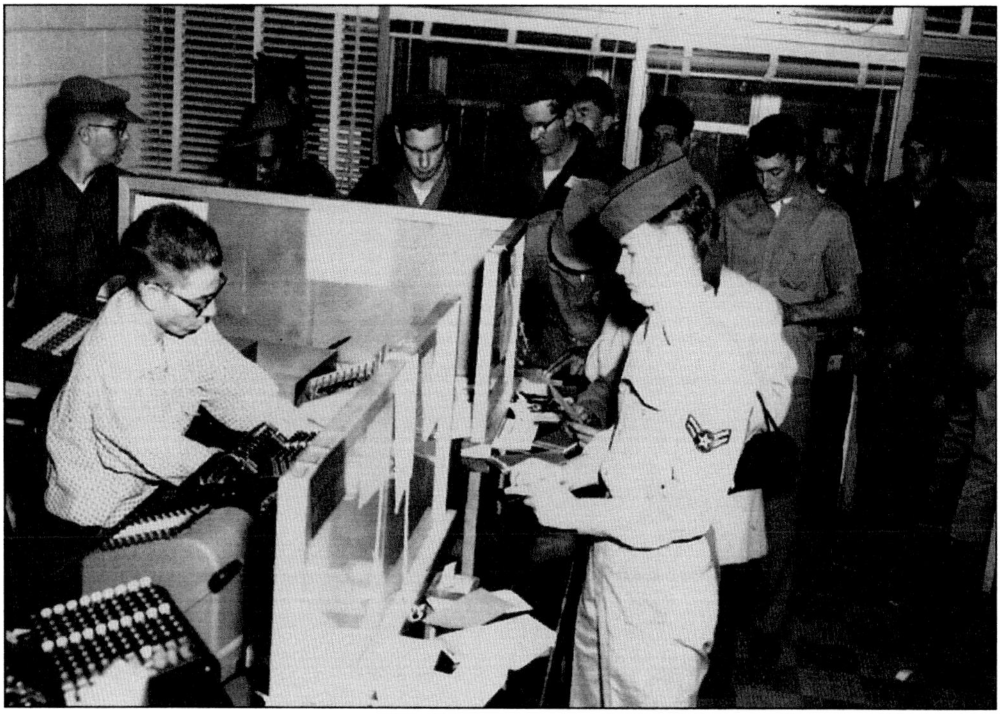

The influx of military personnel brought a huge payroll to Jacksonville. To serve those people, the Jacksonville State Bank opened a branch on base in 1956, after obtaining permission from the Federal Department of Defense. (Otis Stewart.)

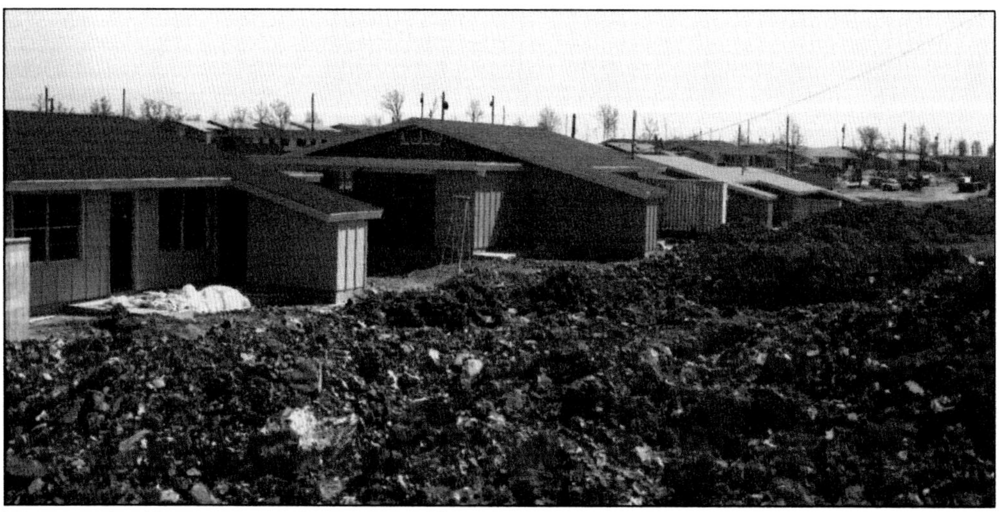

Housing Air Base personnel was a problem from the beginning of the project. With over 5,500 military people arriving in a short time, the need for quarters was apparent. Eventually, 1,535 Capehart family housing units were built and ready for occupancy by May 1959. (LRAFB Historian.)

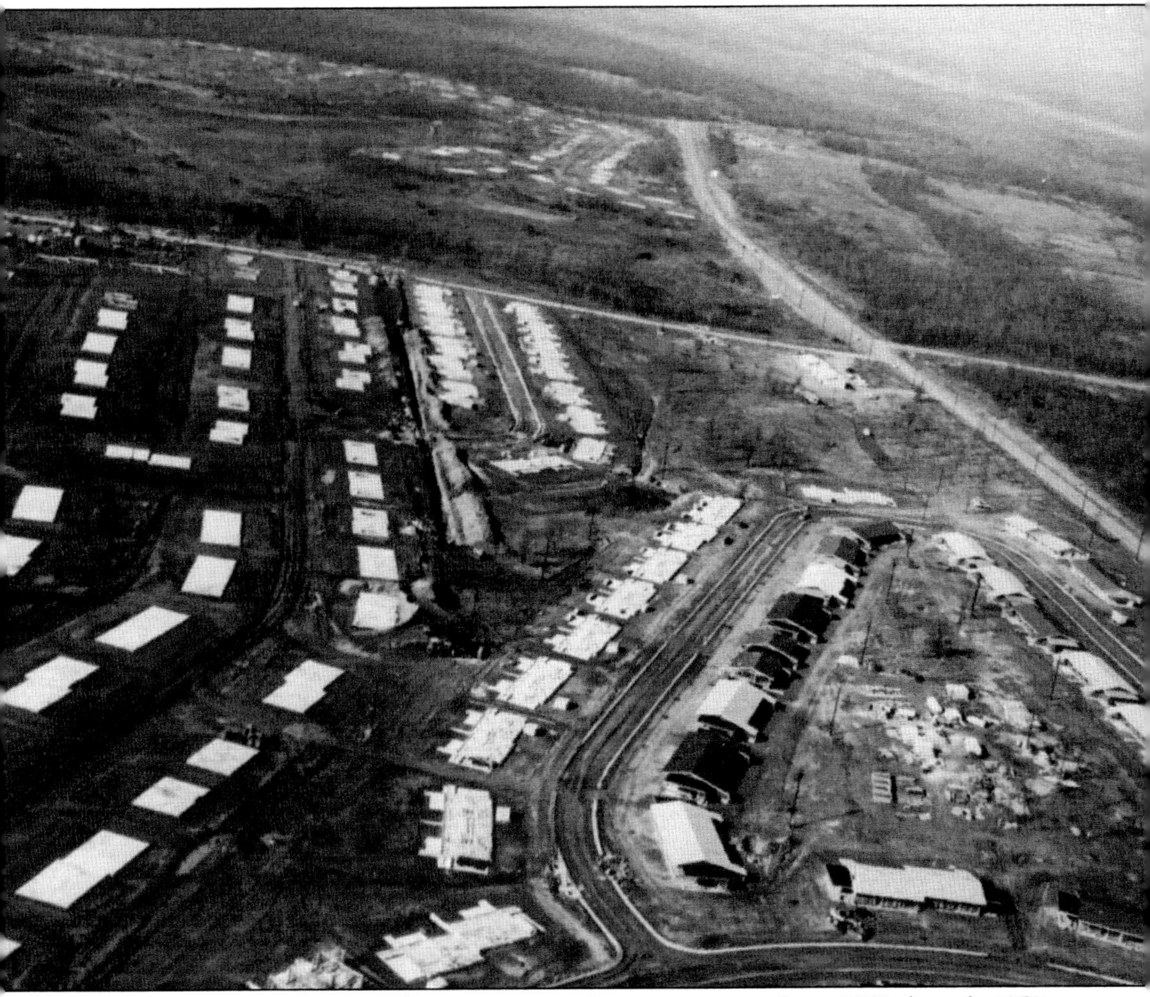

This aerial view shows LRAFB housing units under construction, from 1957 through 1959. (LRAFB Historian.)

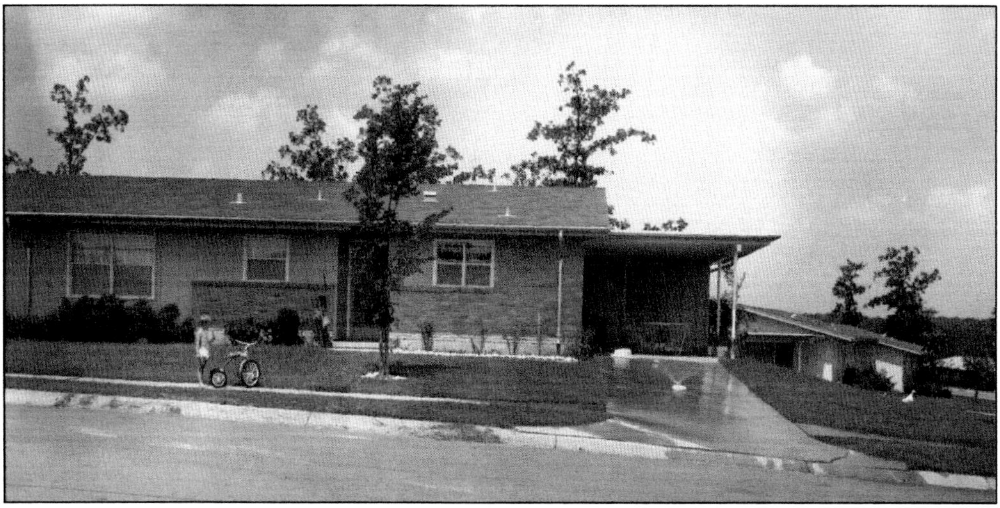

The Air Base is home to many families with children. (LRAFB Historian.)

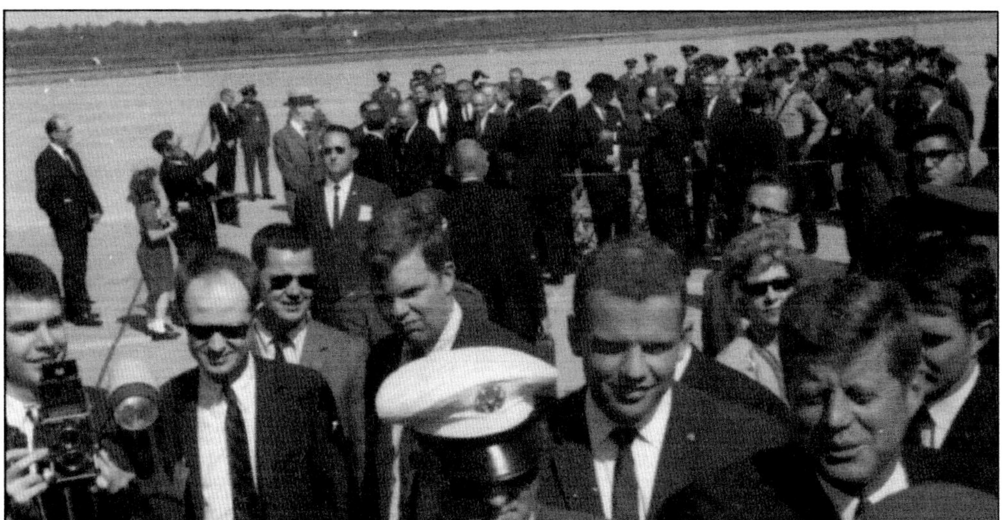

Shortly before he was assassinated, President John F. Kennedy visited Arkansas in 1963, for the dedication of the Greer's Ferry Dam. (LRAFB Historian.)

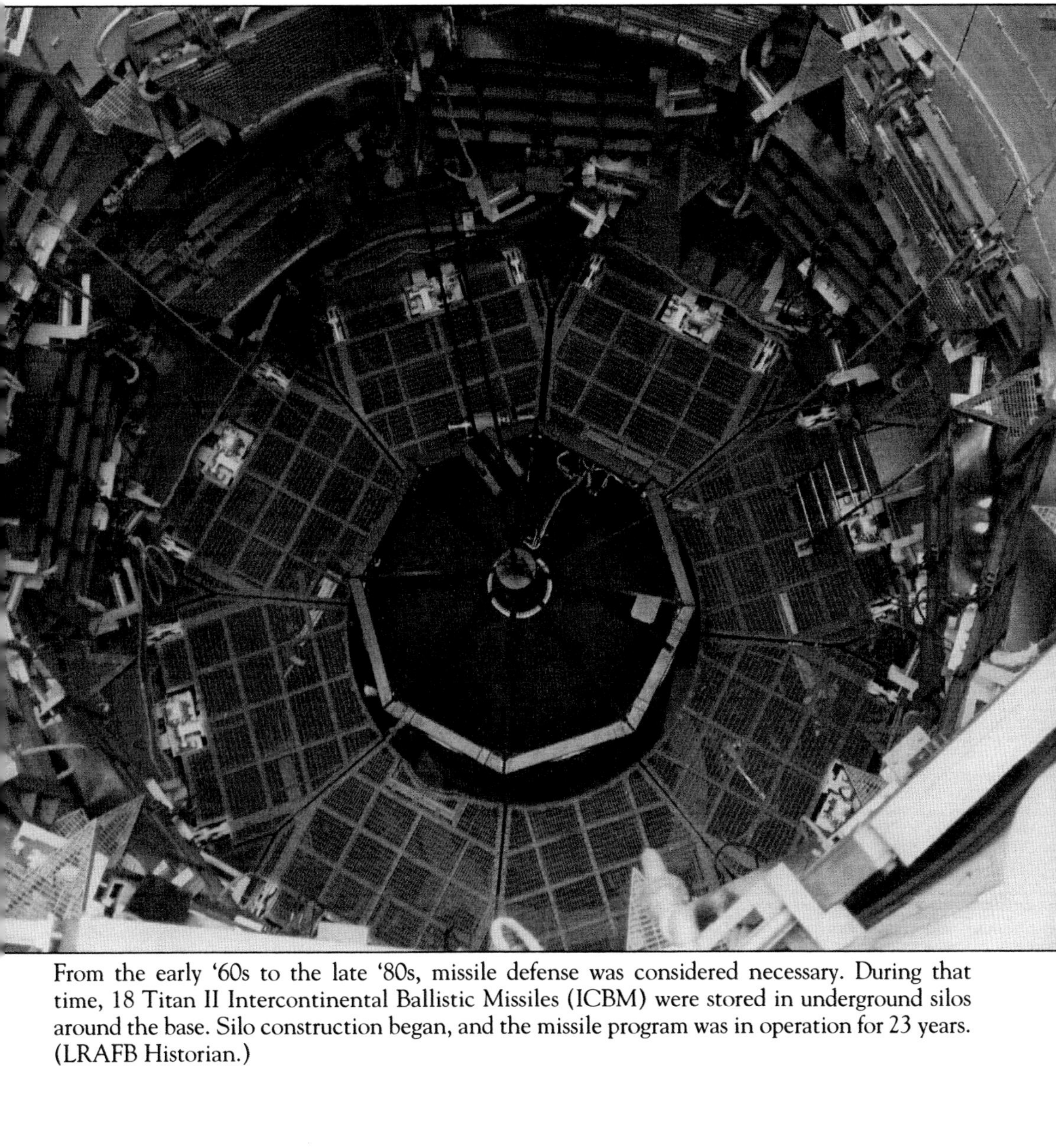

From the early '60s to the late '80s, missile defense was considered necessary. During that time, 18 Titan II Intercontinental Ballistic Missiles (ICBM) were stored in underground silos around the base. Silo construction began, and the missile program was in operation for 23 years. (LRAFB Historian.)

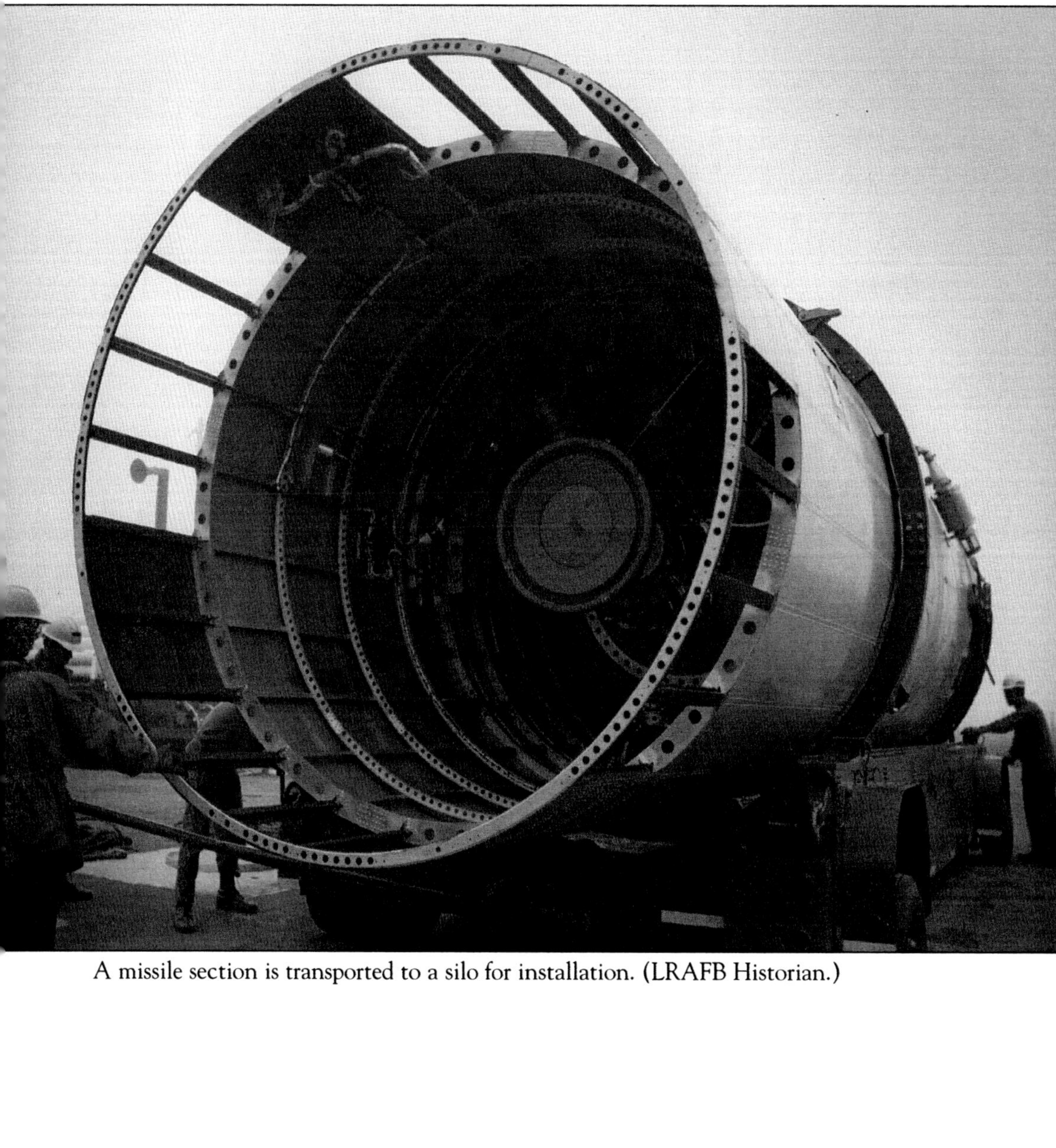

A missile section is transported to a silo for installation. (LRAFB Historian.)

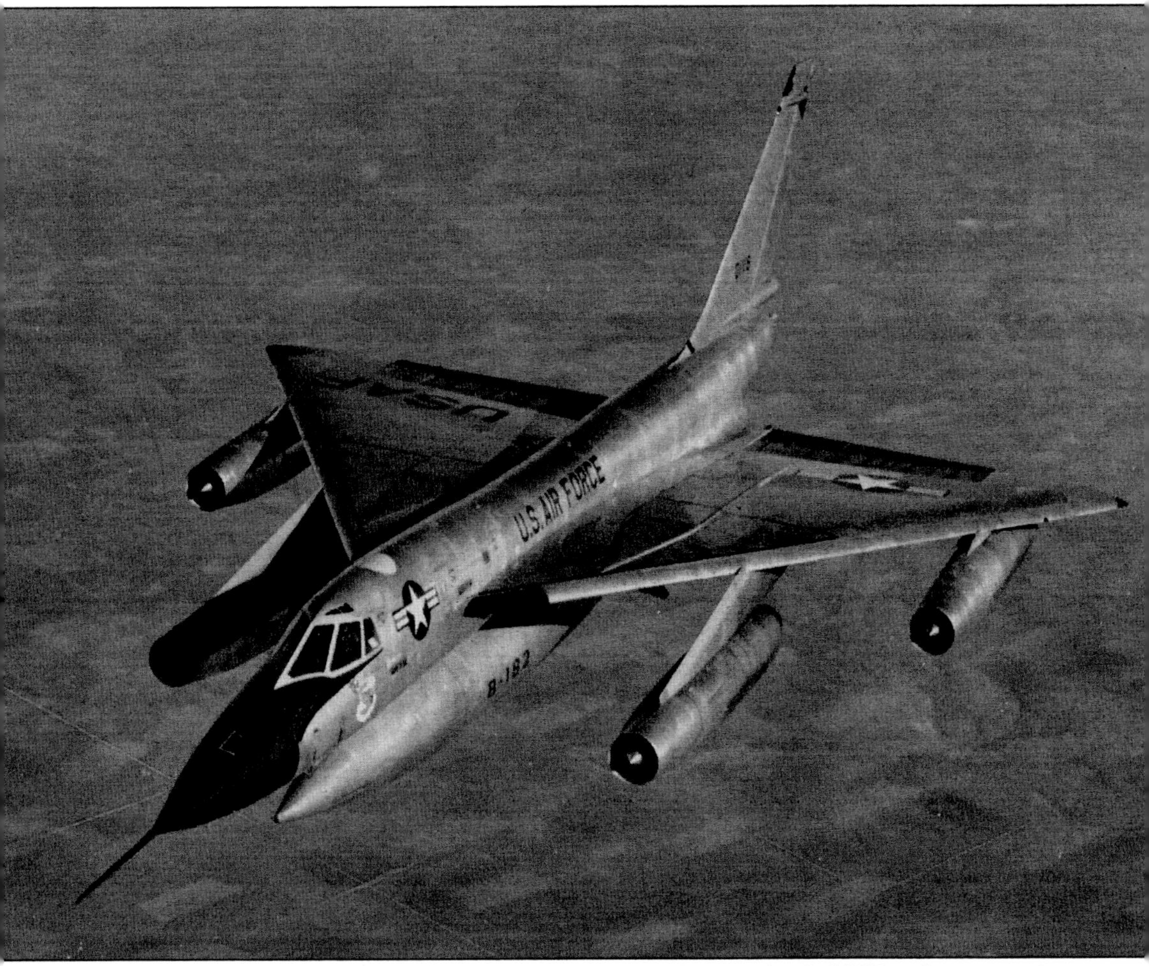

The LRAFB trained B58 Hustler pilots from 1964 to 1970. During the Cold War, these aircraft were on alert as a deterrent to enemy aggression. (LRAFB Historian.)

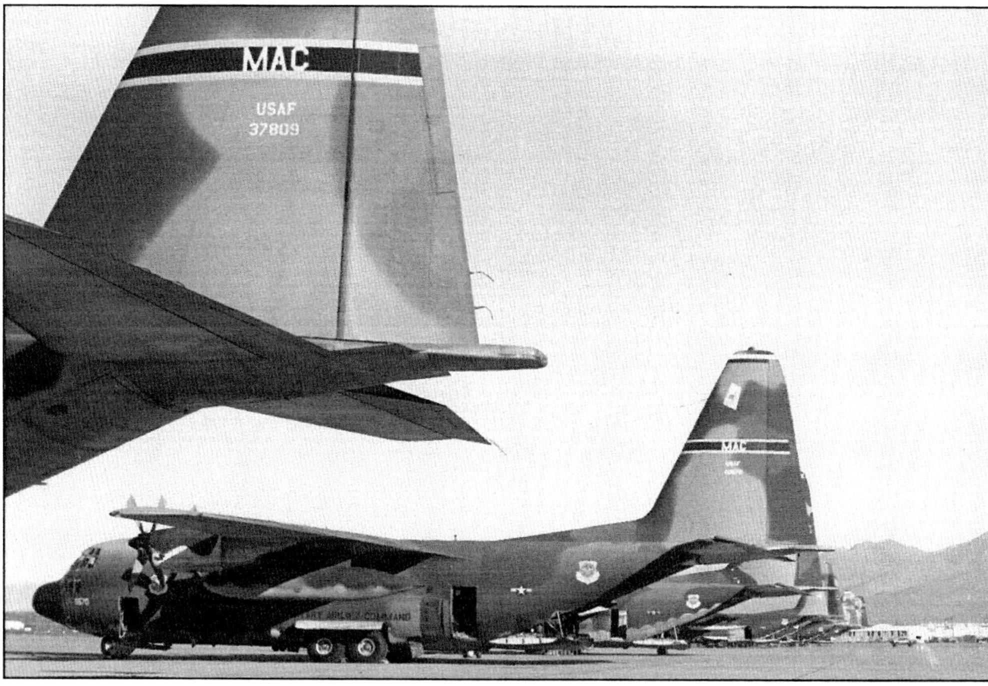

The LRAFB is a training center for the C-130 cargo planes that deliver personnel and equipment all over the world. This particularly useful aircraft will land on a small runway, deliver parachute troops or goods, and roll cargo out the back door. This prop plane has been in production since 1954 and is still in use. (LRAFB Historian.)

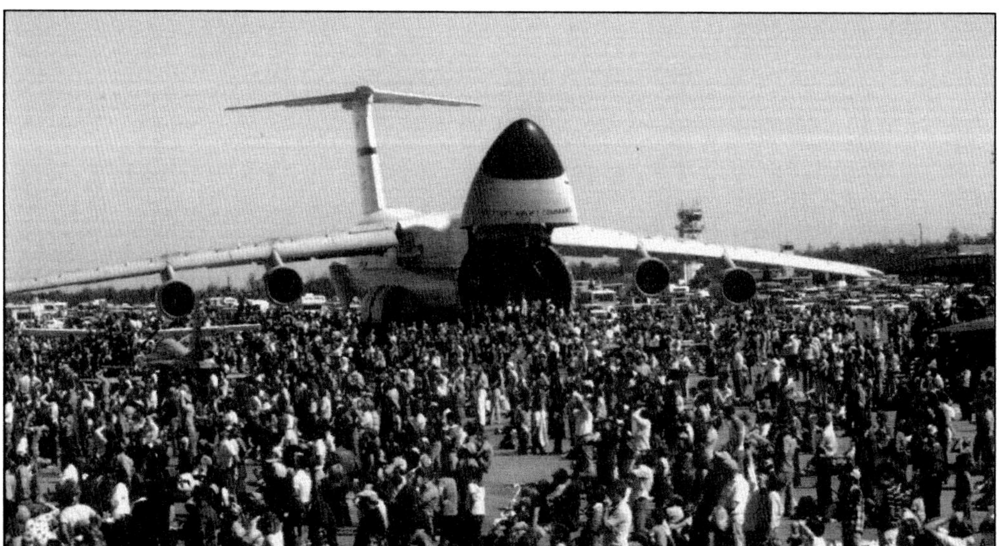

A Little Rock Air Force Base open house draws tens of thousands of area residents. Both the community and the base work at maintaining good relations through the Air Base Committee. (Jacksonville Historical Society.)

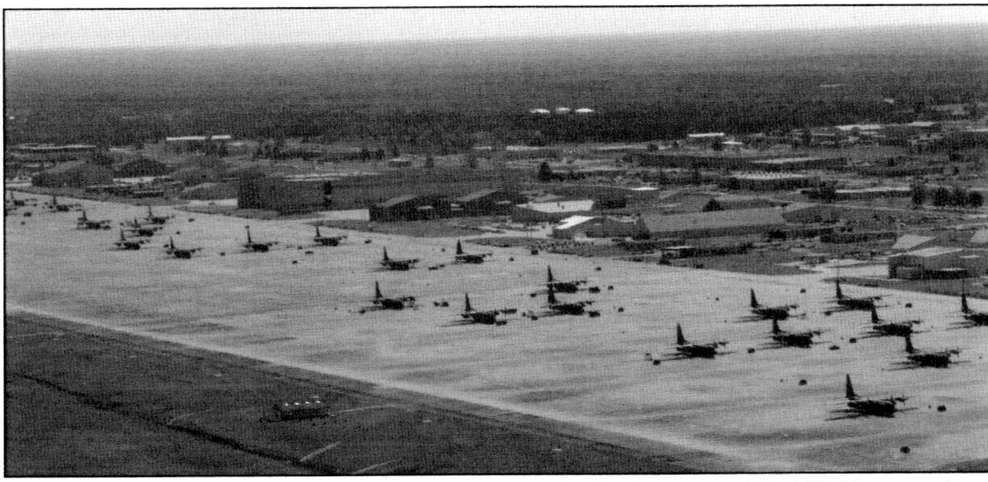

The LRAFB planes are lined up and ready to go on the landing strip. (LRAFB Historian.)

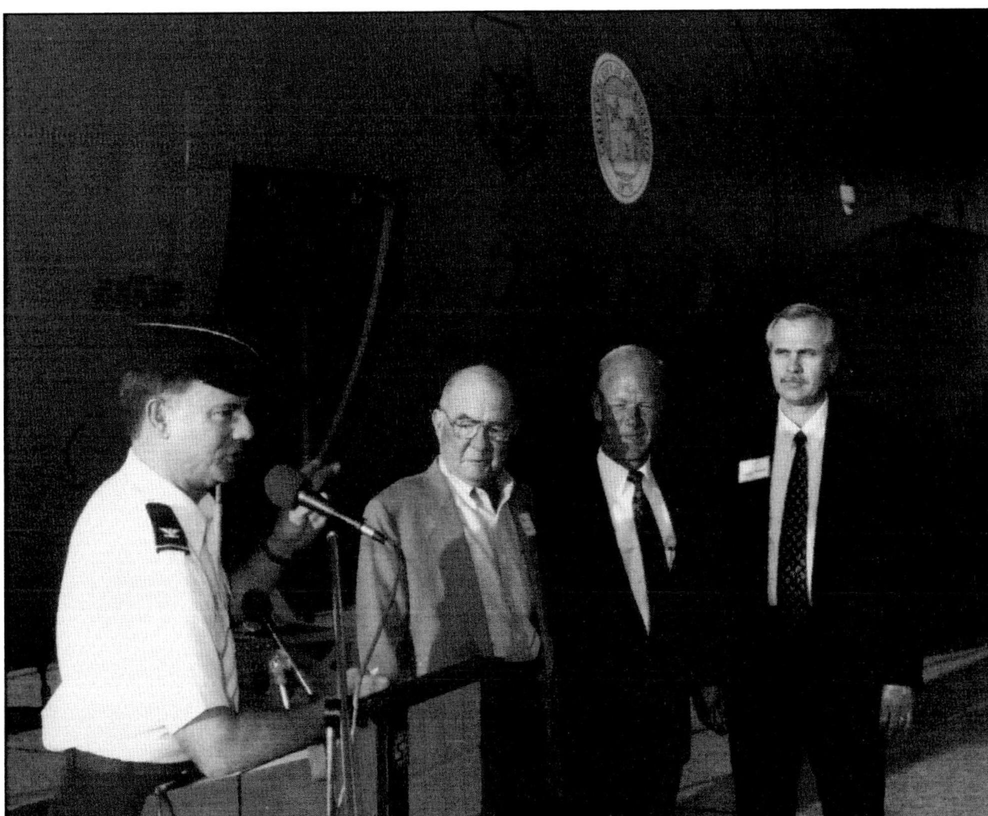

There have been several *City of Jacksonville* planes over the years. This one is dedicated in 1991 with, from left to right: Col. Charles J. Wax, Pat Wilson, Mike Wilson, and Mayor Tommy Swaim. (LRAFB Historian.)

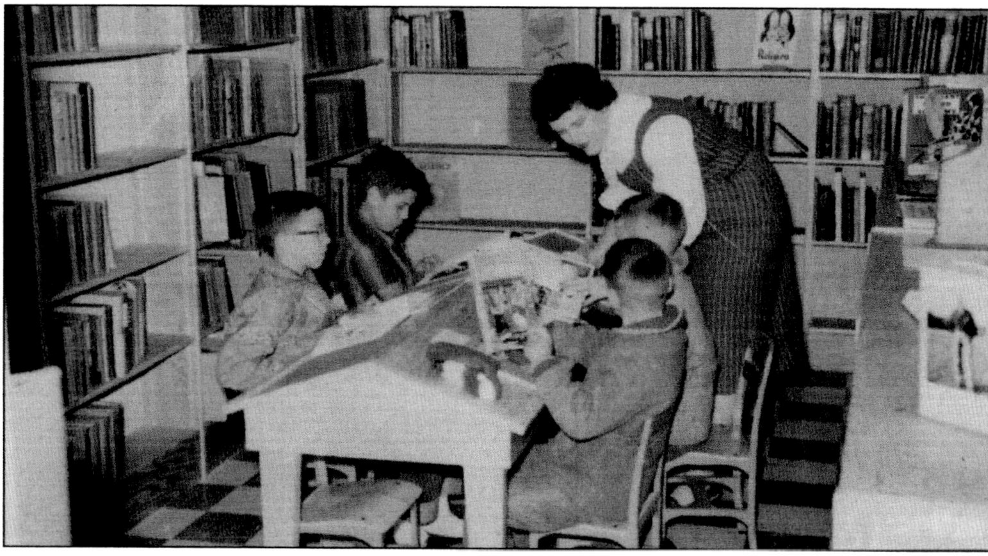

Esther Nixon came to Arkansas from Texas when she married Watson Nixon. In 1959, a library was opened in a single room of the old city hall on Second Street. Esther Nixon served as librarian for 27 years, and when she retired in 1986, the new library on Main Street was named in her honor. (Nixon Library, Jacksonville.)

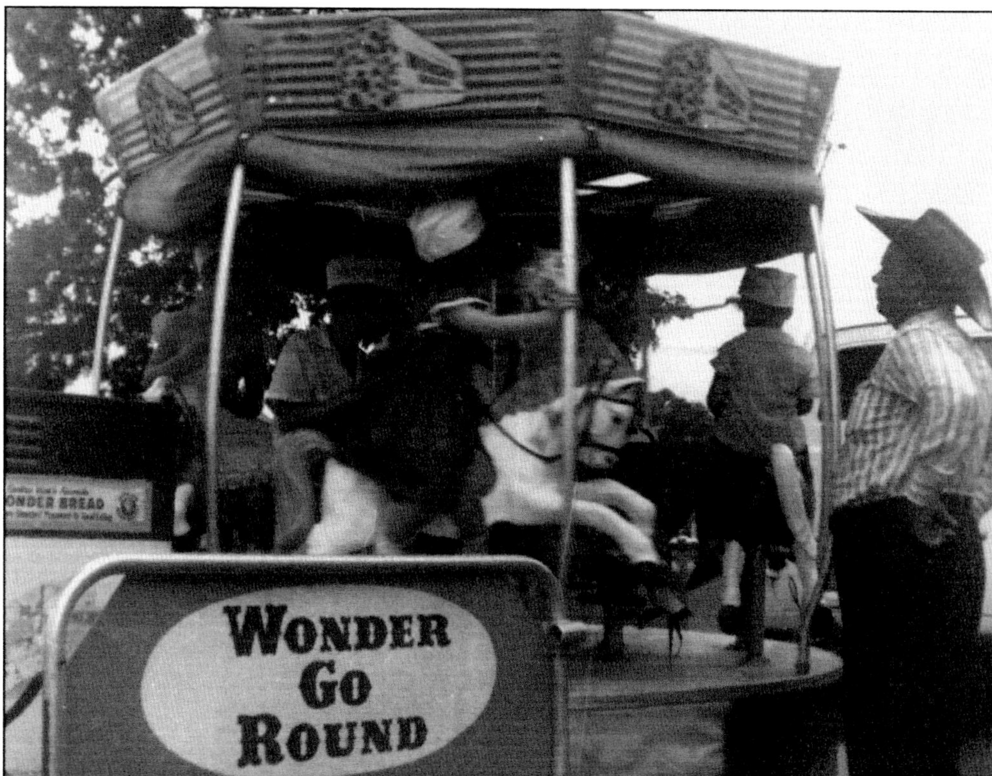

Cactus Vick, Wonder Bread promoter, was a familiar sight at children's birthday parties, as seen in this 1958 photograph. (Mary Alice Lamb Cole.)

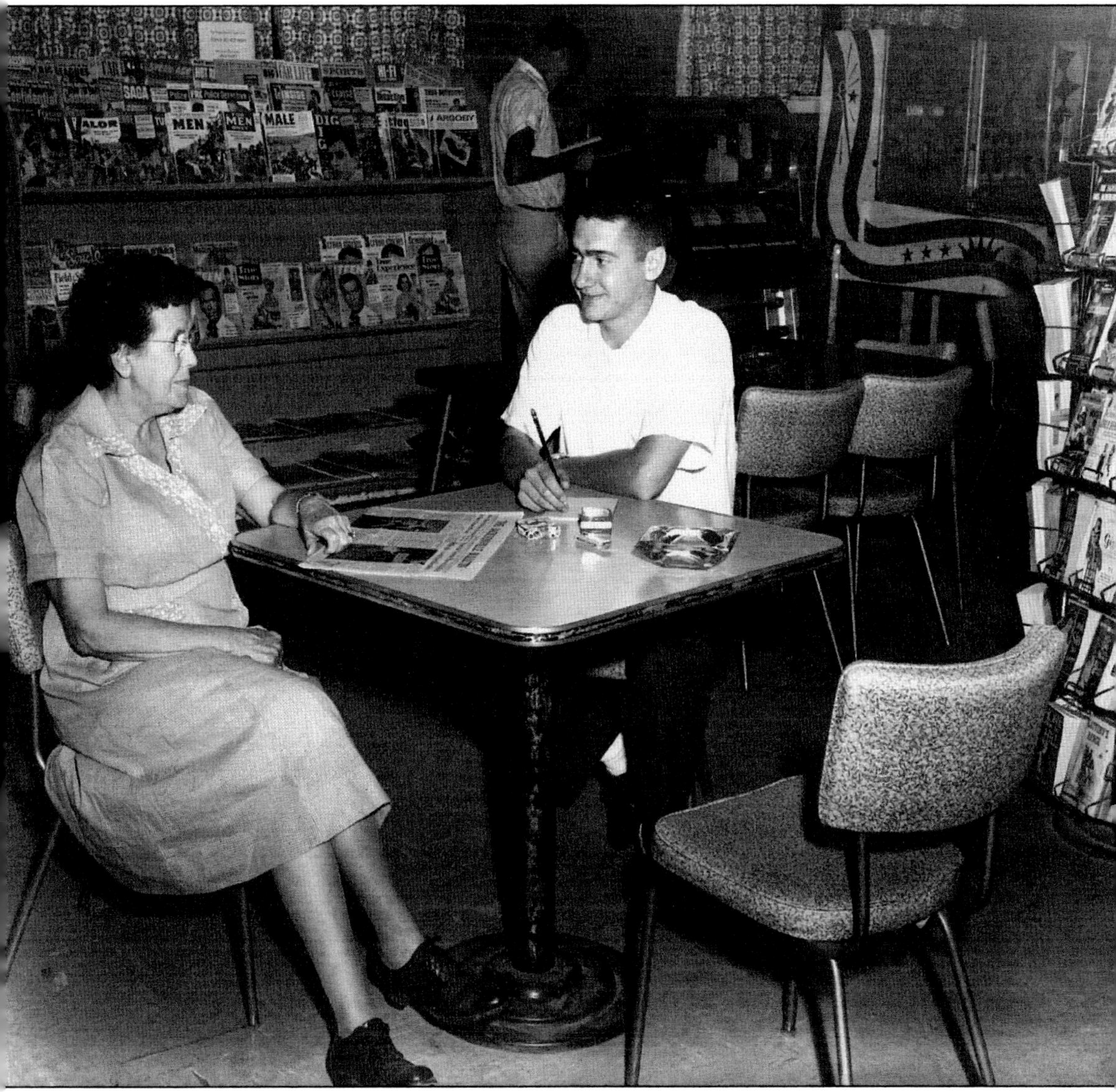

The Confectionery and Bus Station was a long-lived establishment in Jacksonville. Callie Harpole was known as "Mom" to many of the young people who frequented the place over two decades. In 1959, Ben Rice interviewed her for a local newspaper story. (Marie Hackett.)

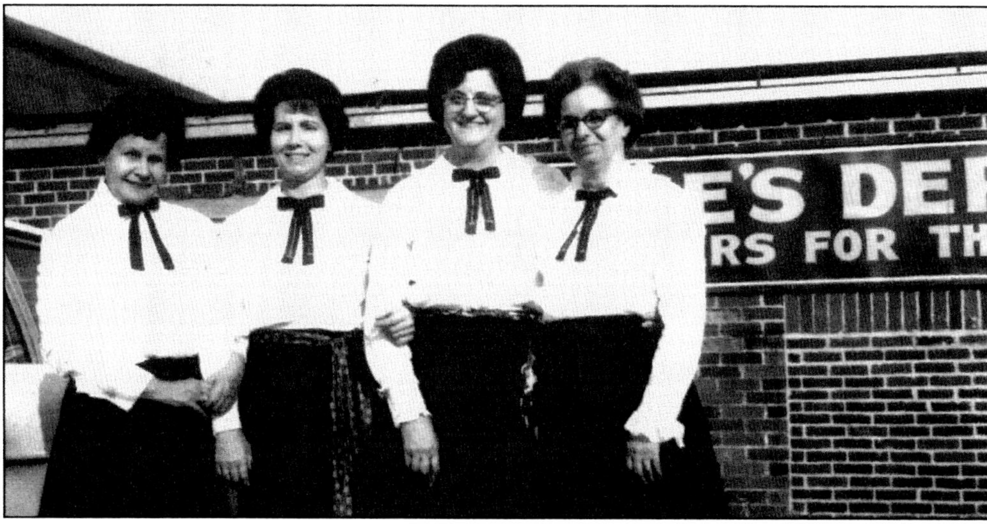

Many will remember the clerks from Pace's Department Store on First Street. They are, from left to right: Imogene Wooley, Juanita Smith, Della Chadwick, and Ola Mae Curtis. (Richard Hibbs.)

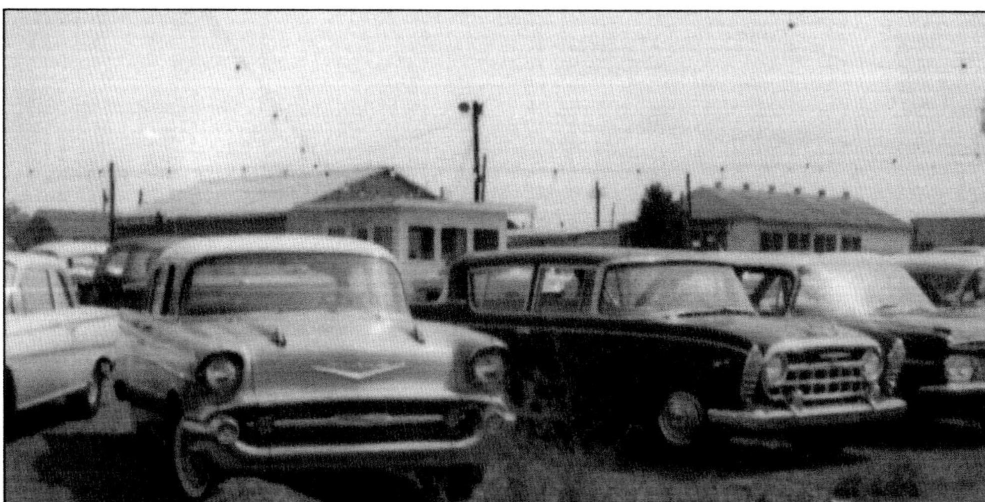

Gwatney Used Cars started small in 1960. The business has grown with Jacksonville, now operating a full-service dealership. (Bill Gwatney.)

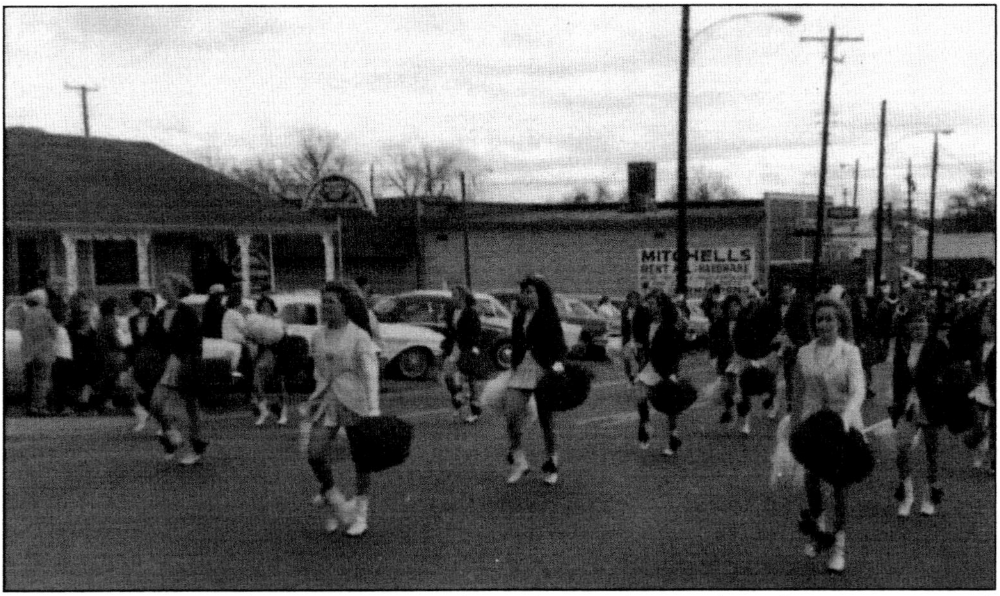

There are different buildings, and fashions have changed, but parades still continue to march down Main Street as seen in this 1965 photograph. (Richard Hibbs.)

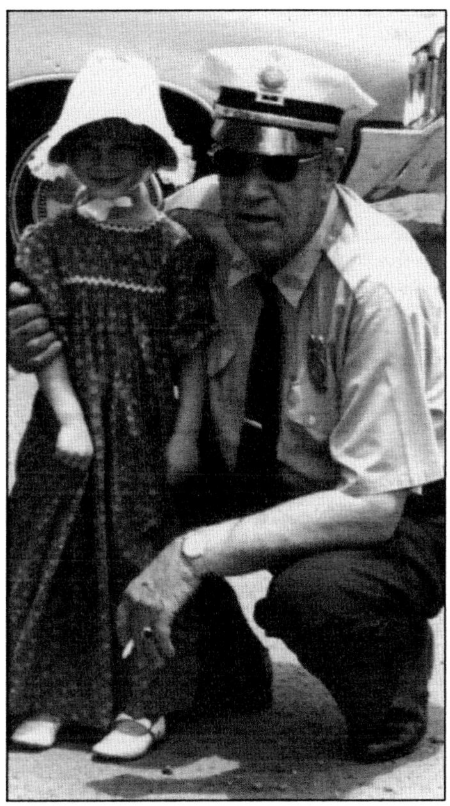

Celebrating the sesquicentennial, Chief of Police Myron Traylor poses with Misty Dupree for a picture in 1976. (Tommy Dupree.)

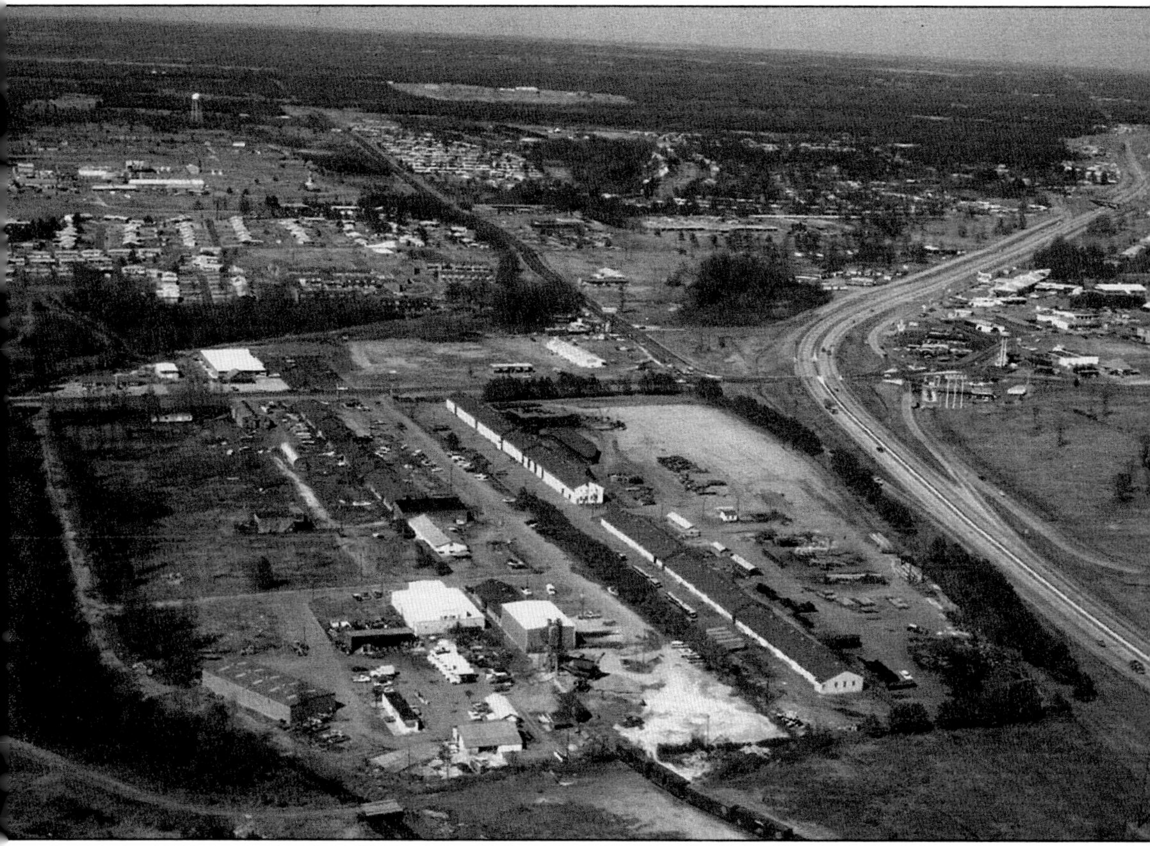

This 1960s aerial view of Jacksonville shows the remains of the Ordnance Plant, the Air Base, the four-lane highway, and some of the housing expansion that continued growth into the next century. (Jacksonville Historical Society.)

INDEX

Air Force 95
Alligator Gar 48
Arkansas Aviation Hall of Fame 82
Arkansas *Gazette* 108
Arkansas River 9, 48
Arkansas State Police 68
Arkansas Territorial Restoration 14
Arkansas Territory 9
Arkansas Treasury Warrant 10
Baggett, Cornelia 74
Baptism 73
Bayou Meto 9, 10
Bayou Meto Cemetery 35, 66
Blodgett, Mr. 92
Bond, Martha (Culpepper) 82
Bond, Morris (Cy) 62, 82
Bond, Thomas Ridgly 82
Boy Scout card 63
Boyd, C. T. 58
Boyd, Caroline Elizabeth 38
Boyd, Carolyn 72
Boyd, Ed 92
Boyd, Haschal 44
Boyd, Jack 89, 96
Boyd, Jerry 104
Boyd, Jewel 30
Boyd, Leroy 58
Boyd, Mildred 72
Boyd, Pick 80
Boyd, R. D. 84, 92
Boyd, Rufus Darby Family 23
Boys in Tree 17
Brown, Mabel 29, 43
Brown, Willie 29
Cactus Vick 122
Caddo 9
Caddo Studio 65
Cairo and Fulton Railroad 11
Carr, C. B. 93
Carr, Charles 93
Carr, James 93
Carr, Kenneth 93
Carr, William 93, 106
Carter, Exie 18
Chambers, Bill 109
Chaney, Essie 53
Cherokee 9
Chickasaws 9
Choctaws 9
City Café 86
Civil War 9, 10
Civilian Conservation Corps Camps 49, 53
Cole, Christine 83, 85, 92
Cole, Mary Alice Lamb 103
Cole, Robert 73, 85, 108
Commercial College, Little Rock 36
Corder, Kathryn Beall 42
Cotton 61
Creek 9
Crook Family 58
Crook, Jim 16
Crook, Joe 16
Crook, Maggie 16
Davidson, Mary 13
Depression 26, 49, 51
Douglas, Margaret 72, 83
Douglas' Station 86
Douglass Minnie Ray 30
Douglass, Inez 30
Dupree Family 17, 23
Dupree General Mercantile Business 17, 21
Dupree, Lorene 71
Dupree, Misty 125
Dupree, P. W. III 73
Dupree, Pete 71
Dupree, Peter Warren 17
Dupree, Tommy 74, 91
Edwards, Dave 92
Eudy, Patricia 81
Eudy, Stephen 81, 98
Evatt, J. W. 90
Evatt, Rose Brewer 90
Federal Building 95
Ferguson, Mary 16
First Baptist Church 28, 36, 101, 102
First Electric 108
First Presbyterian Church 36, 50, 92
First United Methodist Church 35, 36, 41, 107
Flood, 1927 48
Friendship Baptist Church Baptism 49
Gandy Dancers 70
Gandy Mfg. Company 70
Graco Theatre 106
Gray 9
Gray Township 9, 16
Graytown 9, 10
Green, Edgar 84
Griggs, Kenneth 107
Gwatney Used Cars 124
Hackett, Marie 64, 101
Hackett, Marie Harpole 42
Hammons, Thelma 83
Hardcastle, Kathryn 72
Hardcastle, Ruby 53
Harden, John 109
Harpole Brothers' Store 64
Harpole, Callie 123
Harpole, Callie 51
Harpole, Harry 27, 42
Harpole, M. E. 63
Harpole, Marie 40, 87
Harpole, Opal 40
Harpole's Barber Shop 31
Harpole's Confectionery and Bus Station 82, 123
Harpole's Store 28, 42, 86
Hendrix College 17
Henry Brothers' Store 43, 91
Henry, Bobby 42
Hibbs, Mrs. 95
Hudson, Carroll Latta 37
Hudson, Oscar Lorin 37
Hunting, Bear 56
Hunting, Duck 57
Hunting, Rabbit 56
Hunting, Raccoon 57
Indian Chief Motorcycle 80
Jackson Home 12
Jackson, Elizabeth 11
Jackson, Mary Davidson 12
Jackson, Nicholas W. 11, 13
Jackson, Thompson 13
Jacksonville 11
Jacksonville Chamber of Commerce 50, 69, 95
Jacksonville City Marshal 68, 72
Jacksonville Drive-In Theatre 105
Jacksonville Elderly Activities Program 41
Jacksonville Elementary 17
Jacksonville Girls' Basketball Team 100
Jacksonville Junior High School Girls' Basketball Team 72
Jacksonville Main Street 99
Jacksonville Ordnance Plant 69
Jacksonville Phone Directory 97

Jacksonville School 29, 30, 34, 49, 52, 74, 83
Jacksonville State Bank 50, 97
Jacksonville Telephone Company 21
Jacksonville Telephone Exchange 53
Jenkins, John 92
Kennedy, President John F. 116
Killingsworth, Callie 30
La Petit Roche 9
LaForce, Tom 88
Lake Nixon 87
Lamb, Harvey 39, 43, 45
Lamb, Joe 15, 16
Lamb, Mabel 45, 46, 59
Lamb, Mabel Brown 27
Lamb, Marion 45, 46, 108
Lamb, Mary Alice 72, 83
Lamb, Shelly 83
Lamb, Virgil 45, 80
Lamb, Rayburn 106
Little Rock Air Force Base 22, 50, 51, 95, 126
Little Rock Air Force Base, 70th Strategic Reconnaissance Wing 112
Little Rock Air Force Base, Air Strip 110
Little Rock Air Force Base, B58 Hustler 119
Little Rock Air Force Base, C-130 120
Little Rock Air Force Base, Capehart Housing 114
Little Rock Air Force Base, City of Jacksonville Dedication 121
Little Rock Air Force Base, First Command 111
Little Rock Air Force Base, Housing 115
Little Rock Air Force Base, Jacksonville State Bank 114
Little Rock Air Force Base, Open House 120
Little Rock Air Force Base, Titan Missile 118
Little Rock Air Force Base, Titan Missile Silo 117
Lonoke County Warden 68
Madden Homestead 22
Madden-Wilson Homestead 50, 51
Mallett, Robert 97
Mallett,Opal Harpole 42
Martin, Jack 42
Masonic Lodge 35
McCain Family 24
McCain, George 59, 62
McCain, George E. 92
McCain, George Hamilton 24, 34, 47
McCain, Jeanne 83
McCain, Margie Walker 67
Memphis 9
Methodist Church 107
Military Road 9, 10
Missouri Pacific Sunshine Special 70
Mothers of the Bayou Meto Club 46
Mt. Pisgah Baptist Church 36
Murtishaw 52
Neal Bro's Used Cars 104
Neal, C. F. 74
Neal, Fannie 98
Neal, Theo 52
Neal, Willie 52
Nixon Homestead 71
Nixon, DeWitt 90
Nixon, Esther 122
Nixon, Hattie 50
Nixon, Mary Ann 42
Nixon, Wally 90
Nixon, Walter 50
Nixon, Walter Watson, Jr. 37
Oakland, Tennessee 17
Old Mill 87
Ordnance Plant 126
Ordnance Plant 4, 75, 76, 77, 82, 83, 95
Ordnance Plant Fire Department 78
Osage 9
Ostrum, Charles Van 107
Pace Department Store 124
Parade, 1915 32, 33, 34, 35
Parade, 1965 125
Parnell, Lanny 92
Pearson, Bill 109
Petty, Martha 72
Phulinger, Germany 14
Pickard, June 83
Pierce's Café 86
Quapaw 9
Ramsey's Store 14
Ration Dates 79
Ration Stamps 79
Ray, Belle 30
Ray, Penola 30
Rebsamen, Ray 96
Reed's Bridge 9
Reed's Bridge Civil War Battlefield 10, 67
Reeser, Mr. 92
Relocation Act of 1830 9
Rice, Ben 123
Rice, Melda 97
Roderweis Family 14
Roderweis House 15
Roderweis, John Louis 14
Roosevelt 49, 53
Sadler Pond 73
Scamper 101
School Improvement Association 26
Senior Activity Center 106
Sertoma Club 109
Sharecropper 37
Sherer Daughters 59
Sommersville, Tennessee 13
South Bend 84
Spokane, Washington 54
Spool Factory 47
Stanphill, Lenore 30
Stanphill, Tompie 30
Stone, E. C. 17
Stone, Elihu 16, 24
Stone, Leonora 17, 20, 24
Stone, Mancil Euclid 16
Stone, Miles 36
Stone, Minnie 24, 26
Sunnyside 69, 81, 90
Swaim, Mayor Tommy 121
Taylor, Grandmother 25
Taylor, George 54
Taylor, Inez 19
Taylor, Murrell 41
Thomas, Ada Mae 72
Thompkins, Eddie 109
Thompson Sawmill 47
Tomato and Poultry Club 27, 28
Tony Lonesome School 27
Trail of Tears 9
Trailer, Myron 125
Trotter, Lu 88
Uric, Roger 106
Vaughn School 32
War Assets Administration 82
Wax, Col . Charles J. 121
Webb Family 26
Webb, Doyle 89, 109
Webb, Elia 88
Webb, Jim 25
Webb, Noel 88
Webb's Dairy Diner 88
Webb's Grocery 89, 106
Williams, Lefty 68, 72
Williams, Trix 94
Williams-Brown Lumber Company 94
Williford Willie 30
Wilson, Kenneth Patrick 50
Wilson, Mike 121
Wilson, Pat 96, 121
Wonder Bread 122
World War I 43, 44
World War I Red Cross 43
World War II 68, 69, 79, 80, 82
Wright, Johnny 109
Zimmerebner, Earnestine 72, 83